D1352057

Mariane Pearl is an award-winning documentary film director and a reporter who produced and hosted a daily radio show for Radio France International and has written for *Télérama*. She is 'Global Diary' columnist for *Glamour* magazine.

Sarah Crichton is a former *Newsweek* magazine editor and until recently, the publisher of Little, Brown and Company.

A MIGHTY HEART

THE BRAVE LIFE AND DEATH
OF MY HUSBAND, DANIEL PEARL

❧

Mariane Pearl

with Sarah Crichton

Virago

VIRAGO

First published in Great Britain in 2003 by Virago Press
This edition published in Great Britain in 2007 by Virago Press
First published in the USA by Scribner New York, NY 2003

A CIP catalogue record for this book is available from the British Library

ISBN 978-1-84408-459-3

Papers used by Virago are natural, recyclable products made from
wood grown in sustainable forests and certified in accordance with the
rules of the Forest Stewardship Council.

Printed and bound in Great Britain by Clays Ltd, St Ives plc
Paper supplied by Hellefoss AS, Norway

Virago Press
An imprint of
Little, Brown Book Group
Brettenham House
Lancaster Place
London WC2E 7EN

A Member of the Hachette Livre Group of Companies

www.virago.co.uk

A MIGHTY HEART

Prologue

I WRITE this book for you, Danny, because you had the courage of this most solitary act: to die with your hands in chains but your heart undefeated.

I write this book to do justice to you, and to tell the truth.

I write this book to show that you were right: The task of changing a hate-filled world belongs to each one of us.

I write this book because, in suppressing your life, the terrorists tried to kill me, too, and to kill our son, Adam. They sought to kill all those who identified with you.

I write this book to defy them, and in the knowledge that your courage and spirit can inspire others.

I write this book to pay tribute to all the people who helped and supported our family through terrible times, creating an emotional bridge for us to stand on.

I write this book for you, Adam, so you know that your father was not a hero but an ordinary man. An ordinary hero with a mighty heart.

I write this book for you so you can be free.

Chapter One

Dawn will rise soon over Karachi. Curled in Danny's warm embrace, I feel safe. I like that this position is called "spooning" in English. We are like spoons in a drawer, pressed to each another, each fitted to the other's shape. I love these sweet moments of oblivion and the peace they bring me. No matter where we are—Croatia, Beirut, Bombay—this is my shelter. This is our way of meeting the challenge, of confronting the chaos of the world.

As I awaken, I struggle for the right words to describe this place. It is the curse of all journalists, I suppose, to be writing a story even as you are living it. I am not sure I'll ever get to know Karachi. I have distrusted this city from the start, though we are partly here to find out if its bad reputation is deserved. Once relatively stable, even sleepy, Karachi became a nexus for drug and arms trafficking in the 1980s. Now the city is an intricate puzzle, decadent and beastly at the same time, metastasizing into a capital of blind hatred and violent militancy.

The Pakistani people are equally fractured. Those born in their own land hate the Muslim immigrants who arrived from India after the two countries were partitioned in 1947. The Sunni Muslims loathe the Shiite Muslims. Since 1998 more than seventy doctors have been assassinated in Karachi; most were Shiites mowed down by Sunni zealots. And the pro-Taliban fundamentalists, who have been sinking deep roots here, detest the rest of the world.

There are so many people in this city, but no one seems to know how to count them all. Are there ten million? Twelve? Fourteen? Most of Pakistan is landlocked, pressed between India and Afghanistan, with parts of its borders touching southwestern Iran and the farthermost reaches of China. But Karachi, on the brown coast of the Arabian Sea, is the country's major port and, as such, is a magnet for migrants who drift in from the Pakistani countryside and across the border from even poorer places—Afghan villages, Bangladesh, the rural outposts of India. By day you see the poor burn under the scorching sun, selling vegetables and newspapers at dusty crossroads. At night they disappear in the labyrinthine streets, lending the city an air of foreboding. To us, this third-world city may glow with a feeble light, but Karachi draws the desperately poor like a torch draws fireflies.

Very rarely am I awake when Danny is still asleep, especially since I became pregnant. A ray of soft light enters our room, and falling back into sweet torpor, I gradually give up on the mysteries of Karachi and rejoin my husband in this privileged warm space of ours. Together, we can hold on to this night a little longer.

Seven A.M. Danny is pushing back the bedroom door with his foot. He brings coffee and dry—if not stale—biscuits to stave off the fits of nausea I still fight in the morning. Sometimes I have to rush to the bathroom to retch as soon as I wake. The noise alone can turn Danny pale. He seems so unhappy to witness my suffering that I try to muffle the sound track. Danny pretends the pregnancy is making me moody. A few days ago I chanced on a less than discreet email he sent his childhood friend Danny Gill in California:

> Hey! . . . Mariane's belly is getting very pronounced. It's quite a thing to see. Due date is May, ground zero is Paris. She's sick often, moody occasionally, hungry earlier than usual, impatient but only with Pakistanis, horny when other symptoms don't get in the way. . . .

4

To my mind, Danny's moods have become unpredictable, too. I can't tell if it is because he is about to become a father, or because the world has gone amok in the four months since the World Trade Center was brought down, taking with it more than a few certainties. Danny is the South Asia bureau chief for *The Wall Street Journal*. Militant Islamic terrorism may hit anywhere on the globe, but the heart (if you can call it that) of its network is here, in this region, and the work at hand is daunting.

Danny and I have always reported alongside each other. I accompany him on most of his interviews; he comes along for most of mine. Yet I do not kid myself. He is the more experienced journalist, and he works for one of the most powerful news organizations in the world, whereas I work primarily for French public radio and television, which has barely enough money to pay for my métro tickets back home in Paris. But our differences in background and in culture make us well matched. We know naturally when to hold back and let the other speak.

I make Danny laugh to help him forget his worries; I make sure there is silence when he concentrates. And we engage each other in endless philosophical debates—about truth and courage, about how to fight preconceived ideas, about how to learn from and respect other cultures. Still, to try to shed light on the nature of terrorist activities is to plunge into a kingdom of darkness.

Already it is getting hot. To make me feel better, Danny reminds me that today is the last day of this assignment in Pakistan. Tomorrow we will check in to a five-star hotel in Dubai and stretch out on the beaches of the Arabian Gulf. It's a roundabout way back to our home in Bombay, but Pakistan and India are now at loggerheads, and there is no longer a direct connection between the neighboring countries. Battling over the disputed Himalayan territory of Kashmir, the two nations have escalated their historical animosity to the point that the world is braced for either side to unleash an attack against the other. Both Pakistan and India have used Kashmir as an excuse to justify recent military buildups; both possess arms of mass destruction; both strike poses as if they'll use the weapons. I think of the cops of Karachi, patrolling the streets in their pitiful uniforms, batons their only weapons.

The tension is palpable. We hear it in the voices of our Pakistani friends. On December 24 , 2001—the rare occasion that Christmas, Hanukkah, and Eid-ul-Fitr, the end of Ramadan, coincided— Danny received a note from an anxious friend in Peshawar, a relatively unstable city on the Pakistani-Afghan border:

> Happy Eid and happy Crismiss to you. Please also tell us about your wife. Are Indian armies ready to fight with us but they do not know that the Muslims will sacrifice their lives for Islam. In the case of war, India will be divided in lot of pieces and Muslim will take away his [clothes].
>
> My prayer is that OH GOD Save my country from his enemies.
>
> Business conditions in Pakistan especially in Peshawar are not so good. . . .So at the end I say that God may live long for us and whole of yours family.
>
> > With best wishes,
> > Wasim

Wasim is the director of a noodle factory. Danny met him two years ago in the Tehran airport. A very conservative Muslim, Wasim distrusts Westerners in general, but we went to visit him last December, and he treated us as his special guests, plying us with local delights, grilled meats and pastries, and inviting us to visit the marketplaces during Ramadan. Strolling through one store, he randomly picked up a pair of high-heeled shoes, shoes no proper Muslim wife would ever wear, and he insisted on buying them for me. On another night we had the honor of being invited to dinner at his house, a two-story mansion in an overcrowded area of the city. After we arrived, Danny disappeared in a cloud of several men, while seven women swooped in to take charge of me. Sitting cross-legged on carpets and removing their veils, they studied me with intense and unapologetic curiosity as they made me eat three plates of meatballs and rice.

Danny wrote back to Wasim:

> Wishing you a happy Christmas, Hanukkah, and Eid. Mariane and I are taking my colleague and our local Kashmiri carpet dealers out for Christmas dinner. So we'll have three Muslims, two Jews and a Buddhist, which sounds like the beginning of an airplane joke, but may be a good way to wish peace on earth—or at least in Kashmir. Danny.

We are staying with Danny's dear friend and colleague from *The Wall Street Journal,* Asra Q. Nomani, a most unconventional woman. An Indian-born Muslim, Asra was raised in West Virginia, and she is in Karachi to complete research on a book she's writing about Tantra. Tantra is generally associated with the sexual practices taught in *The Kama Sutra;* Asra insists she is focusing on its spiritual side. She is short and feminine but athletic, and striking-looking. Hers is an assertive beauty: Her shoulder-length black hair glistens with the oil that Indians use for daily head massages, and her face is dominated by sharp, broad cheekbones and eyes so dark and large that in repose, she can look like an ancient statue of Saraswati, the goddess who possesses all the learnings of the Vedas, from wisdom to devotion. But in this world she is also outrageously avant-garde. Unmarried women do not, as a rule, live alone in Karachi, but that hasn't stopped Asra, and she has rented a huge house in a district that is, oddly, named Defense Phase 5. Not only that, she has recently fallen in love with one of the sons of Pakistan's elite, nine years her junior. He is an attractive young man whom I immediately find somewhat empty.

To welcome us, Asra has planted flowers at the entrance to the house, which is in a gated community, one of the most luxurious in

7

Karachi. Here, the houses are guarded by a handful of skinny men, who take turns stationing themselves in a guardhouse, the main purpose of which is to protect them from the relentless heat. The neighbors hold good positions in the army and the government, or perhaps organized crime. The terrible gangster Dawood Ibrahim, by reputation a bloody barbarian, is supposed to have property around here. Danny has toyed with the idea of profiling him for the paper.

Inside, Asra has prepared a true honeymooners' bedroom for us. There are flowers and pine-scented candles, a bottle of massage oil, another of bubble bath. To the left of our bed, a small window covered with wire looks out onto a room off the courtyard where a foldout cot occupies the place of honor next to a clothesline draped with children's clothes. This is the property of the house servants, Shabir and Nasrin, who could themselves be called the property of the house, because Asra hired them when she rented the place. I visited their room. They have nothing. They sleep on the floor, and their tiny daughter, Kashva, a doll-like girl with short hair, sleeps tucked between her parents. Nasrin is pregnant. I dare not say "like me," so different will our two children's destinies be.

Danny draws the curtain on the scene, his gesture a perfect metaphor for how one tends to deal with poverty everywhere. Our honeymoon room already looks like a whirlwind swept through it. This is Danny's way of moving in, his trademark. He opens his suitcases and scatters everything within them. Socks. The French comic books he uses to learn my native language (and which he thoroughly enjoys). Shaving equipment. His Flatiron mandolin, handmade in Bozeman, Montana, and more portable than his violin. Upstairs, his tools of the trade have already devoured Asra's office—a laptop, a Palm Pilot with the special keyboard Danny uses when he's traveling, a variety of wired devices, a digital camera, stacks of expense receipts, and Super Conquérant notebooks, which he buys in bulk in papeteries in Paris.

Danny emerges from the bathroom in his shorts, cell phone in hand. He is one of those rare men whose eyes, those chestnut green eyes, always betray him; he cannot hide anything, especially when he's in a playful mood. I smile because I find him beautiful, and because my love for him is absolute. Without dropping the phone, he slips under the sheet. He crawls carefully over my body and reaches my rounded belly, where he starts a private conversation with our child in a tongue known only by the two of them. All I can gather is that he makes many promises for the moment the baby comes out. I weave my fingers through his thick brown hair.

Danny goes to the most unexpected hairstylists. Funny phrase, that. The more picturesque the barbershop, the happier Danny is. Most of the time the barbers don't speak English, but this way one is always assured of a surprising result. This is Danny's way of facing the world: with trust. When we moved to Bombay in October 2000, the first thing he did was go to the barber on our small street. The fellow might have been cutting a white boy's hair for the first time in his entire life, but he had a great ancient barber chair with a dirty white leather seat and red armrests. I sat on the bench just behind Danny, following the action in the mirror. Everything was silent except for the drone of the flies and the snipping of the scissors. Suddenly I realized women were not supposed to be here. Well, blame it on the cultural gap, I thought; I'm staying. The barber began massaging Danny's head so vigorously that it whipped back and forth. Danny looked stricken with shyness, and he fought hard to avoid me in the mirror. I nervously laughed so hard that tears came to my eyes. But they turned into real tears when I was startled by the awareness that we were actually going to live right here, on this very street, which was filled with rats, and where women weren't welcome, and where everyone seemed stern and stiff and cold. Where I was going to be a foreigner. An outsider.

Danny is still talking to "Embryo," as we call him—I think he is telling Embryo that he will be a boy. We found out the day before coming to Karachi, at a sophisticated clinic in Islamabad, Pakistan's capital, where they not only perform prenatal sonograms but claim to be able to influence the gender of the baby.

"BOY! IT'S A BOY! WHOO HOO!! Rock n Roll!! F-in A, man! We BAD, dude, We F-ing BAD!!!" Danny emailed Danny Gill. "Don't get me wrong, a girl would be great too. But IT'S A BOY! HOWOOOO! HOWOOOOO! BOYS RULE!!!"

I actually feel a little strange about carrying the male sex inside of me. When I tell Danny this, his eyes light up, as they always do when he's about to crack a joke. "You know, honey," he says, "that's how it all started . . ."

This morning Danny is more solemn. "It's incredible how much you can love somebody you haven't even met yet," he marvels. He says he wants to study the whole *Encyclopaedia Britannica* to be able to answers those questions kids never stop asking, like "How can you keep the sky from falling?"

Danny gets up and finishes dressing. His glasses give him a serious look, and when he works, he always dresses with understated elegance. He might have a little weakness for beautiful ties, but he doesn't look anything like a *baroudeur,* one of those swashbuckling journalists in their ready-for-action safari jackets.

I have a cold. It is already 95 degrees, but I have a cold and a headache, and there will be a dinner party here tonight, and I don't feel up to doing much of anything. It will take all my energy to prepare for the interview I have to tape for French radio with the director of an organization that tries to protect women from domestic violence. As in India, where the horrifying problem has received more attention, domestic abuse is rife here, with shocking numbers of wives being beaten by their husbands, or worse—attacked with acid, even burned alive.

Danny's schedule today is especially hectic, with meetings stacked up like planes over a crowded airport. It is always this way on the final day of an assignment; there are so many more interviews to conduct, so many more leads to pursue. Among other appointments, he's meeting with a cyber-crime expert, someone at the U.S. consulate, and a representative of the Pakistani Federal Investigation Agency (FIA). He has meetings with the Civil Aviation Authority director to talk about border surveillance as Pakistan tries to prevent terrorists from turning Karachi into their safe haven. Most pressing of all, he is investigating links between Richard C. Reid, the pitifully ugly "shoe bomber," and a radical Muslim cleric in Karachi.

Since Reid was thwarted in his attempt to blow up a Paris-to-Miami flight on December 22, several facts have been established, in particular this: Reid was acting on orders from someone within the Al Qaeda network in Pakistan, and very possibly in this city. Originally, Reid was to fly on December 21, but he was questioned so extensively at the Paris airport, his plane left without him. He then emailed someone in Pakistan and asked, "I missed my plane, what should I do?"

The anonymous reply: "Try to take another one as soon as possible."

Who was the man in Pakistan? *The Boston Globe* reported that Reid had visited the Karachi home of Sheikh Mubarak Ali Shah Gilani, an apparently respected spiritual leader. But was Gilani more than a spiritual adviser to Reid? Was it he who ordered Reid onto the Paris-to-Miami flight? After weeks of trying to track down Gilani through intermediaries, Danny finally seems to have secured an interview with him. They are to meet early this evening.

Danny will be accompanied on his morning round of appointments by a new "fixer," a man named Saeed. The fixer is the lifeblood of the correspondent. In regions where everything from government speeches to body language must be deciphered, they serve as multidimensional translators. Navigators, too. Saeed is not getting off to a good start. He's just called to say that he's lost. This worries Asra. "What kind of fixer is that, who doesn't even know his way around Karachi?" Saeed is a reporter at *Jang,* the major Urdu newspaper. The paper claims about two million readers, which, as Danny notes, is about as many copies as *The Wall Street Journal* sells; comparisons stop there, though. Saeed finally arrives an hour or so late. What is most impressive about him, besides his Western-style checked shirt and pleated trousers, is how jittery he is.

Once Danny leaves, our big house falls into silence. Across the street, parrots of a startling green color talk away, offering a welcome change from the cynical chuckling of the hooded black crows that provide unavoidable company in southern Asia. In the main room, Nasrin crouches on the floor, gathering dust with a handmade broom of twigs tied up with rope. Her daughter, Kashva, follows her like a little shadow. I scare the girl in spite of my attempts to befriend her, but she is fascinated by Danny, who is always more attractive to children than I am.

My headache is frightening. I think with nostalgia about the days when aspirin was permissible. I return to our room to rest a bit, and to daydream about Danny, who is out reporting in the city. I love the way the shirt he so carefully irons in the morning invariably winds up rumpled and falling out of his trousers by early afternoon. Danny erupts into people's offices, his hands always too full, juggling Palm Pilot and pads and pens and documents spilling out of manila envelopes. He wins people over so naturally. I think it is a subtle combination of his boyishness and good manners. Or is it because Danny never lies?

In his early days at the *Journal,* Danny became known for his delightful A-heds, the quirky articles the paper runs in the middle of the front page. He wrote about the world's biggest carpet being woven in Iran ("This is a small town in search of a really big floor"). In Astrakhan he wrote about caviar merchants who are increasing the caviar supply by injecting sturgeons with hormones to make them produce more eggs, which can then be scooped out during a sort of fish cesarean section ("Thus was stitch-free sturgeon surgery born"). Danny can spin unexpected tales straight out of the ordinary.

But I really admire the way Danny has begun to go deeper, further, with his reporting in recent years. The territory he now explores is less certain. He weaves his way through a world filled with narrow, conflicting views. He peers down alleyways, connects the dots, explains the butterfly effect—how the slightest movement in one place can have massive consequences somewhere else. I see Danny growing and taking responsibility as a writer and as a man. He is becoming more genuinely concerned about a world he embraces ambitiously. He makes me believe in the power of journalism.

A year ago in Bombay, influenced by the spiritual heft of India, I rolled my office chair next to Danny's desk and asked him which value he considered most essential—in other words, what did he see as his personal religion? I didn't mean a religion inherited from a tradition, but the values he placed above all else. Danny, who was then working on an article about pharmaceutical products, told me he understood and promised he would think it over. A few minutes later, he rolled his matching chair next to mine. "Ethics," he declared with a triumphant air. "Ethics and truth."

In a few days, that conviction was put to the test when we arrived in the state of Gujarat in northern India. The region had suffered a massive earthquake, and casualties were considerable. Neither of us had ever reported a natural disaster, and as we came closer to the epicenter, the horror almost overwhelmed us. The earth's crust seemed to have crumbled under the force; it was easy to see that hundreds of victims were buried in the rubble. We watched mutely as a corpse was extracted. The smell of death was everywhere.

I was working as part of a reporting team for a French publication. When I kicked in my file, one of the staff writers didn't find my descriptions "colorful enough" and proceeded to invent a series of scintillating details. Back in Bombay, Danny and I had dinner with him. The man was a senior reporter, but all he could talk about was the contempt with which he viewed journalism. He talked about illusions and lies, about news as spectacle. He seemed totally indifferent to any sense of responsibility, to any regard for truth. He seemed half dead.

After the meal, Danny slipped away to his desk, where, depressed, he sat for a long time with his head in his hands. He had already written an article about the economic consequences of the earthquake, but he hadn't been able to shake either the stench of decomposing bodies or the feeling that he'd failed to adequately, truthfully describe what he'd witnessed. So he wrote a follow-up:

What is India's earthquake zone really like? It smells. It reeks. You can't imagine the odor of several hundred bodies, decaying for five days as search teams pick away at slabs of crumbled buildings in this town. . . . Numbers of dead are thrown about—25,000, 100,000—but nobody really knows. And it isn't just the number that explains why the world media are here. AIDS will kill more Indians this year but get less coverage here. In India's Orissa state, reports are emerging of starvation from drought. In Afghanistan, refugees are freezing to death in camps. But an earthquake is sudden death, a much more compelling story. . . .

Lying on our bed in Asra's unlikely house, waiting for my headache to subside, I flip desultorily through a notebook I started writing three weeks ago, when we were last here. We celebrated New Year's Eve with Asra and her young lover, who took us to countless parties of very little interest, where everyone was dressed in black, as in New York or Bombay. In the car, between destinations, I took notes (the irregularity of my handwriting evidence of The Lover's increasingly high spirits):

Karachi, December 31st, 2001, 22:45. Three journalists about to spend New Years in Karachi. All three in love. Happy. . . . Tense about what's about to happen in 2002? Not a single word spoken indicating worries. If bin Laden's name is mentioned, it is for jokes only.

I arrived from Paris this morning. I went half way across the globe to be together with my loving husband and my coming baby. I brought some cheese from my fine food store in Montmartre and some scotch for Danny in a little bottle.

This guy is driving like a nut. . . .

Danny is back before four P.M. for a brief visit. As usual, I run into his arms and bury my face in his neck. I stay there, wanting to get drunk on his smell, wanting to feel some of his sweat. I do not like to be separated from him. Sometimes, after I've gone somewhere, I find him at the front door waiting for my return. He takes me in his arms and tells me how much he has missed me. He squeezes me tight with one hand, and with the other, he caresses my face, calling me "My wife, my life."

Occasionally I like to be separated from him for a few days just to savor this feeling we have—painful but delicious—when the one we love is absent. Just for the pleasure of finding him again when he comes to pick me up at the airport. Of reading the emails he sends me from a stop in transit, for the mere pleasure of hearing him tell me, "I'm on my way." Only when I am back with him do I feel whole.

Conventionally speaking, I am not a good spouse. I can't sew or iron. I can cook only one dish, and I never remember to buy toilet paper. The good news is that Danny doesn't seem to notice (except for the toilet paper). Our complicity grows richer every day, made out of trying moments, new challenges, true joys. Danny loves to be proud of me. Last October, at a film festival in Montreal, I won an award for a controversial documentary I made for French and German public television about Israel's use of genetic screening. Under Israel's Law of Return, almost any Jew has the right to return to the ancient homeland. But how do you make sure someone is actually Jewish? To determine who qualifies, Israeli authorities have used DNA testing to examine applicants' genetic makeup. My film explored the political and sociological implications of this process, which are confusing and disturbing. The moment he heard the news, Danny, who was in Kuwait, shot me an email: "My Baby's an award-winner! signed, Proud Husband."

It is time for all of us to get moving. I'm running late for my interview with the domestic-violence expert; Asra has errands to run before the dinner party; Danny must get over to the headquarters of Cybernet, an internet service provider, to see what information he can gather on Richard C. Reid's email exchange. Then he will move on to two more appointments before, at last, his rendezvous with the elusive Sheikh Gilani. We scurry through the house, tossing our tools into our bags—tape recorders, cell phones, special notepads, Palms. How is it that in a house this big you can still get in one another's way?

Asra calls over to the Sheraton Hotel to line up a car for each of us. In Karachi you don't fool around. Conventional protocol decrees that you hire a trustworthy car and driver to take you on your rounds and wait at each stop. Although he has traveled all over the world and reported from some of its more dangerous corners, Danny is a believer in playing it safe. He is by nature a cautious man. When we moved to Bombay, he drove our car dealer crazy by insisting that seat belts be installed in the backseat of our gray Hyundai Santro. *In the backseat?* They thought it was cute; he felt it was imperative.

The Sheraton has no car to send over. This has never happened before. Asra tries another local service that rents out cars and drivers, but there, too, the wait will be long—at least twenty minutes. If we wait that long, Danny will miss his first appointment, which will derail his second appointment and threaten the third. In desperation, we send Shabir, the house servant, out past the guardhouse to hail two cabs at the corner. As if it will make one come faster, Danny impatiently stands on his toes and hops up and down. He repeatedly checks the fancy silver watch I gave him for his last birthday, his thirty-eighth. At last Shabir reappears on his bicycle, leading two taxis. I signal to Danny to take the first, since he is in the greater hurry. After he tosses his bag in, he cups my neck with his free hand, pulls me to him, and kisses my cheek. Then he dives into the backseat of the cab.

In a matter of seconds, Danny is gone.

Chapter Two

I cook at best twice a year, and always the same dish, the only one my Cuban mother, Marita, could convince me to learn. Her *picadillo* is a perfectly balanced chili, comforting and surprising, with briny bites of capers and sweet raisins hiding in the ground beef and tomatoes and onions. In this Muslim country, I'm unable to buy the pork I usually add, but tonight everything else will be there—red beans if there are no black-eyed peas, plantains, avocados, white rice. This is the right dish, I think, to bring a touch of Latin brio to the heaviness of Karachi, and to celebrate our impending departure. For months we've focused on terrorism, war, ethnic and religious hatred. We've been immersed in it, and we need to come up for air.

Tonight, at Asra's house on Zamzama Street, we will be entertaining some of her new friends, most of whom she's met through The Lover. These are young, handsome, moneyed Pakistanis—financial analysts for multinational corporations, brokers, players in the high-tech world. Asra is particularly pleased that one of her guests is a feudal lord, "a real one." He is a young man born under an old star, the scion of one of the families that has controlled this territory since British colonialists carved it up over two hundred years ago. To be sure, the modern world has chipped away at the old feudal system, and it has evolved since the relatively recent formation of Pakistan. But it strikes me as barbaric that feudal lords continue to exercise a quasi-divine authority over tenants and sharecroppers, limiting access to education, a decent legal system, and, of course, land. Our guest's family, we've heard, owns eighty thousand acres in this province—remarkable, since land reform supposedly limits ownership to 150 acres.

The young man is engaged but permitted only chaperoned visits with his fiancée between seven and nine P.M., so he will be coming alone. As for the others, I am skeptical about the lot of them, but Asra is lonely, and she is trying to make a life for herself in Karachi. Two days ago she was so miserable that she seemed on the verge of falling apart, ready to leave the country altogether. What made her decide to stay was the delivery boy who brought her the chicken biryani she ordered. He'd sworn he would deliver Asra's order in a half hour, and she'd doubted him. "Oh, sure, *insha'allah*," she said with a defeated shrug, God willing. But he'd made it with two minutes to spare.

"You are amazing!" Asra told him. "You saved me from leaving Pakistan." The poor delivery boy didn't have a clue what she was talking about, but her point was this: "I took it as a sign from God. He gave me hope that this society is actually capable of being functional." Thus she decided to stay.

Asra, I have learned, obeys a logic all her own.

Perhaps it's because of the fracture between her two identities. Born in India to Muslim parents and raised in Morgantown, West Virginia, she bears the psychic scars common to all who have pulled their roots out of one land only to discover that transplanting them in another is not easy. In Morgantown (voted "the best small city east of the Mississippi"), she helped her father open the sole mosque in town. Not easy. In 1992 she agreed to return to Pakistan and marry a Muslim. Also not easy, by any stretch of the imagination.

The father of the man she married sat Asra down during her honeymoon and outlined her new identity: "First, you are Muslim. Second, you are Pakistani. Third, you are Urdu-speaking." Asra felt like a cat on a leash. She tried to be a good new bride. She made the rounds, saying little and trying to look pretty in gold Stuart Weitzman pumps.

The marriage lasted less than three months.

Asra was again living in West Virginia when, as she put it, "the region where I was born suddenly became the center of the world," and she felt compelled to return and report the story. But she was on leave from *The Wall Street Journal,* so she lined up assignments from two publications—the on-line magazine Salon.com, and the Morgantown (W. Va.) *Dominion Post.*

The articles for her hometown paper are composed as letters to the classmates of Samir and Safiyyah, her beloved niece and nephew, and they star Merve and Blink. Merve is a small stuffed unicorn; Blink is ... well, that's hard to say. Maybe a donkey. These raggedy animals have traveled with Asra all over South Asia, into the Himalayas, over to Allahabad. They've even been to Afghanistan, though not for very long.

As soon as journalists were permitted to cross the Pakistan-Afghanistan border in late October and November, Asra decided that she, too, should report from the front, which meant, among other things, filing the Kabul-bound adventures of Merve and Blink for the *Dominion Post.* Asra's dispatches are always illustrated by a photo of Merve and Blink on location, so one kilometer into Afghanistan, Asra paused to pull the critters from her bag for their photo op. When she looked up, menacing Afghans were aiming Kalishnikovs at her head. A short time later, her guides began acting surly and rough, contemptuous. What she saw in their eyes terrified her. She was a woman traveling alone, in a country that had not seen exposed female faces in over five years. She turned back and cried tears of frustration all the way to Pakistan.

Asra may be irresponsible sometimes, but I must admit I find her fantasy delightful. Who else would risk her life to take stuffies to Afghanistan?

Danny is still at his afternoon appointment, but I've finished interviewing the domestic-violence expert. When I emerge from my meeting, I find the massively built taxi driver who brought me here waiting out front. When Asra put me in the cab earlier, she demanded authoritatively, *"Kheyal karoe"*—take care of her—and he apparently has every intention of doing so. For the most part, Pakistanis belong to one of four ethnic groups: Punjabi, Baluchi, Sindhi, or Pathan. My driver is a bearded Pathan, with staggering shoulders and a broad smile. At regular intervals, he earnestly studies me in the rearview mirror and asks, *"Teek hay?"*

Yes, I'm okay. My head still aches, but I'll live.

Asra and I need to shop for the dinner we're throwing tonight, so the kindly driver and I swing by Asra's to pick her up, then move on to Agha's, a grocery store frequented by foreigners and the Karachi elite. Shopping is much easier here than in Bombay; we find all the ingredients we need. While filling up our basket, we discuss the virulent anti-American sentiment in the air. It's getting on our nerves. It's systematic, little constrained by fact or analysis. It pours out of people, and not just Islamic conservatives. It is a comfortable anger, an easy conversation piece for The Lover's set, as they relax around a weekend campfire on French Beach along the Arabian Sea. Tonight at our party, in their Armani suits, AmEx corporate cards in their wallets, they will not miss an opportunity to vent, regardless of our feelings. It is turning Asra and me into the most unlikely pair of flag-wavers, even as we're aware that Americans are doing an equally good job of reducing culture to a caricature.

As we shop, Danny phones. He's finished his meeting at Cybernet. "I think I've found the shoe-bomber's email address," Danny reports excitedly. He's en route to his seven P.M. meeting and will be a bit late to dinner but home by nine P.M., he figures. He loves me a lot. He calls me "baby."

The conversation is clipped. At dusk in Karachi, everything grows rushed. The street vendors pack up, traffic congestion gets worse, believers quit the mosques, and the town, which is overwhelmingly masculine, gets even more crowded. I can picture Danny somewhere in this mass of human beings, eager to record just one more voice before his day is over. I smile at his boyish intensity.

Earlier, he met with Randall Bennett, regional security officer at the U.S. consulate in Karachi. The consulate is a cluster of buildings set off the road next to the Marriott Hotel, tucked behind concrete barriers. There, Danny solicited Bennett's advice for his meeting with Sheikh Gilani.

"Will it be safe?" Danny asked.

"I stated that the only way he should go would be if it were held in an active public gathering place," Randall will recall later. "He stated that they planned to meet at the Village Restaurant, and that he felt comfortable with that. I concurred."

Danny then met with Jameel Yusuf, a highly successful Karachi businessman who heads up an unusual organization called the Citizen-Police Liaison Committee (CPLC). Yusuf formed the group in 1989 when he grew infuriated by the wave of kidnappings for ransom menacing the business community. The Karachi police were ineffectual in combating the threat, so Yusuf mobilized fellow businessmen, and they transformed themselves into a sophisticated band of crime fighters. The CPLC has tackled 275 kidnapping cases since its inception, and kidnappings have been reduced by 75 percent.

If anyone understands risks in Karachi, it's Yusuf. "Is meeting Gilani safe?" Danny asked him.

"As long as you stay in a public place," Yusuf answered.

Danny then called Asif, the fixer he used back in Islamabad. It was Asif who originally put Danny in touch with the contact who promised to lead him to the cleric. At six-thirty P.M., Danny asked Asif, "How dangerous is it to see Gilani?"

"It depends on where you meet," Asif told him. "Is Mariane going?"

Danny directed his taxi driver to drop him off at the Village Restaurant by the Hotel Metropole. Back in the 1960s and '70s, before former prime minister Zulfiqar Ali Bhutto tried to appease the fundamentalists by cracking down on alcohol and clubs, the Metropole was *the* place to drink and dance. Today it is a sad hotel for low-budget travelers. It is here that Danny is to meet the man who will lead him to the elusive Sheik Mubarak Ali Shah Gilani.

* * *

After weeks of walking Pakistan's dust, I want to feel pretty tonight, like a woman. I pull from my luggage the one dress I can still fit into that is modest enough for Karachi. It is black, and over it falls a white crocheted chemise; I look not unlike a penguin. Asra slips into a pair of black nylon pants that have white Nike swooshes at the ankles. She owns ten pairs of these pants. They're perfect for hanging with the Pakistani elite—loose without being too loose, sleek enough to feel festive, especially with her fancy high heels.

We put on Springsteen's *Live* album, Asra lights candles, and I confront the mountain of ingredients waiting for me on the kitchen counter. Around eight P.M., I call Danny to check in. That's how we always proceed: If one of us goes alone to an appointment, the other calls every ninety minutes or so to check in and ensure all is well. His phone is off. There might be dozens of reasons for Danny to turn off his cell phone, but he doesn't usually. "Your correspondent cannot be reached at this moment. Please try again later," says the cheerily robotic, feminine voice, which then repeats the message in Urdu. I will come to detest that voice.

The guests begin to arrive. They walk in waving lit cigarettes, the men clean-shaven and beautifully tailored, the women elegant in black outfits, with proper pumps and modest makeup. I greet them, but I am distracted. They gather in the living room, their rapid Urdu and English punctuated by laughter. Most are childhood friends and marvelously comfortable in one another's company. As the guests settle back with bottles of Murree Brewery beer that we bought from a bootlegger, Asra busies herself in the dining room. I am in the kitchen seriously overcooking the *picadillo*. I have been calling Danny every fifteen minutes, and I keep getting the same damn message.

Asra leads the young feudal lord on a tour of the house. On the second floor she points to the sweet sitting room where she works. The room is bizarrely shaped, a parallelogram gone wrong. Her desk is one of the smallest rolltop desks I have ever seen, so small that Danny's ThinkPad looks beefy on it.

"So, this is the CIA cell?" the feudal lord asks with a guffaw.

Asra doesn't answer, but I don't think she finds his witticism any more amusing than I do when she tells me about it later. Why is there always this suspicion that reporters are spies? The feudal lord may have said it as a joke, but in a country as tense and paranoid as Pakistan, such an aside is never funny.

It is now ten o'clock. An impatient Lover appears by the stove. "Hey, everybody's got to work in the morning," he says. I realize that the sooner we usher our guests to the table, the sooner they'll be out the door. A few minutes later, I hardly hear the polite compliments of the diners gathered around the table. I play at eating and feel lucky—the guests expect little from me. Instinctually, I place my hands on my belly and, in my heart, unite the three of us—Danny, our child, and me. Tuning out the boisterous chatter, I pray, silently formulating *Nam Myoho Renge Kyo,* the Buddhist mantra I have chanted for more than eighteen years. To my intense relief, the guests eat quickly, and all but The Lover are gone by eleven P.M.

Ignoring the party's debris, we head to Asra's office to take stock. The Lover stretches out on one of the sofalike beds and pulls Asra down beside him. Holding her in his arms, he lights up some hash. In a pinched drawl, he says, "Maybe they've taken him to a *madrassa* where there are no phones. Or maybe he's out of town. When you get out of Karachi, you get out of reach. Happens."

He really irritates me. What he doesn't understand is that this has never happened, not in Kosovo or Saudi Arabia or Iran. No matter where Danny has been, he has always found a way to get to a phone and call me.

Asra and I leave the young man to his smoke and huddle before Danny's computer, searching for clues. We scan his calendar and emails. "Chaudrey Bashir Ahmad Shabbir," I read out loud. Asra writes down the name and phone number.

Bashir. Of course. He's the one who was to introduce Danny to Gilani.

We find several emails in Danny's archives from Bashir, under the email address "nobadmashi@yahoo.com." "That's weird," says Asra. "Why?"

"*Nobadmashi* means 'no wrongdoing' in Urdu."

The whole exchange is weird. We study the messages intently, not yet able to grasp their full significance. Bashir and Danny have obviously been in touch for a while. On January 16, when Danny and I were in Peshawar, Bashir wrote:

> Thank you very much for your articles—I enjoyed reading them and I have passed on the print-out to Shah Saab [Gilani]. He has now gone to Karachi for a few days and I am sure that when he returns we can go and see him. I am sorry to have not replied to you earlier, I was preoccupied with looking after my wife who has been ill. Please pray for her health.
>
> > Looking forward to seeing you,
> > Adaab,
> > Chaudrey Bashir Ahmad Shabbir

Three days later, Danny received another email, an uncommonly chatty one:

> Dear Mr Pearl,
>
> I'm so sorry to have been out of touch with you earlier . . . I've managed to misplace your phone-number . . . I think I gave you my older brother's number last time only to return home and find out he has sold it! We have applied for a home line and as soon as we pay the "relevant people" we will get it. Such is Pakistan! My wife is back home from hospital alhamdolillah and the whole experience was a real eye-opener. The poor people who fall ill here and have to go to the hospital have a really miserable and harassing time. It made me realize once again that our

family has a lot to be grateful for. The Shaikh says that gratitude is the essence of faith.

I spoke to the Shaikh's secretary yesterday and he told me that the Shaikh-Saab has read your articles and that you are welcome to meet him. However it will be a number of days before he returns from Karachi. If Karachi is in your program you are welcome to see him there. . . .

Learning this, Danny changed our plans and made Karachi part of our "program," even though we had been intending to leave the country very soon. Bashir responded to the news quickly:

It is sad you are leaving Pakistan so soon—I hope you have enjoyed your stay. I will arrange an appointment with the Shaikh in Karachi for you on Tuesday or Wednesday, depending on his time-table. . . . He will give me the number of one of his mureeds [disciples] whom you can call when you get there. The mureed will take you to see him. Please give the Sheikh my regards and respect and ask him to continue to remember me in his prayers.

Ah. So now we know Bashir was not the go-between Danny was meeting this afternoon. A *mureed* was. Who, then? Who, for that matter, is this sheikh? Does he even know his name is being used?

We Google "Gilani." For someone who has been described as the "secretive" leader of an "obscure Muslim sect," there's an awful lot online. Danny and I had, of course, discussed Gilani to a certain degree, but I didn't know that a 1998 U.S. State Department report defined his organization, Jamaat al-Fuqra, as "a terrorist group committed to waging jihad, or holy war, against the United States." Or that the FBI holds its members responsible for at least seventeen bombings and twelve murders in the States. Gilani founded the group in Brooklyn, New York, twenty-odd years ago, and since then, cells of radical Muslims, mostly African-Americans, have spread across the U.S. from rural corners of Virginia to the Colorado Rockies to the foothills of the Sierras in California. He has brought more than a hundred American disciples to Pakistan for religious and military training, and other supporters can be found in the Caribbean and Europe.

Did Danny know all this? Did he know that "terrorism specialists suspect that Fuqra is supported—or at least condoned—by influential Pakistani governmental officials"? Or that Gilani has been suspected of having ties to the terrorists who bombed the World Trade Center in 1993?

"Just because it's on the Internet doesn't mean it's true," Asra says, sensing my alarm.

I am frightened all the same. Gilani's hands are stained, directly or indirectly, with the blood of several victims. And our most plausible assumption is that Danny has been forcibly retained in a *madrassa* by this man or his subordinates.

The Lover's voice floats from the couch again. "They probably made him stay for the night. Those people are very hospitable."

I want to push him off his perch.

Asra tries to calm me. "Oh yes, I bet in the morning they'll feed him a Pakistani omelette with green peppers and onions, and give him some roti, and then send him home. He'll come home through the gate all pissed off that he wasn't allowed to call."

"I have to go to work in the morning," whines the thick-voiced Lover from his chaise.

"Go to bed," Asra says gently. "We'll get you up in time."

Danny has downloaded the January 6 *Boston Globe* article that prompted his pursuit of Gilani. In it, reporter Farah Stockman established the connection between Reid and the cleric. Nothing Stockman reported makes me any more sanguine.

"Over the years," Stockman wrote, "Gilani has sent young men to wage jihad against Indian rule in Kashmir, against Russians in Chechnya, Serbs in Bosnia, and to fight Israelis. He set up training camps in Abbotabad, Pakistan, about a three-hour drive from the capital, and other parts of the country." One of the places where Gilani's followers study and train is in Lahore, "on the eastern-most edge of Pakistan that has been home to a number of spiritual leaders, Kashmiri militants, and madrassas, schools that have groomed Taliban leaders."

" '[Reid] was there,' said [an] official, referring to Gilani's walled compound in Lahore. . . . A member of Gilani's large extended family also said that Reid had visited the home."

In the article, Stockman quoted Khalid Khawaja, a close friend of Gilani, who denied any connection between the two. " 'He is not a follower, and he is not known to any of the people within our system,' " Khawaja said of Reid.

The denial is pro forma, but the mention of the "close friend" chills us. Khawaja is a fascinating but dubious character, one of those people who seems to know everybody, at least in militant Islamist circles. A former Pakistani intelligence agent and air force officer, Khawaja loves nothing more than to entertain journalists, especially Americans. He loves to watch their faces when he tells them he is a friend of Osama bin Laden. Danny and I have interviewed Khawaja several times, as has Asra, and found him to be, in Danny's blunt terms, "Nice guy, but a bit of a psycho."

Danny and I met with him in Islamabad shortly after the 9/11 attacks, and more recently in early January, in an office he uses in a relatively empty house in a gated district apparently reserved for military. Asra visited him at his real home in September, when she was staying at her paternal aunt's house. "You might want to interview our neighbor," her aunt had said helpfully. "He's a religious man, a friend of bin Laden's and the Taliban. He fought with the Afghan resistance." And so, escorted by her aunt and uncle, Asra paid a call to Khalid Khawaja, and the three of them sat and listened politely as he ranted and raved about the righteousness of the Muslim jihad against America.

Asra would watch him every morning as, after prayers, he headed down the street, hands clasped behind his back, for a daily stroll around the little local park. One day she joined him, and as they walked, he described how he, along with the influential Pakistani-American businessman Mansur Ejaz and former CIA chief James Woolsey, had tried to hammer out an agreement that would have averted war between the United States and the Taliban. The effort failed.

Khawaja spun a similar story to Danny and me, and while we were never able to nail down all the facts, we were inclined to believe a part. But much of what Khawaja told us was total and ugly fabrication: "You know who was behind the attack on the World Trade Center and the Pentagon?" Khawaja asked us in September. "The Jews did it, the Mossad, it can only be them."

That was not the first time we'd been exposed to "the Jew theory." We'd heard it the day before from Hamid Gul. The director of Inter-Services Intelligence (ISI), Pakistani intelligence, from 1987 to 1989, Gul is considered the architect of the Afghan jihad, the man who masterminded the war financed by the U.S. Central Intelligence Agency and waged by the mujahideens against the Soviet occupiers. A decade ago, Gul was the most powerful man in the region; some called him the "godfather of the Taliban." But power, like an unfaithful mistress, had left him without turning back. New alliances had been formed, and Hamid Gul wasn't part of them.

I could feel the bitterness behind his assured diatribe. Gul manifested the same fanatical exaltation we saw in Khawaja, and in so many others we met in the days after September 11. It was a craving for revenge that had been unsatisfied for too long. It was a dominating and burning desire.

After an hour-long monologue during which Gul insisted that Osama bin Laden couldn't have had anything to do with the attacks, he had leaned in toward us conspiratorially. "Do you know," he said, "that the four thousand Jews who normally worked at the World Trade Center were all absent on that day?"

To the day I die, I will love the cool with which Danny responded. "Really?" he said, without any perceptible trace of irony.

The "theory" was that the perpetrators had secretly notified all the

Jewish workers in the Twin Towers so they would fail to show up for work and thereby be spared the terrible fate. The allegations apparently originated on Al Manar, the TV channel of Hezbollah, the Lebanese Islamist party, not long after 9/11. Once the ugly rumor hit the Internet, it found dedicated converts throughout the fundamentalist world.

In an article Danny filed just ten days after the attacks, he wrote, "A theory that Jews or Israelis engineered the September 11 attacks on the United States is gaining credibility among Muslim intellectuals, in a disturbing sign of how little globalization has bridged gaps in perception."

In Pakistan, Danny reported, pilots, scientists, and experts had gathered for analysis, and they had all concluded that the attacks could not have succeeded without the help of American intelligence services or the Israelis. "Pakistani air force officers casually opine that 'Mossad is the only one that could do it.' Respected newspapers in Saudi Arabia, Pakistan and the United Arab Emirates run news items suggesting authorities suspect some Israelis of involvement in the attack. . . . One Pakistani commentator told the BBC Friday that America's belligerent attitude 'gives credence' to conspiracy theories spreading on the Internet."

Here is the same old hatred, the kind that makes you wonder if humanity will ever draw the lessons of its own history. Still, Danny and I refuse to let it defeat us in our work as journalists. We see ourselves as tightrope walkers, careful and insistent in our quest to bridge the world. In his work, Danny struggles to keep free of dogma and allegiance. It's not easy to remain impartial, but it sharpens Danny's vision and independence. He doesn't represent a country or a flag, just the pursuit of truth. He is here to hold up a mirror and force people to look at themselves. What better way is there to respect humanity?

The Wall Street Journal never ran Danny's article on the Jewish conspiracy. Danny emailed his boss: "The story didn't run today and isn't on the Sked 1. Please tell me this is because it got overlooked somehow, or there wasn't any space, and not because people are scared to tell our readers what people here are really thinking!"

He was more emphatic in a message to a friend: "Pisses me off that we're ready to pick apart the Eastern psyche to no end, except if it might offend our Jewish readers. . . . Maybe I'm just paranoid," he concluded, "or engaging in my own Jewish-conspiracy theory."

Who knows what theory Khalid Khawaja was preparing to concoct when, in the course of lecturing us during our meeting, he suddenly sprang a tangential question. "What are you?" he asked Danny. "A Christian?"

Without a moment's hesitation, Danny answered, "I'm Jewish."

The answer startled Khawaja. "*Are* you?"

We were prepared for the question, if not this day, then some other. Whenever you travel, and especially in less developed countries, people try to categorize you, neatly, swiftly. Whose side are you on? Or, more pertinently, *Are you my enemy?* Am I yours? In our case, this has always been an irrelevant question with only one answer: We have come here as journalists.

Both of Danny's parents are Jewish. His mother, Ruth, was born in Baghdad, Iraq, a descendant of Iraqi Jews dating back either to the destruction of Solomon's temple (586 B.C.) or somewhat later—the second exile (70 A.D.). His father, Judea, was born in Israel, but his family were relatively newly returned to the Middle East. Judea's grandfather, a Hasidic Jew, moved to Israel in 1924, after selling all his possessions in Poland. He joined twenty-five families in establishing a super-kosher dairy in a new village called Benei Beraq. Judea's mother fled Poland and arrived in Israel on the eve of Chanukah, 1935. (Her parents, brother, and sister stayed behind and were sent to Auschwitz. Only one sister survived.) Ruth and Judea met at the Technion-Israel Institute of Technology in Haifa and, after marrying, moved to the United States, where Danny was born in 1963.

It's a rich history, and Danny is proud of it. He is not a religious man, but he once told me that if he ever did feel the need to speak to God, he would turn first to the religion his ancestors practiced. Still, he resists being defined by his heritage—or by anything else. Yes, he sees himself as a Jew and he sees himself as an American. But Danny is also a journalist and a musician. The way I see him, Danny is a free man.

Around midnight a car pulls up on the street. Asra and I run onto the white-speckled veranda, praying we'll hear that too-loud doorbell. We don't.

If Danny isn't back by two A.M., we will call the authorities.

But which? Corruption is endemic among the Pakistani police; that's a story Danny and I have been researching for months. In fact, it's possible that calling the police is precisely the wrong thing to do now. Can we call Pakistani intelligence? ISI, Inter-Services Intelligence—the role of the agency is so murky, frightening. We've heard it called "a kingdom within a state"; we know that little happens in this country without ISI knowing about it. But what if they're involved? Should we call the U.S. consulate first?

We decide to place our faith in our own kind. Asra calls a reporter for *Jang* whom she met in Peshawar. He has news, but not about Danny. Ghulam Hasnain, a stringer for *Time* and CNN, is missing. Connection? Hard to know. "Can you give us his home number? Can we talk to his wife? Compare notes with her?" Asra asks.

"It's too late to call," the *Jang* reporter says. "She shouldn't be disturbed."

It is after midnight, and he is heading over to the Karachi Press Club to spend the night. When he gets there, he'll query his colleagues, but he doubts he'll learn much. We suspect he's right, especially if the rumors we've heard are true: that most of the Press Club night owls are there to watch porn videos smuggled in from the airport in Dubai. (You can buy anything in Dubai.) The journalist invites us to check in with him, and Asra takes him at his word. She calls him all night long, waking him up each time. He never has any news.

We phone the American consulate. A sleep-heavy voice answers, "Corporal Bailey, how can I help you?"

Fearful of sounding fearful, we explain the situation with exaggerated calm. But no matter which tone or words we use, we cannot make Corporal Bailey understand that we are serious and that this is an emergency. He clearly expects Danny to reappear at dawn, drunk and disoriented, having had too much of a good time too far from home. Such calls are not rare at a consulate, even in a Muslim country. "Call back at six A.M.," Corporal Bailey commands wearily. "Ask for Randall Bennett, regional security officer."

Bennett. That's one of the men Danny met with today. At least he'll know who Danny is.

Huddled in front of the small secretary, Asra and I do not utter a single unnecessary word. I can feel she is with me. Our two brains are turning at a thousand RPM, but our actions are controlled and our voices do not shake. I call and call Danny's phone; it is never answered. We alert *The Wall Street Journal*. I watch Asra study my rounded belly as she explains the situation, gingerly, almost soothingly, to foreign editor John Bussey, Danny's boss.

Bussey asks us the question we had hoped to ask him: "What do you think we should do?"

We need allies here, urgently. For the moment we seem to have none.

"The Musharraf government is trying to be clean," Asra says. "The military can be trusted. I think." The other day, when Asra rescued a stray kitten from the clutches of the neighbor's son, she spoke at length with the boy's mother. During their conversation, the woman revealed that she is related to the corps commander for Karachi, President General Pervez Musharraf's top military representative in the province. "She'll wake up with the morning prayer," Asra says. "We can go over to her house and ask her to introduce us."

Bussey is going to send us Danny's fellow foreign correspondent Steve LeVine from his post in Kazakhstan. Steve has lived in this country and knows it well. It will be good to have him here.

I keep talking to Danny in my head. "We're going to get you out of this," I promise, but I have to acknowledge that we have few clues to go on, and what my intuition is telling me is not reassuring. I refuse to let my emotions go, I refuse to let in the fear that's pressing on me. My eyes have developed a tic, and I'm very cold, which is a peculiar pleasure because it is an acceptable pain, compared the fear that Danny might be harmed. I'm reminded of the old joke about the man who bangs his head against a concrete wall because it distracts him from his terrible toothache.

It is pitch black out. There are still several hours before the muezzin's call, marking the end of the night. I would give everything I have to be with Danny at this moment, wherever he might be. I know he is not free to move as he pleases. Why didn't I pay closer attention to the nature of his rendezvous? Why wasn't I more vigilant? Why didn't I go with him? I wasn't feeling that sick. Why . . .

Stop, I tell myself. Stop this chain of thought. Regrets will just waste energy—don't question reality.

If this goes on much longer, I will have to inform Danny's parents. They are worriers, and it will be painful, but they have to know. A few months ago, when we were visiting Paris, Judea found an item on the Internet claiming that two hundred Arabs had attacked people of Jewish origin on the Champs-Élysées. Danny could never confirm this. Nevertheless, it concerned Judea enough for him to exhort us to leave Paris. In his email to Danny, he added pointedly, "This is your sober dad speaking, not panicky Mom."

In the Pearl family, it is usually Ruth who sounds the alarm. When Asra and I scan Danny's emails for clues to his disappearance, we chance on a mother-son exchange from yesterday morning. Danny wrote, "We're in Asra's beautiful house in Karachi, feeling like we're on holiday—though I'm actually working on the same old terrorism story. . . ." Ruth had recently undergone surgery, and he asked, "Everything okay with you?"

"Yes," she replied, "as good as new." Then she added: "I read that stress, especially in the 26th week of the pregnancy, when the brain develops, can cause autism in the child, take good care of your wife and make sure not to stress her out (including not to tell her about this). . . . Love, Mom."

Before dialing the number of their house in Los Angeles, I isolate myself in Asra's room, trying to calm my frantic heartbeat. I dig the fingernails of one hand into the back of the other. Physical pain will help me to get myself together. Where did I ever learn that? Ruth and Judea get on the line together, as usual, she on a telephone in the kitchen while he sits in his office on the first floor. They ask me precise questions that I try to answer as best I can. "We'll wait to hear from you," they say.

I know they are dying of fear, but they control their feelings. They are courageous people. Before hanging up, however, Ruth asks me the question that, I am certain, was the first to cross her mind: "Does anyone know we are Jewish? Does anybody know about us?"

I tell her, "Don't worry. Nobody knows."

But that isn't the truth, I remind myself as I hang up the phone. Someone does know: Khalid Khawaja. Former ISI agent, friend of Gilani, friend of Osama bin Laden, or so he claims.

It is 5:58 A.M. We have decided to call Khawaja, not because he can be trusted but because we cannot figure out who can be, and we might as well get as close to Gilani as we know how. "*As-salam alaykum,*" Asra says. "Peace be upon you."

"*Wa'alaykum as-salam,*" answers Khawaja.

Asra doesn't waste any time. "You know my friend Danny Pearl. He was scheduled to meet Sheikh Gilani last night at seven, and he never returned. We need your help in finding him."

"Hah," says Khawaja. This is clearly some sort of setup—"maybe another CIA conspiracy"—because Gilani would never agree to meet with a journalist, much less a foreigner.

Asra tries her best not to lose patience with Khawaja, because we need him. She pleads with him to put politics aside and help for my sake. "His wife is sitting here. She's been up all night, she's so worried, and she's expecting a baby."

Khawaja cannot resist the temptation to preach. "Think about the plight of the Afghan women whose husbands are being killed by America's war on the Taliban," he says. "Think about the innocent children and women who are being killed by American bombs. Think about the Pakistanis who are missing, too, and you do not hear about them. Think about—"

The muezzin's call to morning prayer cuts through the air and saves us from Khawaja's litany. A furious Asra slams down the phone and lets go a mouthful of curse words; I add a few of my own. She covers her head with a *dupatta,* and we slip outside, where it is still dark, because the morning prayers start before sunrise and the light hasn't emerged yet. In the dim glow of the lamppost, we make our way to the neighbor's house and press the buzzer anxiously.

No one answers. We press it again and again, then run back to our shared boundary wall and boost ourselves up in order to peer into windows, searching for signs of stirring. We feel self-conscious, vaguely guilty, like kids trying to steal apples from a neighboring tree.

Asra goes back to the front door and resumes buzzing, and a woman finally emerges on the veranda, with a *dupatta* over her head, as if she was about to pray or has just finished. She is a silhouette in the dark; we can barely see her features as she stands unmoving, listening to Asra's appeal for help.

At last, she speaks. "First I have to go work," she says. She works at a local school. "I will try to reach him when I get back."

Hearing this, we know we cannot expect any help from this woman.

I walk away while she's still speaking. In the office, I wake The Lover. He leaves the house without combing his hair, without even asking if our inquiries have yielded any result.

It is late enough to try Randall Bennett at the U.S. consulate. Bennett confirms that he met with Danny yesterday. He doesn't reveal any alarm, but advises us to immediately call the authorities, whom he considers like "trusted brothers."

"Call Tariq Jamil, deputy inspector general. He conducts police operations on the field. Then contact Jameel Yusuf at the Citizen-Police Liaison Committee. We're the best of friends."

It takes Tariq Jamil under a minute to understand what is happening. "Give me your address, I'll come right away."

When we hang up, Asra and I look at each other as if we've heard really good news. What else can we do? It has been twelve hours since I heard from Danny.

Chapter Three

MY FATHER was a brilliant man, a mathematician and speaker of seven languages. But he was also a sad man, and he committed suicide when I was nine. My mother, on the other hand, oh, she loved life. She loved people and music and she loved, above all, to dance. When my mother danced, nothing mattered except the pulse of the moment. You could see her absorb the rhythm and start moving in a subtle way, quietly sensual. An involuntary smile would cross her lips as if she could not refrain from sharing her pleasure, and she would radiate serenity and contentment. Those dances of fulfillment illuminated my childhood.

In recent years, my mother had become a well-known figure in Paris, because of the clandestine Cuban parties she threw on Sundays, parties so popular that four to five hundred people would line up to get in. Rightists, leftists, old men in suits and hats and shiny shoes, women in white gloves and skirts with flounces. Some people brought children, others brought dogs. Everybody danced.

That was my mother's mission, to banish the loneliness that could sweep through Paris over a weekend, and to gather everyone under the banner of the Cuban music she so loved. Marita based her parties on *guateques,* the traditional peasant fiestas in Cuba. Every Sunday she'd occupy a space—a garage, say—and turn it into a kind of movie set. She'd suspend a laundry rope from the ceiling and hang items of clothing—T-shirts, underwear, you name it—as a reminder of the community houses of Havana called *solares*. She'd set up bars serving *mojitos* and tables laden with roasted pork and manioc, arroz con pollo. Musicians of all caliber would climb onstage and rip into song:

> *Sanduguera tú te vas por encima del nivel*
> Party girl, you're just going over the top
> *No te muevas más así*
> Please stop moving like this

From noon to midnight my mother would pass from one person to the next, triumphant, a regular woman who had achieved a humble yet noble ambition.

I was dancing with my mother when I spotted Danny for the first time in the fall of 1998. He had already spotted me. It was in a studio apartment facing the Élysée Palace. A mutual friend had thrown herself a birthday party, and Danny was standing alone, a glass of whiskey in his hand, surrounded by a joyful crowd. Wearing a conservative dark blue suit and small round glasses, he watched us, my mother and me, absorbed in our dance. He was fascinated by our complicity. He looked to me like an elegant extraterrestrial casting a delighted but somewhat perplexed glance at the earthly specimens. His body bent slightly forward, as if he wanted to give us something, or perhaps, catch something we might have.

"You're both journalists. You should meet," someone said in introduction. Danny gave me his business card. I was impressed—by the gesture, and by what I read: "Daniel Pearl, Middle East Correspondent, *The Wall Street Journal*." By contrast, the information on my business cards seemed pitiful, but I handed him one just the same. It only mentioned my name, Mariane van Neyenhoff, and a phone number.

He told me his home base was London, but he traveled constantly, with an avowed preference for Iran. I told him about the radio program I had developed and now hosted for Radio France International, *Migrations,* built around the concept that international migrants are both the great adventurers and the real citizens of the twenty-first century. Ah, another coincidence! He happened to be working on a story about immigrants in Saudi Arabia.

Leaning against a wall, we discussed how people who leave their homeland also leave their frame of reference. How foreigners are eternally seen as intruders. How, as the world becomes a global village, it has been necessary to evolve new roots.

Danny's eyes traveled between my mother, still dancing, and me, singing my theories to him. "You should come to Iran, report from there," he said, flashing his shy but attractive smile.

"Forget it," I said. "The station has no money to send me there."

"Maybe I can help you figure out a way to come."

It was only when he was ready to leave that I noticed Danny was accompanied. His friend was my exact physical opposite, tall, blond, and blue-eyed. A German lingerie designer, I later learned. With an air of possession, she took Danny with her, leaving the smell of her perfume behind.

Two weeks later, Danny sent me two of his articles detailing the situation of immigrants in Saudi Arabia. His brief note renewed the invitation to Iran. I could picture him, dressed in that same suit and tie, casting the same charming and curious look, sailing through exotic countries. He was an amusing mystery to me, and I entertained a desire to see him again, in spite of the woman with him that night.

Sometime later, Danny made another brief appearance. On a layover between two flights, he escaped from Charles de Gaulle Airport to bring me a book he thought I should read, *Shah of Shahs,* by the Polish journalist Ryszard Kapuscinski, about the last shah of Iran and the events leading up to the 1977 Islamic revolution.

"You know," he said, "I'm trying to get a house in Tehran," and I thought, Man, this guy is crazy, which is too bad, because I like him.

Then he was gone, and I curled up with the book, and I became entranced. I thought, Well, he might be crazy, but I've never read such original and vivid and free-flowing journalism. That Danny so loved the book—and thought I would love it, too—made me think,

God, we really do have something in common. What it was I couldn't yet see. But it was strong.

Returning to Paris from a trip to Cuba, I reciprocated with a letter, an extensive one scribbled on a handful of paper scraps. I told him about the pope's visit to the island, remarkable because until his visit, Catholics were liable to be jailed in Cuba. I wrote about the scramble for greenbacks in a country where anti-imperialistic diatribes still cover the decaying walls of an ever more worn-out Havana. I told him how people in the street took me for a prostitute because I looked Cuban but was seen hanging out with foreign friends. I told him about the extraordinary cost of meat. I discussed the rare gift Cubans have for savoring the present in spite of everything.

I told him I would like to see him again.

I heard nothing for months. And then he called, urgency in his voice. My letter, it seemed, had gotten mixed up in a stack of bills that he'd ignored as he traveled. It wasn't until he had returned to London that he'd spotted the return address on the envelope and rescued it from the pile.

"When can I see you?" he asked.

He had plans; I had plans. But he soon called from Spain with a concrete proposal. He would take the night train from Madrid to Paris and arrive in time to cook breakfast for me. I was amused, because I could read his mind: If, by chance, I turned out to be the wrong destination, he would still have time to catch a train home to London later that afternoon.

The following morning, at eight o'clock, my door swung open to receive Danny, looking tanned and in great shape in a Freddy's Pizza T-shirt. In one hand he held a bulging suitcase; in the other, a bulging shopping bag. A mandolin case was tucked under his arm. He greeted me with a giant smile, then ran straight to the kitchen, where he extracted from the bag a half-dozen eggs, a jar of sun-dried tomatoes, onions, a pair of red peppers, and Spanish blood oranges. Realizing he'd left aromatic herbs in his suitcase, he dragged the bag to the middle of the living room (rendered immaculate in his honor), and as he rifled through its belly, he proceeded to scatter every-thing—*everything*—across my wall-to-wall carpeting. Notebooks, mismatched socks, wrinkled shirts. He found the herbs and raced back to the kitchen.

Hovering over the stove, Danny was like a conductor directing a symphony. His hair stuck straight up from the effort and the heat. Still grinning, he handed me a plate, upon which lay his steaming masterpiece. "Here it is," he announced with a flourish of unbounded pride. My kitchen was in a state of chaos. Speechless until then, I burst into laughter.

That evening Danny didn't take the train for London. When the time for sleeping came, we fixed him a bed on my living room floor. We were too shy to even admit how shy we were. Danny disappeared into the bathroom and emerged wearing a very serious expression and green pajamas with red stripes. I burst out laughing again. He helped me make up the mattress by seizing two edges of the sheet. Then, tak-ing a moment to aim well, he threw himself down, arms stretched out in a cross, trying to catch two mattress corners at once, like a cartoon character. Suddenly I understood what was attracting me so much: Danny gave his all to everything he did.

How many different beds have we slept in during the four years since we met? They blur. In the marriage contract we wrote together and read at our wedding in 1999, we proclaimed, "We promise to discover new things, places, and people together, to view our life together as a work of literature." We have discovered much together in a short time.

In Danny's computer he keeps a list entitled "Places We've Been."

> Paris
> London
> Wales
> Port-Vendres
> Barcelona

Los Angeles

North Adams, MA

Rhode Island

Washington, D.C.

New York

Seattle

Vancouver

Istanbul

South Turkey

Lebanon

Croatia

San Francisco

Greece

Holland

Israel

Cuba

Basque Country

Dominican Republic

Hong Kong

Singapore

India

Qatar

Pakistan

We first came to Karachi four months ago: September 12, 2001. We flew in from New Delhi, where the airport was almost terrifyingly tranquil. I watched Danny struggle to contain his emotions by finding comfort in familiar acts. He wandered the aisles of the duty-free shop, inspecting the rows upon rows of Ganesh, the familiar Hindu elephant god. You could have a Ganesh of ceramic, wood, plastic, fuzzy polyester, any material your mind could conjure. I told Danny that the reason Ganesh is such a favorite of cabdrivers is because he supposedly removes all obstacles. Danny tried to appear interested, but he just seemed spacey. Everyone was spacey that day.

He balanced boxes of chocolates in his arms. In every big airport, Danny stocked up on candies, intending to distribute them to the children of new acquaintances. He'd always forget, though, and in the end, the candy would be left in the hotel room, stale or melted.

There was only one other customer in the duty-free shop, a German journalist, also on his way to Pakistan. He was buying whiskey, which he planned to smuggle in. With a strange grin, he told us, "I have my sources. War starts next Tuesday, and *pffffit.* Erased from the map, Afghanistan!"

We just stared at him.

Two days before, we'd been in a Mushahar village in Bihar. Bihar is the land where Shakyamuni Buddha was enlightened and where Gandhi acquired the name Mahatma (great soul); I was there to profile a disciple of Gandhi's for a French magazine. Nowadays, Bihar has the distinction of being the poorest and most anarchic state in India. If such things are really quantifiable, the Mushahar villages are perhaps the most desperately deprived. Their name means "rat eater," and the Mushahar people do make a dish of the rodents. After centuries of inbreeding and a lack of iron in their diet, the villagers have turned monstrous-looking, with giant goiters protruding from their necks. We felt as if we had been transported back in time to the Middle Ages.

In the aftershock of 9/11, we were struggling to rocket back to the twenty-first century, where the "civilized" world was in chaos. We had witnessed the attacks almost as they happened on CNN. And we had stood frozen before the television as John Bussey—"It's my boss! My boss!" Danny had cried out—movingly and graphically reported what he was witnessing from the windows of the *Wall Street Journal* offices.

The *Journal's* offices were just across the street from the World Trade Center. Bussey wrote a terrifying account of that morning, published on page one of the *Journal* the next day. He vividly captured what he could see from the ninth floor, what it sounded like when the first plane hit, what it looked like soon afterward. "Great clouds of smoke pushed skyward. Intense flames were consuming higher floors above the crash site. Debris was falling onto the streets—huge chunks of metal that echoed blocks away when they hit. Office papers littered the ground. Cars in a nearby parking lot—a full two city blocks from the explosion—were aflame." He described, plainly and terribly, the people leaping "in a flight of desperation."

He stayed in the office reporting the scene for the *Journal*'s television partner, CNBC, and he almost stayed too long. The South Tower collapsed, and the *Journal* offices "filled with ash, concrete dust, smoke, the detritus of South Tower." Managing to get out of the building was a dangerous challenge. But nothing compared to what happened next: "[As] I walked down the street, getting my bearings . . . the second tower was weakening. I heard a pressing metallic roar, like the Chicago El rumbling overhead. And then the fireman next to me shouted: 'It's coming down! Run!'

"Run where?"

John could so easily have become among the thousands who died that day.

Even though we were on the other side of the world, we knew it, and we were shaken by it, and here in the Pakistan International Airlines lounge, we frantically tried to get an internet connection to make contact with our friends and colleagues. When we finally got through, more than a thousand emails waited for Danny.

Danny had arranged for a personal security guard to pick us up at the Karachi airport. Even under "normal circumstances," Karachi's airport has a reputation as one of the most violent in the world, where highway robbers regularly intercept and attack business travelers. And these were not normal times.

You could not miss our guard. In one hand, he gripped a piece of cardboard reading "Mister Peul," in the other, an AK-47. He wore military clothes and combat boots, and his eyes were an arresting turquoise. He led us to a 4 X 4 that looked less like a jeep and more like a tank. Inside, another man, also armed, sat motionless. As we drove into the city, those turquoise eyes darted around in an otherwise impassive face. It was like being guarded by a large high-strung cat.

A fog of hostility weighed over the city. We were here to ask the big questions: Who was responsible for the attacks? Who financed them? Who protected the terrorists? In the days that followed, the United States had the tenuous support of Pakistan, but if the German journalist was right and the U.S. was about to bomb Afghanistan, would Pakistan support it? Would Musharraf fall victim to a coup d'état, as rumor had it?

Everywhere we went, we faced Karachi citizens who felt stung by what they perceived as a powerfully negative Western prejudice against Islam. Danny emailed a message to a friend on September 17, "Hi from Karachi, which would be a great city if we weren't scared to go out of the hotel."

We wanted to understand this world, but it wasn't easy to know where or how to begin. You could hardly stroll up to strangers on Karachi's streets and lob questions at them. We turned to a local fixer for assistance. Saeed had been recommended by a man we knew, but we didn't much like him, and he wasn't much help. Still, he managed to set up a meeting for us with a group that essentially served as the women's auxiliary branch of the militant Islamist Jaish-e-Mohammed party. We never quite understood their specific function, but we couldn't fail to miss their fury.

We met them in a two-bedroom apartment in a larger middle-class section of Karachi. One bedroom was completely bare; in the other, simple chairs lined the perimeter. All save one were filled with women covered head to toe in black burkhas, which hid their look but not their anger. There was also one man, Karachi's municipal mayor, dressed in a white *salwar kameez*. Two seats had been placed in the middle of the room. Those were for us. We wore color.

For what felt like many minutes but was probably only seconds, no one made a sound. At last Danny spoke. "Where should we start?" he asked softly. "We'd very much like to hear what you are thinking these days."

The women responded aggressively. The sounds coming from them were raw. One woman, particularly incensed by CNN's coverage of the September 11 attacks, assailed the Western press for ascribing responsibility to a network of militant Islamic groups. Groups like hers.

"What proof do they have?" she demanded. "They have no proof."

As they questioned us, they also studied us. Danny was white but on the dark-complected side. I looked a bit like them. Nobody asked me about my origins or religion, but I appreciated once more the advantages of our being a mixed couple. No one can peg a mixed couple. They cannot assume they know anything about you, individually or together. And it's not simply that you are no longer restricted by conventional boundaries, it is that borders are meaningless to you. You are free to create something new. "My mulatta," Danny calls me.

In the middle-class neighborhood in Paris where I grew up, people often assumed my brother Satchi and I were Algerian. We weren't, but that didn't stop racist bullies from chasing my poor brother. One night, after he had gone out dancing, he staggered home, his face covered with the blood that flowed when they hit him over the head with a crowbar. But most of the time, the two of us—half-Cuban and half-Dutch, with more ethnic strains running in us than anyone could ever figure out—were labeled "exotic."

My father was the illegitimate son of a Dutch Jewish diamond merchant, an unpleasant homosexual who made love only once to a woman—and managed to get her pregnant. He confirmed this extraordinary tale to my mother on his deathbed. He showed little interest in his son or the mother. When the Nazis threatened to invade the Netherlands, my grandmother and my father walked all the way to the South of France to escape, and that is where my father grew up. The rest of his family died in the Holocaust. My father became a revolutionary wanna-be, traveling from one world hot spot to the next, landing in Havana in the 1960s in time for the

Cuban revolution. That's where he met my mother, Marita. She came from a poor family, she was colored, and she had a Chinese grandfather. Clearly there was Spanish and African blood in her, and who knew what else. I felt like history had worked really hard for me to enjoy being a bit of everything.

Early in our relationship, Danny decided that coffee-drinking epitomized the French part of me, and he considered it his duty to provide me the precious black nectar. Only once did he fail on this mission. We were in Dubrovnik, Croatia, and we had to catch a plane for Zagreb, the capital, at six in the morning. War was raging in neighboring Kosovo, and the hotel was empty. The man at the front desk refused to open the kitchen; surly and muscular, he wasn't a person you'd dream of arguing with. Danny seemed so crushed that I bravely took off for the airport without the dose my system was craving. But this bitter experience taught us a lesson: After that, we went nowhere without a traveling coffee kit of Danny's own mak-ing—kettle; French press; coffee, bought in enormous quantities in Paris or Dubai, personally ground and stored in little containers; sugar and sugar substitutes.

So I knew something major was up the morning in June 2000 when Danny burst into our bedroom without bringing me my morning cup.

"Hey, baby! Want to go live in Bombay?"

"Sure," I said, even if I wasn't.

As Danny sat at the computer, confirming his candidacy to become *The Wall Street Journal*'s new South Asia bureau chief, I studied the Eiffel Tower through our living room window. It had been clothed in tiny blue lights since the celebration of the new mil-lennium, but you couldn't see them in the bright spring morning. The job, as Danny had explained it, was to cover all of South Asia—Sri Lanka, Pakistan, Bhutan, Nepal, Bangladesh, India and its billion souls. I had known Danny for two years and I had immense trust in him. And it was clear to me that after five years of covering the Middle East, his career was at a standstill. He needed a new and wider challenge. At the same time, I was terribly afraid of India. A patchwork of images streamed through my head: sacred cows and placid elephants; hungry children, hands outstretched, begging, filling miles upon miles of slums.

Our October arrival in Bombay made my apprehensions look like a child's sweet dream. Danny and I didn't exchange a single word while our plane flew over a landscape of utmost misery. Below were mountains of garbage, and the corrugated metal roofs of huts undulated for miles. It sounds harsh, maybe, but the image I couldn't shake as I looked down was of pock-marked skin, or worse, a leprous face.

Our plane landed at the international airport Chatrapati Shivaji, named after a seventeenth century warrior king whose life was a symbol of progress and security. Danny had booked us into a five-star hotel in the Bandra district in the north of Bombay, where the jet set of Bollywood lives. (I've always had a weakness for Indian films. I find them hilarious, with their ellipses and their scenarios that take such license with reality.) We were told that our room was "on the fifteenth floor," but it was a seven-story building. Our bellman seemed bewildered by our bewilderment. It was a matter of prestige for a hotel to have a large number of floors, he explained.

Our windows looked out on the saddest seaside I had ever seen. The sea, a dirty brown color, smelled of sewage. Greasy papers drifted along the shore. The only touches of color in this ashen landscape were the saris of women, walking with bent backs. A little boy flailed a monkey with a stick, forcing it to perform somersaults in time to a scratchy recording of Michael Jackson's "Beat It." I doubt the song was chosen intentionally.

Danny came up beside me at the window. He smelled of the mosquito repellent in which we had drenched ourselves. To give each other courage, we spoke of those who had already jumped in before us. About a BBC correspondent who, in our situation a few years ago, had realized he was supposed to cover a country where he was afraid of even walking the streets. About the many couples we had heard of who hadn't been able to survive moves like this one.

"We'll be fine if we keep our sense of humor," Danny said. That was another of the vows in our wedding contract. We referred to that contract a lot. Danny had a copy in his Palm Pilot; I had one in my computer:

> On the ninth day of the twelfth month of the year five thousand seven hundred fifty-nine since the creation of the earth, corresponding to the twenty-first day of the eighth month of the year one thousand nine hundred and ninety-nine, as time is commonly reckoned in the country of France.
>
> In the presence of treasured family and friends, Mariane van Neyenhoff and Daniel Pearl enter into the following covenant:
>
> We promise to grow old together, while keeping each other young, maintaining our sense of humor, sharing love and secrets.
>
> We promise to discover new things, places, and people together, to view our life together as a work of literature.
>
> We promise to share our happiness with our friends and relatives.
>
> We promise not to let money, lack of money, or passage of time change us.
>
> We promise each to treasure the other's happiness at least as much as our own, to support each other's creativity, and always to keep faith in the strength of the other's love.

Even with such a pledge, Bombay remained trying. We struggled to find an apartment, and we shipped our essentials from France, including Danny's oversize blue leather Barcalounger. A lot of his best thinking had been done in this elephantine chair, and it had followed him around the world. He worried that its overwhelming leatherness might offend his cow-revering Hindu hosts, so he had gone so far as to email friends and query them. They assured him the chair would be fine, as long as he hadn't actually killed the hide's original owner.

India turned out to be a major producer and consumer of leather, as Danny went on to discover and write in an article entitled "How Many Ways Can You Skin a Cow? In Hindu India, Plenty." It takes "some effort to accommodate business and religion when it comes to cowhide," he wrote. "The Hindu religion forbids eating beef and slaughtering cows, but permits taking the hide of a 'fallen' cow, or one that has died naturally. Muslims, who can slaughter cows, work in slaughterhouses and butcher shops. But in the case of 'fallen' cows, a low-caste Hindu does the work, because it is against Islamic belief to skin an animal that has died naturally."

Yes, there was much to learn here, and we were trying hard to figure it out. But we didn't have time to really settle into Bombay. One month before Danny's first anniversary as South Asia bureau chief, the world seemed to lose its center of gravity. First New York, then Afghanistan, India, Pakistan . . . *Le monde ne tourne plus rond,* I thought, the world has ceased to turn around. And South Asia had become its hottest corner.

Chapter Four

"It is seven o'clock," says Asra, as if I didn't know.

Asra has the most captivating gaze I've ever seen. She looks perpetually astonished, and with the lack of sleep, her eyes seem wider and blacker than ever. They're almost disturbing. I never catch her blinking, although she must.

She has showered and dressed as if she's going on an expedition—cargo pants, a tight black Nike tee, and Caterpillar construction-worker boots. I have slipped out of the dress I had chosen to please Danny, and put on a similar battle uniform, down to the boots. Asskickers.

I do not for a moment imagine that Danny has been in a car accident, or been robbed and left by the side of the road. I know he has been captured by Islamic militants. I know this. I know in my heart that he has been kidnapped by men who have kidnapped their own god, by which I mean men who have twisted the concept of jihad, of holy war, into something warped and wrong. Numerous Muslims have described jihad to Danny and me as the most courageous process a person can undertake. A jihadi fights with himself to overcome his own limitations in order to contribute to society at large. This slow and difficult battle, the true jihad, is what Buddhists call the "human revolution."

The respite of dawn is past, and the heat has again captured Karachi in its embrace. It penetrates all the rooms and makes the dust dance in the rays of sunlight. We listen to car doors slam up and down Zamzama Street as neighbors start leaving for work.

Asra and I continue to huddle together before Danny's laptop as we try to reconstruct his last moves before he disappeared. We find the name of the disciple who was to meet him at the Village Restaurant and take him to Sheikh Gilani: Imtiaz Siddique. We dial the phone number Siddique gave Danny. It's been switched off.

Asra has begun to draw up a chronology of events. And together, we make a large chart to help us keep the names straight and visualize the sea of information in which we swim. At the center of a large piece of white paper, we write DANNY. Alongside his name, we write "Sheikh Mubarak Ali Shah Gilani." We add Bashir's name, and Siddique's. Then we start going further afield, adding Khalid Khawaja and Mansur Ejaz, the well-connected Pakistani-American businessman who suggested Danny contact Khawaja.

"Call Danny's regular fixer," Asra says.

Ah, plump Asif in Islamabad. He probably doesn't have the faintest idea what is happening to us. His wife answers the phone and gets flustered when I demand to speak to her husband. He is still in the bathroom, she says.

"I must talk to him this instant."

I ask Asif to answer my questions directly and not make any other comment. What he hears wakes him better than any cold shower.

Yes, he says, he arranged the meeting. Danny insisted on meeting Gilani, and the only way Asif could make that happen was by enlisting someone "well connected with that kind of people."

"*What* kind of people?"

Jihadi movement people. In this case, a rather young man of frail constitution who serves as a spokesman for Harkat-ul-Mujahideen, a militant group recently outlawed by President Musharraf. What is this spokesman's name? Arif. Between Asif the fixer and Arif the terrorist spokesman, my head pounds. I decide to call one Asif-le-fixer and the other the Jihadi Spokesman. It helps. "What does he look like?"

"A bit sophisticated, with a long beard."

Asra asks if he wears his loose trousers, his *salwar,* high—an odd but telling question, since it has become the fashion among fundamentalists to hike up their pants. The prophet Mohammed, it is said, suggested this habit so his disciples might avoid dirtying their clothes in the mud of the roads. Muslim fundamentalists, in their never-ending quest to prove their orthodoxy, have adopted the look. The Jihadi spokesman did wear his *salwar* high.

"Was he clean?" demands Asra.

I cringe, but it's another instructive question, because Pakistanis habitually complain about the personal hygiene of Afghans. Before she can continue down this path, I break in with a question that has been eating at me: "This Jihadi Spokesman, does he have connections to Al Qaeda?"

Dead silence. I can hear Asif breathe heavily, but he doesn't speak.

"Did Danny know?"

More silence. More breathing.

"Why didn't you say anything? It is your job to protect us. *Why did you betray us?*"

A fixer should know how to navigate the hard-to-define borders between what's safe enough and what's not. You should be able to trust your fixer and depend on him. Fury scrambles my brain. I am almost mute with rage. "Get ready, Asif. The police are on their way." I hang up the phone.

Asra and I occupy so little space, here at the petite roll-top desk, that the house around us feels immense. As she surfs Danny's computer for more information, I flip through stacks of his little notebooks. On each he has stapled his business card and methodically noted where we were at the time. From Jaipur to Doha, all of our wanderings have been scrupulously recorded, but they've been recorded in the shorthand Danny invented as a journalism student at Stanford. I cannot decipher it. In time I'll come to find that *no one* can. The FBI will hire some of the world's greatest code breakers to try to decipher the singular Pearl shorthand. No one will crack it.

In the backup for his Palm Pilot, we find lyrics for dozens of songs—"The Harder They Come," "What a Wonderful World," Bob Dylan's "Love Minus Zero" . . . "My love she speaks like silence / Without ideals or violence . . ." And countless random, funny lists. *"Things to like about Germans:* curious, good beer, took lots of refugees, punctual, produced Beethoven, not as bad as Austrians, earnest women, apologetic about war." Ever the optimist, he has a list entitled *"Cool things in Bombay."* It is short. There are lists of books read and French phrases learned. That list grows longer all the time.

> forcenées—maniacs
> suppot—henchman
> la risée—laughing stock
> boucher un coin—floor somebody
> la branlette—masturbation
> se goinfrer—pig out
> prendre des gants—treat with kid gloves
> frémir—shiver

When I first discovered Danny's compunction for making up lists, I found it a little disconcerting, especially when I learned that he'd started one on me. My pride was singed. Did he need to be reminded what I was about? But he explained that the items would make prime material for a song he intended to write for or about me. What's more, he said, if he kept adding to it, by the time we grew old, it would become an epic ode to the woman he loved.

Fair enough. Now I paused in my research to see how many entries had thus far made it to the list. Sixteen.

THINGS I LOVE ABOUT MARIANE

Plays Led Zep in the morning
Says doesn't want commercial wedding shit
Dances with or without music
Doesn't think you have to give up certain things when you
    get older

Is shy the next day

Is not afraid to cry

Likes typical stuff—fires, sailing—without being typical

Lets me be as silly as I want without getting embarrassed

Doesn't take Dad too seriously

Rides with pilots

I can talk to her about anything

Likes getting stuffed animals

Climbs on me while I'm working

Wears same shirt 2 days running if she feels like

Little step walk

Has incredible ability to see herself and ourselves with clear
   perspective

"It is nine o'clock," says Asra.

Almost three hours have passed since we called the police; they should be here soon. We get up and stash last night's beer bottles in a kitchen cabinet, and we hide Danny's computer and our own so we can retain control over key pieces of information. We know that Pakistani men do not always welcome the collaboration of professional women. It is essential that we remain involved and free to do as we see fit to find Danny. We are on guard.

Asra pulls off her boots and slides back into heels. Not me. I stay dressed for battle.

Tariq Jamil sits on the edge of the living room sofa, surrounded by half a dozen of his men, none of whom will look at us. They won't sit down, either. Deferential, they keep their heads lowered until Jamil addresses them in Urdu, at which point they nod. "*Ji sir.*" Asra tries to pretend she doesn't understand, but her eyes give her away. "Shhhh," she hears Jamil tell one of his lieutenants. "She can hear us."

Jamil is Karachi's deputy chief of police. He's short, and dressed in the olive green uniform of the Pakistani police. His mustache is carefully trimmed, and his eyes are small and round, like black marbles. In slow, measured words and a silky voice, he asks us to tell him what we know. As we work our way through yesterday and our discoveries of the night, he studies us. The more we progress, the more preoccupied he seems. "And you are pregnant," he finally says, fixing his eyes on my belly.

"Man, you're a shrewd detective," I mutter to myself.

Outside, the street has been taken over by a phalanx of dilapidated police jeeps and unimpressive military vehicles. Again and again the doorbell rings, and yet another strange man steps into the house. How many can one house hold? Jamil's men greet their compatriots with a salute. The new arrivals, most dressed in Western-style civilian clothes, wander from room to room as if the key to Danny's disappearance has somehow escaped the others. In the kitchen, they take note of the remains of last night's dinner; in the living room, they slyly open drawers and riffle through papers stacked by the phone.

Why aren't they out combing Karachi for Danny? I observe the entire scene in disbelief. It reminds me of those TV series I watched as a teenager, bored on Sunday afternoons: Police arrive, collect evidence. Victim's wife appears, arms folded across her chest, voice choked with grief, face awash in tears.

Desperate to goose Jamil into getting his men out in the field, Asra grabs the phone and calls John Bussey as a demonstration that Important People in the United States are also waiting for action. Over the phone, she manages to mangle Jamil's acronyms, prompting a smile from the chief. I don't think that man smiles a lot as a rule.

Asra hands Jamil the phone. I hear him assure Bussey that "the police will make every possible effort to find Danny." The use of the cliché erodes what little confidence in him I have clung to.

A shorthaired elf navigates through all these men, her black eyes big as if she never conceived of seeing that many grown-ups at once. It is Kashva, the daughter of the servants. Dressed in a long skirt, barefoot and dirty, she wanders around with her mouth open. I realize that the scary otherness of her looks comes from the way her eyes are made up. Pakistani mothers line their children's eyes with smoky black kohl to protect them from bad spells. It makes them look like evil angels. As soon as someone speaks to her, Kashva flies back to her mother, who is busy sweeping the carpet. Using a totally inefficient method—crouching—her mother goes everywhere, brushing back and forth with her primitive homemade broom. At this pace, it will take her the whole day to sweep the house.

Though no one raises his voice, several of the men in our midst cannot conceal their excitement. This is a high-profile case, and they are elated to be included. Asra does her best to keep track of the comings and goings. Solid journalist that she is, she chases after the men, demanding family names and professional titles and recording them in a tiny notebook. Some of the men are clearly taken aback. They are not used to being questioned, especially by a beautiful, Urdu-speaking, Indian-born American woman who rents a house costing a seemingly irrational forty thousand rupees per month, by herself, in crazy, lawless Karachi. SSP, DIG, DSP, CID—all she gets are acronyms. Her notebook looks as if she tossed the alphabet up in the air and randomly scattered ABCs. The only acronym I know for sure is ISI—and while it seems reasonable to assume they are here, those men don't like to reveal their true identities.

A short man in a uniform and beret enters, each step preceded by the ominous tap of his walking stick. He is presented to me as Kamal Shah, the inspector general, or IG. Calm and soft-mannered, he listens to Tariq Jamil's whispered and respectful report. A policeman steps forward and drops a few additional words in the IG's ear. They all act as if they're sharing personal secrets. I begin to find these little mysteries irritating, but I force myself to stay calm. I study the chain of command. Clearly, Jamil reports to the IG, and the IG reports to the governor of Sindh province, whom he now phones. Their conversation is in Urdu, but the IG punctuates his sentences with English—"This is important, sir, this is important. . . ."

Men step forward to interview me. Why did Danny want to meet Gilani? How did he get himself into trouble? As Interior Minister

Moinuddin Haider will accusingly inform me a few days later, "Pakistan has welcomed three thousand journalists during the whole war in Afghanistan, and none has gone missing until now." The implication is clear: Danny has somehow brought this on himself. He must be reckless, or he has gone too far.

"Hardly," I tell them, "and if you want, I can prove it." For starters, if Danny were some kind of cowboy, we'd be in Afghanistan. The moment it became clear that the U.S. was going to retaliate for September 11, journalists began jockeying for position to get into Afghanistan. Not us. We were expecting our child, and we agreed it would be too dangerous to go. Besides, Danny had gotten a solid taste of war reporting when he was sent to Bosnia in 1999. There, he witnessed the aftermath of massacres and saw what life is like in a world filled with snipers and mine-infested fields. He had no hunger for the adrenaline rush that can come from reporting in danger zones.

Still, *The Wall Street Journal* did not want to be left out. We were reporting from Islamabad when news editor Bill Spindle sent Danny an email in which he asked, "by the way, how tough would it be for you to apply to a visa for afghanistan? just in case. . . . bussey is very hot to have someone go into afghanistan—too hot, if you ask me . . ."

Danny replied quickly and firmly:

My understanding—from latest Reuters story—was that foreign journalists who had been covering the aid-workers-arrests have now left Afghanistan . . . You can easily get a visa in Delhi for northern Afghanistan, but then you have to go through three countries to get there and you end up in the enclave controlled by Massoud, who's now dead . . .

I would refuse to go to Afghanistan, and I'd do so partly on the basis that I sent Bussey a detailed memo on reporter safety more than a year ago—things like procedures for checking in regularly and whether editors know what to do if a reporter goes missing, whether we need the war-conditions training that some journalists get, whether we should all be taking basic first aid kits and so forth—and he hasn't responded. I'm not trained to be a war correspondent, and don't think it's responsible for a newspaper to send people without proper training into situations like that.

Of course, I'm no one to lecture to Bussey now, since he's been through something more hairy than anything I'll experience [the attack on the Twin Towers]—insha'allah.—DP

War held no appeal for Danny or for me. What interested us was the challenge presented by peace. People often see peace as the simple absence of war, but it is instead the result of courageous actions taken to initiate a dialogue between civilizations. Both Danny and I saw our profession as a way to contribute to the dialogue, to allow voices on all sides to be heard, and to bear witness.

Our journalistic ethic was strong, but our vulnerability was great. Back when he was reporting from the Balkans, Danny had called New York to discuss with his editors the content of an article he was writing. "Ah! Danny, where are you, by the way?" his editor asked. Basic question, innocently asked. But it infuriated Danny to realize he had been sent into a war zone without the hierarchy troubling to remember where he was.

[Thank you] for all of the excellent Kosovo coverage you got into the paper . . . ," one of the top editors emailed him in the summer of 1999. "You did it artfully, and kept us looking really good on the story. . . . So thanks. We'll keep you in mind for the next war."

That wasn't what Danny was looking to hear.

As soon as he got back home to Paris, he composed a detailed document entitled "Memo on Protection of Journalists," the one he mentioned when deputy foreign editor Spindle queried him about going to Afghanistan. The memo would prove remarkably prescient and instructive.

MEMO ON PROTECTION OF JOURNALISTS

First, a general point: many of us have heard the refrain that the *Journal* "doesn't send people to dangerous places." There's some truth to that. A *WSJ* correspondent is less likely than an APTV or Reuters correspondent to be riding a military convoy out of Freetown. We don't feel the pressure that TV or wire correspondents feel to be first into a warzone, and that's good. But it can also lull the paper into a false sense of security. The fact is, we sent people to Kosovo while there was still shooting going on—and without the kind of preparation the paper would have had if we were more used to this sort of thing. We went to Chechnya as well. . . . Foreigners are increasingly becoming targets in places like the Middle East and Southeast Asia.

If something like a kidnapping or arrest occurs, do we know how to react?

Danny was ambitious enough to know that a hot dateline was a hot dateline. But for him, the point was to manage the risks of the road instead of letting the risks manage him.

CHECKING IN—In the past few years, we've had reporters detained in various places. Fortunately, it hasn't lasted more than a day. But there is a danger that a reporter could go missing for days without anybody realizing it. Several times, I've told my editor or the news assistant that I'll be checking in daily, and that they should call if they don't hear from me, but when I went a few days without checking in, I never got a call. . . . At the very least, it should be made part of editors' job descriptions to keep track of a reporter who is going into a hazardous situation. They should have a system . . . to remind them to check up on a reporter, and a list of numbers to call if there is any doubt the reporter is safe. . . . [The] first contact (after spouse) would be the translator/fixer, then other journalists in the country, then whatever government agency is responsible for visiting journalists, then the U.S. embassy or interests section. Those numbers should be available to whoever is tracking the reporter or is woken up in the middle of the night by somebody worried about the reporter.

There are additional numbers that should be called if a reporter goes missing: first, the International Committee of the Red Cross, at 011-41-22-734-6001 (24-hour switchboard), 730-2088 (press secretariat), or 734-8280 (fax). The ICRC can canvass prisons to see if the reporter has been arrested, and can arrange for messages to be passed back and forth. Second, the Committee to Protect Journalists, at 212-465-1004—they know how to put public pressure, if needed, to get somebody freed. . . .

GUIDANCE—The more time a reporter spends out in the field, the more of a risk he or she takes. So, one way to reduce risk is to discourage reporters from doing reporting that New York doesn't want or can't use anyhow. But in places like Kosovo, your decision on where to go and what to do is made by 8 a.m., and the advice from New York may not come until too late to be of use. Obviously, it's too much to ask for Page One to make instantaneous decisions, or for the foreign editor to make decisions at 2 a.m. But if there were a way to get expedited responses in cases where someone is in a hot zone, it would be of great help. . . .

MONEY—There are still plenty of countries where an AmEx card and a Citibank card won't get you anywhere. Carrying U.S. dollars is mandatory in Iran, carrying deutschmarks is mandatory in much of former Yugoslavia. But we don't have a good system to get money to journalists quickly before trips. Besides costing the *Journal* money ($50 every time I cash a $1,000 check to get francs here, plus the exchange rate loss when I exchange the francs for dollars) and time (waiting for money to begin a trip), this can pose safety problems. If you run out of money in a nasty place, you may stick around longer than you need to waiting for funds to arrive. In Montenegro, journalists were actually making full-day runs to Dubrovnik to hit the cash machines, and thus exposing themselves to hostile situations en route for no good reason. Also, if you start running out of money, you may cut corners by dropping your regular driver, going places without a fixer, moving outside the main hotel—all potential safety risks. Suggestions: Keep a standing account in a few strategic locations, where a reporter could quickly get $5,000 or $6,000 for a trip. Work out a system . . . allowing an editor to wire-transfer money to a reporter without going through days of paperwork or having to put cash on the table at Citibank. Western Union is another option, but it's costly, and you'd have to keep a pile of cash in New York that somebody would have to walk to a Western Union. . . .

TRAINING—There are at least two training courses available to journalists covering wars. A few people are put off by the military overtones—should reporters really be getting training from former special-forces soldiers? But Craig Copetas, who took a course some years ago, says it has come in handy several times and thinks it should be mandatory. Others who haven't taken the courses agree. The courses cover things like basic first aid (e.g., how to tie a tourniquet), armaments (e.g., how to recognize whether the gun pointing at your face is "locked and loaded"), human psychology (e.g., how to reason with hostile people at checkpoints), driving (e.g., how to drive out of bad situations) and miscellaneous things like what to wear to keep from becoming a target, how to deal with extreme weather, how to stay safe during demonstrations, how to avoid mines. One course that has won good reviews among journalists is done in the UK through a company called Centurion Risk Assessment Services (*The New York Times* and BBC have sent people there). Copetas's course was by Andy Kain Enterprises (CNN and BBC reporters have gone through it), and is offered in the UK and elsewhere. The three Reuters correspondents caught in the Sierra Leone ambush apparently had Centurion training; two survived, one died. The cost seems to be about $500 a day for a course, which can go three to five days. I enclose a story from *The New Yorker* on the Centurion course.

EQUIPMENT—Flak jackets make people nervous, but if we're going to have them, we should be serious about them, instead of going through the last-minute "I think there was a flak jacket in the Paris bureau five years ago" routine. Cons—they're uncomfortable, heavy (six pounds), hot. Pros—the right kind can protect against grenade and shell fragments as well as handguns, and you don't need to wear them all the time. Example—you might keep one in the car if you're traveling anywhere near a battle zone, and then put it on if shells start flying. Several colleagues say there were times when they wished they had one handy. The problem is, you need one that's the right size, and you have to know how to use it.

From this point on, Danny's memo grew *even more* specific.
It was not adopted.
Sitting on the sofa next to the chief of police, I find it hard not to replay the memo point by point in my head.

As Tariq Jamil whispers into the phone in Urdu, another official-looking man, in his mid-thirties, polite and smiling and dressed in a suit, summons me with a discreet gesture. He tells me he is from an acronym's police branch—like Asra, I've lost track of them—and he asks for a photo of Danny "for the needs of the inquiry." We happen to have made identity photographs recently and I riffle through Danny's computer bag for his. When I pull it out, Danny's sweet and slightly ironic glance crosses mine, and something suddenly starts screaming inside me. I experience an instant of pure panic. I feel a devastating urge to charge into the streets shouting his name, demanding that he be given back to me *now*.

I am Danny, I am our son, I am revolted.

The anger that rushes through me goes well beyond the hellish night I've just lived through. In a flash, I feel a terrible bond not only with the victims of September 11 but also with the kids brainwashed to become instruments of death in the name of an invented Islam. The terrible absurdity of it all overwhelms me.

Two men stand watching me from across the room. One, in his

mid-forties, is remarkably elegant. He smokes like an actor in a 1940s movie—not hungrily or with attitude but with total composure. His clothes are tailored to perfectly fit his slender frame, and his hair and mustache are flecked with gray. There is something noble about the man. His companion is younger, equally elegant and handsome. He holds a notebook but doesn't use it. Both seem to be patiently waiting for all the turmoil to quiet down before they start to work. I sense they are steeping themselves in the scene. How could we not have noticed them before?

I walk up to them, and the older gentleman takes my hand.

"I am the SSP, CID."

"Right."

"And this is Dost MI," he adds, nodding at his companion while never losing eye contact with me.

"Yeah."

They have a gravitas that I think I like. Remembering Asra's favorable opinion of the military, I ask if that's where they're from.

"I was," the elder says, smiling. "I was once a captain in the army, but I am now the chief of CID."

I wait, praying he will explain what on earth "CID" stands for, but he doesn't. The young man comes to my rescue: "The unit in charge of counterterrorism."

Et voilà. In spite of our sleepless night, I have never been so awake in my life. Baby, I think, this is it. This is what we need. The chief of counterterrorism to run the search for Danny—good news if you ask me, though those are just my instincts speaking.

An invisible tie has always linked me to Danny. When he is afraid, I am afraid; where he aches, I ache. I am emboldened by the courage he is showing wherever he may be. "Captain," I say brusquely, "listen, we're running out of time. We need to find my husband fast. You are a professional—but I am your best ally."

I explain why Asra and I should stay at the center of the inquiry. I walk him through the work we've already done. I take him to see our chart. I ask him to stay close to us. He looks me straight and deep in the eyes, thoughtfully, radiating an Olympian calm. I cannot tell if this is astonishing composure or simply professional detachment. "We will work together," he finally says, adding, "You haven't slept last night."

Asra meets us in the corridor, and I quickly introduce her. Since their arrival, Captain and Dost have studied the efficient way she has monitored the scene in the house. Without our being aware of it, she has already earned their esteem.

Captain points to Asra's high heels. "You take those off," he says firmly. Shoes like that may be acceptable among the Pakistani elite, but to others they're provocative. Impractical, too. Asra sheds them.

Later, talking to a male friend, I refer to "Captain" by this spontaneously given nickname. My friend is appalled. "You've demoted the man by three grades," he protests. But I do not know or, frankly, care much about military hierarchies. To me, Captain is the man who will guide me through a system I have good reasons to distrust. He is the commander of our ship.

Lunchtime must be nearing, for the house is emptying. Captain and Dost sit at the dinner table, where we have brought out Danny's laptop from its hiding place. Asra and I have decided to share with them our finds of the night, as well as some chicken biryani. Captain will later tell me, "I think, 'Something so serious has happened in the house, something must have gone wrong, but these two ladies are trying to behave normally. And they're trying to stay hopeful.'" We win his heart. "And you show me the chart you have made, and I know at that moment that you are going to help me. These ladies don't know how, but they will help me, I know that from the outset."

Captain's phone rings incessantly, mostly calls from superiors who are feeling the pressure rise. I continue to dial Danny's cell number every fifteen minutes, always jolted by the mechanical voice. I also regularly call Siddique, the man Danny was supposed to meet. The same voice from hell is at the other end. We can use only our cell phones because we have decided that no one must use the landline in the house anymore, in case Danny calls. A page torn from a notepad has been taped to the receiver: "Do not touch. Danny's phone." The one piece of equipment Dost has brought is an answering machine, there to record a kidnapper's call. The problem is, the phone is plugged into the machine, which is plugged into the living room socket, and somewhere along the line a connection is faulty, which means that every twenty or so minutes, we have to jiggle all the cords to make sure the phone still functions.

Asra starts chatting with Dost as if they're dinner partners at a banquet. Both Dost and Captain have been to the United States. In fact, they were both in New York on September 11 for an international antiterrorism conference.

"Oh, that's *hysterical*!" says Asra. "What exactly is your function?" she asks him. His background is intelligence, he answers. Which is good in this case, I suppose.

"Tell us what you know of Gilani," I tell Dost.

"We don't know anything about him," he answers. How can they not know this man? My beautiful trust begins to falter.

The Gilani family, he explains, were the caretakers for a historical Sufi shrine in an area of Lahore. Gilani is "a very respected figure of Lahore. That's all we know."

My heart sinks. I think, These fuckers don't know anything. Only then does it occur to me that American authorities have not yet deigned to pay us a visit. Exhausted, I grab the telephone and call Randall Bennett at the United States consulate.

"How are you doing?" he asks in a preoccupied tone.

"I'm great, just great! My husband has been kidnapped and no one knows shit about the guys he is with, you're sitting in an office somewhere instead of helping, so yeah, I feel great!"

Patronizingly, Bennett asks me to calm down; he pretends he has the situation under control. When I tell him I am about to raise hell in Washington, he says that, appearances to the contrary, he is not sitting in an office but is working on Danny's release, and that he'll be there within two hours.

Dost and Captain have listened to my altercation without saying a word.

"We need him to come over," Captain says plainly, and then he begins to interrogate me, this time on health matters. How pregnant am I? When did I last sleep? What have I eaten? He orders me to lie down on the couch. "I am a married man," he informs me, "and I am a father. I know everything about pregnancy. I know about sentiments and hormones. I know everything. And I will tell you this: We will find your Danny. But you must take care of yourself and the baby."

While obeying him, I realize nobody has spoken to me that way since my father's death twenty-seven years ago. His voice, forgotten after so many years, comes back in my memory. It was a voice made thicker by the cigarettes he smoked endlessly, a voice my brother and I obeyed without discussion, not simply because it was so authoritative but also because there was some sweetness there, too. Normally I do not like being ordered around, but this is different. It's okay, I think, I can trust Captain.

I am afraid of falling asleep, as if sleep is going to make things more real, and reality is already a nightmare. Dost tries his best to help me. "If you fall asleep," he says, "maybe it'll only be a dream and Danny will be here when you wake up."

There is a ring at the door. I see we have become a team when, together, the four of us emerge from the dining room, carefully shutting the glass doors behind us to keep indiscreet glances from charts and such. Shabir, the servant, announces Najeeb, a reporter from *Jang*. It is the man Asra called earlier who told us about the missing *Time* magazine stringer.

Asra turns to Captain and Dost, not knowing if we should talk to Najeeb. Dost delivers his first order in what will become our intensive training in police tactics, in this awful mix-up of intelligence agents, real cops, terrorists, and well-intentioned people: "Go ahead, but don't tell him anything. Ask questions and just listen to what he has to say. Make mental notes."

Najeeb, tall and lean, stays at the door. "I am the crime reporter for *Jang*," he says. He has the look of a Pathan and wears a white *salwar kameez*. I distrust all the Pakistani press, which seems to have no tradition of objectivity or neutrality. Beyond that, I instinctively dis-trust Najeeb. He is doing a poor job at disguising the fact that Danny's abduction represents a real scoop for him. He intends to make his mark with this story. He tells me he's just returned from the Village Restaurant, where he heard from "people I know in the field" that Danny left the place accompanied by two bearded men.

"I'll tell you more if you answer some of my questions," he says.

For a brief moment, I hallucinate. I see Najeeb turn into a vulture, with his little eyes emptied of all humanity. I walk back into the house without even bothering to answer.

I tell Captain what Najeeb has proposed. He might know some-thing more, but I cannot deal with him; I want him interrogated by the police. But Captain is in no rush to ask him questions. "It is bet-ter," he says, "to keep journalists out of our way.

"Let us start with what we know," he says. "We have three tele-phone numbers. We have the cell-phone number for Imtiaz Siddique, who was to take Danny to Gilani. We have the cell-phone number for Bashir, who introduced Danny to Siddique. And we have Danny's cell-phone number. From here, we take our start."

"But," I protest, "that's so little to go on."

Captain lights another cigarette and nods.

Chapter Five

ASIF-LE-FIXER arrives from Islamabad at five the next morning. The usual sleepy look on his face is totally gone. His eyes are so wide open, so bloodshot, he reminds me of Alex in *A Clockwork Orange*. When I first open the door, his terrified expression makes me step back. His temples throb so visibly that I am embarrassed for him. He enters the house without acknowledging it; the hand that he extends, which I don't take, is shiny with sweat. "I meant no harm," he says. The panic that has taken hold of him almost softens my anger. "I just gave Danny what he wanted. That's all."

Asra rises from the living room couch, where she's been resting while staying close to the phone. She presses hard on her weary eyes, grabs her notepad, and leads us to the terrace, where we can talk without being overheard by our police guards.

We tell Asif it's time for us to call his friend, the one who introduced Danny to the Jihadi Spokesman. "What is his name? What is his number?"

Asif shakes his head. "I can't tell you that. I promised him his name would never come up."

"How much does Danny pay you?" demands Asra.

His head bowed, Asif confesses that Danny pays him a hundred dollars a day. Such a salary is almost indecent for this region—who makes a hundred dollars a day in Pakistan?—and he knows to neglect us would be unforgivable.

It's way too early in the morning for me to be diplomatic. Asra and

I are both in our baggy T-shirts and sweatpants; our hair sticks out, and our faces bear the sad signs of sleep deprivation. We don't look good, and we don't look friendly. "Give me the name and number!" I bark.

Asif surrenders.

The man's name is Zafar, and he is yet another journalist for *Jang*. He's an old friend of Asif's. "I begged him to help me," Asif says. "I told him that if I did good work for Danny, I could become a stringer for *The Wall Street Journal* in Pakistan. I said, 'Please help me.' We help each other as journalists. I begged Zafar, but I never told Danny about him."

In her notes, Asra begins to sketch a family tree: Asif → Zafar <___> the Jihadi Spokesman → Bashir → Imtiaz Siddique → Gilani.

In other words, Asif-le-fixer turned to Zafar for assistance. Zafar lined up the Jihadi Spokesman. Who introduced Danny to Bashir. Who then introduced Danny to Sheikh Gilani's disciple, Imtiaz Siddique. Who was to take Danny to Gilani. Who may have played a major role in Richard C. Reid's attempt to blow up American Airlines transatlantic Flight 63 with a bomb in his shoe.

"How well does Zafar know the Spokesman? And what group does the Spokesman represent?" we ask.

Zafar and the Spokesman apparently were introduced at a Harkat-ul-Mujahideen meeting a year ago, Asif tells us, "but he's just a spokesman." This is supposed to reassure me. It doesn't. Harkat is one of the most militant Muslim groups operating in Pakistan.

Asra and I need to talk to Zafar. With great reluctance, Asif dials his number. His tone is curiously deferential. "I am with Danny's wife and their friend. They know who you are," he says. "They will make sure you are protected and questioned by American police and not the Pakistani. They'll make sure your name won't be made public. They are about to call you from another line."

"Bullshit," I say when Asif hangs up. "He'll be questioned by the Pakistani police as well."

Asif falls silent. Asra and I plug a microphone into the telephone to record our call. On the phone, Zafar seems far less frightened than Asif, and he willingly answers all the questions we shoot his way.

He explains his relationship with Islamist extremist groups.

To understand it, one must first know a bit about the long and deadly struggle over Kashmir. In 1947, when India and Pakistan gained independence from Britain, the future of the Himalayan state of Kashmir was left murky. The majority of those living in the region were Muslim, but it was ruled by a Hindu maharaja, and according to the settlement with the British, the maharaja would decide whether it became part of predominantly Muslim Pakistan or predominantly Hindu India. Before he had made a final decision, Pakistan moved to claim the state, and the maharaja, in response, decided Kashmir would join India. The ensuing dispute has raged for over a half century.

Three wars have been fought over Kashmir; as many as sixty thousand may have died trying to claim it. The United Nations brokered a cease-fire to the first war in 1948, and the territory was divided in such a way that roughly a third was put under Pakistani control, while the remainder was left to India. Both the British and the United Nations called for a plebiscite to be held, to allow all the people of Kashmir to have a say in its status and future, but it never happened, and so the tug-of-war has continued all this time. Now the desire to see all of Kashmir brought under Islamic rule has become a national obsession for Pakistanis. A million men are mobilized along the Kashmiri border, known as the "line of control," and the entire world braces for yet another war, one that, horrifyingly enough, may involve nuclear weapons. Both nations have them; both seem willing to use them. So intransigent are the two countries that they even maintain positions on the Siachen glacier, in the far northeastern corner of Kashmir. The glacier is so remote it was never assigned to either country, so of course both demand it. Siachen boasts many things. At 20,700 feet, it is the highest battlefield in the world; it is the largest glacier not found on either pole; and it is regularly 70 degrees below zero (many of the soldiers live in igloos). Both sides appear to be spending up to one million dollars a day to fire at each other across the paralyzing terrain, although far more die from the unholy conditions than from gunfire.

What have caused passions to escalate in recent years have been the rise of both Islamic and Hindu fundamentalism and, in particular, the intensified efforts of Islamic fundamentalists to stake a claim to the region. In 1989, when the Soviets pulled out of Afghanistan and the Taliban seized control, jihadi groups turned their attention to Kashmir.

Now covering Kashmiri groups is a hot beat for a journalist like Zafar. Car bombs, mined fields, suicide bombers. . . . "These people came to the surface, and these activities became more intense. I am working for *Jang*. I am covering defense. Diplomatic organizations, Kashmir and Afghanistan. I often come across these jihadis. I contact them to find out what is going on."

His sources are people like the Jihadi Spokesman. "What's the Spokesman like?" we ask. "Who is he? Where does he live?"

"He's a simple activist," says Zafar. "He looks like a responsible person," maybe twenty years old, educated (which, in a country with an almost sixty percent illiteracy rate, is not insignificant). As for the Spokesman's private life, Zafar knows little. It is his impression that the Spokesman spends most nights in the organization's headquarters in the city of Rawalpindi. Former military headquarters of the British colony, Rawalpindi is both the twin city to and the antithesis of Islamabad, just a few kilometers to the south. Where Islamabad is formal, Rawalpindi is crammed, crumbling, chaotic.

The Spokesman is a well-connected young man. "He also seems mixed up with Jaish-e-Mohammed. When their camp was bombed in Afghanistan, the Spokesman invited me, along with other reporters, to a ceremony for the dead."

This is why Zafar reckoned that if anyone might be able to contact Sheikh Gilani, it would be the young Spokesman.

"You know," he says, "until not long ago, there was no harm in visiting these organizations."

This is an important point. It was only a few weeks ago that President Pervez Musharraf banned any of the jihadi groups. Danny wrote about it in "Pakistan Has Dual Goal in Crackdown on Islamic Militants," which ran on January 2. He reported, "Pakistan, in rounding up leaders of militant Islamic groups, is trying to kill two birds with one stone: avoiding a war with India and addressing Pakistan's own domestic terrorism problems."

Since the September 11 attacks, the United States had been pressuring Musharraf to seize control of terrorist activity based in Pakistan, but wary of possible political repercussions, he had resisted taking action. Then came a terrorist attack on the Indian parliament on December 13, 2001. Bursting into the parliament in New Delhi, five Kashmiri militants managed to shoot nine people dead before being killed by the police.

We were in Islamabad at the time. By phone, Danny mobilized coverage in India, then we headed out to collect reactions from Pakistanis in the street. What we discovered was disconcerting, to say the least. Most people we spoke to sincerely believed that India had staged the attack so the world would turn against Pakistan. Everyone was engaged in a conspiracy theory. It felt as if mental chaos had become the norm. If Pakistani citizens could believe such a highly unlikely plot, how far could they be manipulated? How deep did the ignorance and paranoia go?

India threatened military retaliation unless Pakistan cracked down on the groups that were most likely to be have been behind the attack: Harkat-ul-Mujahideen (HUM), Jaish-e-Mohammed (JEM) and Lashkar-e-Taiba (LET). Musharraf agreed to ban the three groups, but crackdowns on extremists are more easily announced than implemented. Pakistan shelters many organizations that carry on terrorist activities. Almost fifty are known to authorities, and many are interrelated. And extremist groups tend to be in a constant state of revolution, whether they're being shut down or not. Groups go underground, take new names, form new permutations. JEM is an offshoot of Harkat-ul-Mujahideen; Lashkar-e-Taiba has its roots in the fundamentalist Wahhabi sect of Saudi Arabia, which has links to Lashkar-e-Jhangvi, an outlawed group of Sunni Muslims that has been responsible for the murder of untold Shiites. If Pakistan wants to rid itself of terrorists, it will have to untangle a web formed by twenty years of intrigues and bloody alliances.

After the Indian parliament attack and the ensuing crackdown, Danny and Asif-le-fixer traveled to Bahawalpur, a cotton-farming district in Pakistan's Punjab province, where Jaish-e-Mohammed has its headquarters. A few days before, Pakistani police had rounded up much of JEM's staff, but JEM knew the authorities would be coming, and they'd moved their files and computers to a secret location before the police arrived. In addition, the cops left behind enough JEM members to keep the office running.

Danny and Asif easily found the JEM office in an unmarked house in a dirt road neighborhood of Bahawalpur. Parked outside were double-cabin Hilux trucks for the use of JEM members. Some, Danny told me later, had Pakistani government plates. On the wall of the recruiting office, the group's name had been painted over, but posters urging holy war were still everywhere: If you don't rise to the occasion now, the Muslim nation will be finished. Danny stepped into the office marked FINANCES, where he interviewed a member of the JEM central executive committee. The man settled himself behind a desk, lined up his three switched-on cell phones, and proceeded to pontificate about the cause of the Kashmiri "freedom fighters" (which, Danny noted, is what the Indians call their guys, too). It was jihadi business as usual.

As part of the crackdown, the banned groups' funds were supposed to have been frozen. But when Danny visited the local branch of the bank, he found that JEM had never actually had a bank account. Instead, the organization stored its donations in "personal" accounts—thousands of them. Since none technically belonged to Jaish-e-Mohammed, the money just kept flowing.

Jaish-e-Mohammed means "Army of the Prophet." The organization is young: It was founded in early 2000 when Maulana Massood

Azhar, once a leader of Harkat-ul-Mujahideen, was sprung from an Indian prison. How extremist is the JEM? And how wealthy can such a young group be? When he launched the group, Azhar flew to Afghanistan, where he met with Osama bin Laden, who, it is said, provided the group significant funding. Azhar is under arrest again, but as Danny recently wrote, the group "is unlikely to suffer from the arrest of the 33-year-old [Azhar], who, after all, rose to fame in prison. . . . Now the group claims to have sent thousands of fighters into Kashmir and says its bi-weekly magazine has a circulation of 50,000 in Pakistan and abroad."

On January 12, 2002, a month after the crackdown on the three primary jihadi groups, President General Musharraf announced a ban on all other Pakistani terrorist organizations. Danny and I were in Peshawar, and we went to the Khyber Bazaar to listen to the announcement. Danny found the only restaurant in the area with a television set. Smiling and polite, he ordered fried chicken and sweet chai and asked for a little space on the crowded bench so we could watch the TV. We were the only foreigners, and I was the only woman. I brought out my radio equipment and taped Danny's conversation with a man on the bench who wanted to please the inquiring American with his answers but couldn't figure out what the "right" answers might be. Similarly, the crowd, watching us work, knew that we were exercising a freedom of movement and thought that to them was almost exotic. On the television, General Musharraf occupied the full screen, which made him look both dignified and tiny. He spoke of a bright future for Pakistan. We will have a democracy, he told his people. But it will be our *own* democracy.

Staring up at the DANNY chart on the dining room wall of the house on Zamzama Street, I recognize that almost every name we've written down in the thirty-six hours since Danny disappeared is a name Danny mentioned in one article or another over the last four months. I find it chilling, even if I don't know what to make of it.

We have been talking with Zafar for a half hour, and he tells us something that disturbs us even more. He spoke with the Jihadi Spokesman yesterday morning, and the Spokesman said he'd lost his address book and thus would be unable to give us Bashir's number. At the same time, Zafar promises he will help us find Bashir—provided, that is, we remain discreet about his participation.

We lie, promising to stay quiet, but in truth we have no reason or desire to hide his identity from Captain.

The doorbell rings; the police are back. I pocket the tape on which I've recorded our talk with Zafar. Asra says to Asif-le-fixer, "Your interrogation is about to start." Then she adds a little more gently, "I know you're scared. But you're not in danger, Asif. Danny is. And so it is Danny we must protect."

Steve LeVine and Danny originally hired Asif in September to help them on a story on Bashiruddin Mehmood, a prominent Pakistani nuclear scientist with scarily strong ties to the Taliban. Asif had been working for Jiji Press, the Japanese news wire. Signing on with *The Wall Street Journal* was clearly a step up for him. Image-conscious and reasonably good-looking, if plump, Asif had a tendency to be lascivious, but aside from that, he seemed all right. More important, he appeared to have the contacts that Danny and Steve needed. When all the big international media are pitted in competition, the quality of the names in your fixer's address book is what really counts.

Danny met with Asif for daily briefings in the lobby of the Islamabad Marriott. The Marriott was a scene back in September as the war in Afghanistan was about to start. Heavily armed soldiers stood guard on nearby street corners, sheltered by piles of stacked sandbags, while inside the five-star hotel had been transformed into a temple of worldwide information. Seemingly the entire planet was represented in this media Tower of Babel, and of its 290 rooms, 270 were taken by an international battalion of journalists.

The elevators spat out and swallowed a continuous wave of reporters, cameramen, and technicians poised to jump on info, *any* info, one might stumble across in the aftermath of the terrorists' attacks. All the icons of reportage were here—"Look, there's John Burns of *The New York Times*." The weary war correspondents looked like they'd seen it all, while the jittery young freelancers chomped at the bit. Veterans swapped tales from not so old times in the Balkans, while a stream of people paced the marbled lobby, cell phones glued to their ears. There were reporters from Croatian radio and Aztec TV, more dailies than you knew existed, and of course the BBC and CNN. These last two had rented most of the hotel's top floor, thus reigning over us all.

There was just one problem: There was nothing to see or report.

September, October, November, the action was elsewhere, in inaccessible Afghanistan. Back home, editors pressured journalists into speculation. *The Wall Street Journal* had little historical presence in Pakistan, and suffered from a lack of institutional clout, but that wasn't what the higher-ups wanted to hear. On November 14, John Bussey rapped the knuckles of Danny and his colleagues: "comrades, i'm very keen to get pakistan/musharraf on page one . . . any way to do that? . . . every major publication and tv channel has had an interview with the guy. is our request still standing?"

Yes, very much still standing.

Western cameramen, desperate for content and pressured by their organizations, filmed the Islamic militants who regularly regrouped in front of the hotel. Some Pakistani spokesmen, if they showed the slightest level of eloquence, granted up to ten interviews a day. I wrote about the journalists and the hothouse of the hotel. The truth is, most journalists don't like being interviewed. One world-famous star of the Marriott constellation loudly chastised me as I approached, reporter's notebook in hand. "Do you know who I am?" she snapped. To be fair, she hadn't had her morning coffee. Danny, who had stayed at our table, gleefully flashed me two thumbs up—"Great quote, baby, great quote"—as I beat as graceful a retreat as I could.

Islamabad became an abyss of boredom. I struck up a relationship with an old man selling umbrellas. He sat in a field at the intersection of two roads. Around him, he had built a system of laundry ropes on which he hung his umbrellas. It didn't rain during the four months we were in Islamabad, but the little man persisted all the same.

We abandoned the hotel and moved into a guest house called Chez Soi, which also housed journalists almost exclusively, though this lot preferred to keep a lower profile. Chez Soi looked exactly like a bourgeois home you would find in Bordeaux, filled with tasteful reproductions of tasteful Parisian scenes. What gave the difference away were the Inmarsat Thrane & Thrane sat phones on every terrace, their gray-on-white antennas pointing south toward the Indian Ocean satellite. The Chez Soi boasted Internet connections even better than those at the Marriott, and the staff was used to accommodating the needs and desires of journalists, however bizarre. Here, the guests were courteous to one another. But we were also all competing, and we never forgot it. Breakfast conversations were held in whispers.

Danny's work never let up. It led us to Kuwait; to Qatar, for the Islamic Countries Conference, where Danny interviewed one of the most respected spiritual leaders in the country, Yussef Qaradawi; to Peshawar, on the Afghan border, in Pashtoun country. The work was fascinating, but there were countless frustrations. At first Danny was pleased with his new fixer's work, but before long, it became clear that Asif wasn't the best, and in certain respects was a washout.

It looked as if a bloodbath would erupt any day in Kashmir, but Pakistani authorities were denying Danny access unless he agreed to join an organized trip for journalists (he refused). There were rumors that Pakistani nuclear-weapons scientists, like Bashiruddin, were collaborating with the Taliban and Al Qaeda, and reporters everywhere were chasing the story, but *The New York Times* locked it down first. The email Danny and his colleague Steve LeVine received from *The Wall Street Journal* foreign desk in December was to the point. "See the *NY Times* story today." No signature, no comment. One wasn't needed, really.

On such evenings Danny was depressed. Steve LeVine , too. The head of the Central Asia office for the *Journal* out of Kazakhstan,

Steve is a discreet and serious-looking man, blessed with a gift for observation and a quiet but strong sense of humor. He and Danny worked well together; they shared a directness and a distrust of knee-jerk judgments. Steve's fiancée was here with him—the lovely-looking Nurilda from Kazakhstan, who, like me, was pregnant. Because our situations were similar, a part of me hoped to find in Nurilda an Islamabad buddy, but she was younger and showed a disarming disinterest in the conflicts surrounding us.

The official questioning of Asif-le-fixer has begun. "All right," says Captain, exhibiting his regal calm. "I would like to hear about this again. When was Danny's first contact with these people?"

As Asif explains it, early this month, Danny and Asif hired a car and driver from the Islamabad Marriott and, as they had arranged with him, met the Jihadi Spokesman at a spot somewhere between Islamabad and Rawalpindi. The Spokesman was waiting for them on the side of the road. He was alone. He climbed into the car and directed Danny and Asif to what he said was Sheikh Gilani's house. He'd been there just a few months before, he told them, but when they pulled up to the house, it was empty. Neighbors said Gilani had moved out.

The Jihadi Spokesman assured a disappointed Danny and Asif that he would track Gilani down. The second meeting took place January 11. This time the Spokesman promised to introduce them to Bashir, a man who could lead them to Gilani. The introduction would take place at the Akbar International Hotel in Rawalpindi, on Liaqat Road.

Once again Danny and Asif picked up the Spokesman by the side of the road. This time he brought along a man he identified as a school friend from Karachi, with whom he planned to continue on to Murree Hills, a local resort, later that evening.

The Akbar was a ten-dollar-a-night hotel of seventy-five rooms. When Danny and Asif got to the hotel, they took the elevator to the fourth floor, as instructed, but the room they were supposed to meet Bashir in was locked. So Asif-le-fixer and the Jihadi Spokesman left Danny and the friend on the fourth floor and went down to the restaurant to look for Bashir. Which is where they found him, sitting with two friends. It was seven P.M., and he had ordered dinner.

"Your guest is here," the Spokesman said.

The men talked for two hours, Danny scribbling his mysterious shorthand in his Super Conquérants. He can take perfect notes without ever glancing down or breaking eye contact. Bashir, who was apparently Punjabi, spoke "fluent English," Asif told us. "Bashir said he was in the stitching-garments business in Pindi. He seemed balanced. He seemed educated. He mentioned nothing about his personal life in conversation; there was no conversation of a wife."

Danny asked Bashir about Gilani—his personality, ideology, preachings, actions. Bashir asked Danny nothing. "He showed no signs of curiosity about Danny," said Asif.

Defying Pakistani tradition, Bashir offered no food or drink to his guests, until Asif insisted on ordering sandwiches and coffee from room service. The food was served with visible ill will. When the interview drew to a close, the group got up. Danny slid a business card from his wallet and gave it to Bashir. In South Asia, people exchange cards as soon as they get acquainted. Bashir didn't reciprocate.

As they were leaving, Danny asked Bashir if he thought he could arrange an appointment with Gilani. Bashir answered that he would try, but Danny would have to prove first that he was "neither anti-Islamic nor anti-Pakistani" by sending a selection of his articles. Another hurdle. If the articles passed muster, the meeting would take place in the capital after our return from Peshawar.

When Danny came home that night, I was already asleep. He crawled onto the bed, still dressed, to let me know he was back and that he had missed me.

"How was your meeting?" I murmured.

"Interesting," he said. "It's always interesting to see how other people's minds work."

We were heading to Peshawar the next day for a documentary I was producing for French radio on a prestigious *lycée français* in

Kabul that had been shut down by the Taliban, moved to Pakistan, and, with the Taliban's fall from power, was about to return to Afghanistan. Before we left, Danny honored his promise to Bashir by sending an array of recent articles. Many, if not most, reporters would pick through their articles and weed out those that might ruffle the feathers of the recipients. Not Danny. Faithful to himself and the work he does, Danny did not hide any of the topics he had been writing about, no matter how potentially touchy. He emailed Bashir his stories on Kashmir and the crackdown on Islamic extremists. And he sent features on less controversial topics, too—stem cell research in India, and the race for an AIDS vaccine in the subcontinent, where the authorities have just begun to acknowledge the extent of the damage done by the deadly virus. "Hello, thank you very much for arranging the meeting with Pir-Sahab [one of the honorific titles of Gilani]," Danny wrote in a short note. "Here are a few of my articles from the past year. Best regards."

Thus began the unusual email exchange between Danny and Bashir that Asra and I studied so intently earlier. Bashir's first email to Danny came two days after Danny sent him his pieces, three days after they met. It was an ingratiating response:

Dear M. Pearl,

Thank you very much for your articles—I enjoyed reading them and I have passed on the prints-out to Shah Saab. He has now gone to Karachi for a few days and I am sure that when he returns we can go and see him. I am sorry to have not replied to you earlier, I was preoccupied with looking after my wife who has been ill. Please pray for her health.

Looking forward to seeing you.
Adaab,
Chaudrey Bashir Ahmad Shabbir

Adaab? As Asra and I showed Danny's emails to Captain and Asif, they both looked startled by the use of the word. That was a formal greeting, they said, commonly used by scholarly Muslims but not by the general Pakistani population. It could prove significant. Then again, the word is also sometimes used by Muslims to greet non-Muslims. It could be nothing more than that.

The email was sent eight minutes after midnight on January 16. After having struggled for an hour to obtain an Internet connection from our room in Peshawar, Danny had given up and gone to read his emails at the reception desk, thus raising the curiosity of the hotel staff. He swiftly replied to Bashir's message: "I wish a speedy recovery for your wife, and look forward to seeing you in Islamabad—I'll be back Friday. Best regards, Daniel Pearl."

We returned on January 18. The following day, Danny received yet another email from Bashir, who had good news: The sheikh had read the articles and was willing to meet with Danny. Just one catch: He was no longer in Islamabad.

Dear Mr. Pearl,

I'm sorry to have not been in touch with you earlier . . . I've managed to misplace your phone-number. Please mail it to me. Or you can call my brother's mobile no. I think I gave you my other brother's number last time only to return home and find out he has sold it! We have applied for a home line and as soon as we pay "the relevant people" we will get it. Such is Pakistan! My wife is back home from hospital alhamdolillah and the whole experience was a real eye-opener. The poor people who fall ill here and have to go to the hospital have a really miserable and harassing time. It made me realize once again that our family has a lot to be grateful for. The Shaikh says that gratitude is the essence of faith.

I spoke to the Shaikh's secretary yesterday and he told me that the Shaikh-Saab has read your articles and that you are welcome to meet him. However it will be a number of days before he returns from Karachi. If Karachi is in your program you are welcome to see him there. Or if you want to put some questions

to him you can mail them to me and I will pass the printout to
his secretary. Or if you want to wait until he returns here that is
fine also.

Wish you the best and look forward to hearing from you.

Adaab, Bashir

Odd, I think, going again over the emails. These are so much
more personal, warmer, than the interaction Asif describes having
had with Bashir at the Akbar International Hotel.

The following day, Danny and Bashir made plans for Danny to
meet with the sheikh in Karachi. By going to Karachi, we could score
two goals, Danny told me, grinning. He could finally land Gilani, and
maybe, just maybe, I could "help Asra figure out her love life."

Bashir wrote Danny that Gilani "will give me the number of one
of his mureeds, whom you can call when you get there. The mureed
will take you to see him. Please give the Sheikh my regards and
respect and ask him to continue to remember me in his prayers.
Tell him we miss him very much and hope to see him back soon." He
then sent the name and number of Imtiaz Siddique. Danny's trip was
set.

Captain studies the emails with a preoccupied air. "I need a copy
of them," he says.

"Why don't you ask someone to print them for you?" Asra snaps.

Captain gives her a pained smile but doesn't answer. A single
glance outside to the battered jeep parked at the curb, and to the
underfed driver attending it, and we understand what the captain is
trying to say. He doesn't have a printer at his disposal.

I have felt the bone-rattling power of F-16s soaring overhead to
bomb the bearded men clustered in the caves of Afghanistan. But I
had no idea—few do—what the front line of this war against terrorism really looks like. Here on the ground in Karachi, the verita-
ble safe house of the Al Qaeda network, those who are battling the
bad guys on behalf of the entire world—the people conducting the
raids and brushing off death threats—do not have the most rudi-

mentary printer, let alone computers, access to databases, cell phones. They don't even have decent cars.

"What do you need?" I ask Captain.

"Your trust," he says. "And technology."

Asra recognizes the job at hand: We need to establish a bona fide antiterrorist headquarters here at the house. She starts drawing up a list of necessary supplies that she will ask *The Wall Street Journal* to provide. We need cell phones; at least two more for us, and several others to equip the men Captain has sent out to track Gilani in Lahore; to Rawalpindi to find the Jihadi Spokesman and Bashir; and all over Karachi. We need a laser printer or two, preferably ones that can also serve as fax machines. We need file folders to organize documents; pens, Scotch tape, paper for the ever expanding chart. We need a new answering machine, one that doesn't have to be glued together. We seriously need landlines—for Internet access, the fax machine, international calls. And we need a technician to get it all going.

Steve LeVine shows up with boxes of equipment: sky-blue one-inch binders, notebooks, a hole puncher, a stapler, Post-its, even a pencil holder. A new recruit of Captain's, an unassuming young man named Imran, goes out and buys a huge laser/fax printer. "This is not the one I wanted!" grumps Asra, inspecting the box. Imran tries to justify his purchase, but Asra turns icy—until, that is, he swiftly connects it to Danny and Asra's computers and it begins to spit out information we desperately need. She loves Imran from there on.

Getting more landlines isn't as easy. In Pakistan it can require months, even years, to get a new phone line. It takes a few days to hit upon how to score new lines, but once the authorities develop their method, they are ruthless in using it. They check the status of our neighbors' phone bills, and in any household that is the faintest bit late in making a payment, the police step in, plug up those phone lines, and *riiiipppp,* hand them over to us. Preferably in the daytime, when no one is home.

"Oh my God," Steve moans when it becomes apparent where the

phone lines are coming from, "we're going to need extra police protection just to save us from our neighbors!"

I wonder how Captain is able to maintain his dignity in the middle of such absurd obstacles. "What else do you need?" I ask him.

"I need *their* trust," says Captain, by which he means the FBI. It is as if the two groups—the Pakistanis and the Americans—inhabit entirely different worlds. The distrust is endemic. But neither side is going to succeed without the other, and we need them to willingly cooperate in the field—now.

We appeal to the FBI. The lines of communication have got to be open, we tell them, and a system for sharing information devised.

We send Imran out to buy a speakerphone, and that afternoon, the heart of our team gathers around our coffee table. There are three Pakistanis, Captain and Dost, and Zahoor, who works for Randall; and four Americans—Randall, two FBI computer experts, and Maureen Platt. Maureen is an official woman, big and brusque. She is clearly someone more used to giving orders than receiving them.

When she strides through the door, she immediately takes note of the three French attachés who have arrived from the French consulate to offer their services. "What are they doing here?" she snaps. "What have you told them?" This isn't exactly the collaborative spirit we had in mind, and clearly, asking Maureen to share and share alike with the Pakistanis is pushing her to her limits. Reluctantly, we ask the French to leave.

"Is there something we can do for you?" they ask us.

Yes, we say. "We'd really like some French food." Later that day, they drop off a glorious array of tartes that their wives have made us— porkless quiche Lorraine, tarte à l'oignon, tarte Tatin, tarte aux poires, and meringues, too.

When the phone rings, it is the FBI headquarters in South Brunswick, New Jersey. Now Maureen insists that Asra and I be evicted from the room. It strikes us as silly, but we shrug it off. We have gotten Captain what he needs—vital cooperation from the FBI. We can handle a little indignity.

A man presents flowers addressed to me. There is so much tension in the house that Dost and Captain grab me as I reach for the bouquet. They study the little card stapled to the wrapper, then pass it my way. "Best wishes," it reads, "Syed Anwar Mahmood, Secretary of Information and Media Development." Danny and I interviewed him a few days before at PTV's headquarters for an article on the Pakistani media and their coverage of the conflict with India.

The sight of the flowers brings a nauseating taste to my mouth and the brutal recollection of a memory, carefully tucked away. My beloved mother, two years before, sick with cancer. Around her bed, visitors had left armloads of flowers. "Can you take them away?" my mother asked me. "All these flowers. It looks like . . . a cemetery."

I drop the secretary's bouquet in the kitchen. I do not want to think about my mother right now. I suddenly recall the journalist for *Time* magazine, Ghulam Hasnain. What has become of him?

Asra and I join Captain on the sidewalk in front of the house. These are my first steps out of the house since Danny's disappearance. My legs are unsteady. The sun blinds me painfully. Asra asks the question delicately: "Are the people involved in the *Time* journalist's disappearance also involved in Danny's?"

Captain whispers his answer: "Between you and me, they are not."

"Who took Hasnain? Pakistani intelligence? ISI?" I ask just as quietly.

Captain does not say, but he tells us that Hasnain has been released, and that the reporter fiercely refuses to divulge—to anyone—what he experienced during his thirty-six-hour "disappearance." Now only two things are clear: Danny was not with him, and whatever Hasnain underwent has traumatized him forever.

Dost and Captain have left to join their families for dinner. Asra fluctuates between her computer and Danny's, a plate of chicken and rice between them. The mere sight of food makes my stomach shrivel.

Asra throws an oblique glance at my belly, and I sit down next to her and try to eat something. I eat with my fingers like they do in Pakistan. While I swallow the chicken, much too spicy, I pray that Danny is being fed: May they treat you decently.

From his belongings, I have extracted a photo Danny cut out of the newspaper the day before our arrival in Karachi. It is of Danny's favorite animal—a giraffe with her baby. While kissing him, the mama seems to be swallowing up his right eye. It makes the baby look as if he is winking, and the photo is winning and comical. I tape it up, imagining that my husband is winking at me, telling me not to worry.

Up in the office, Asra lies on the couch with The Lover. I hear their voices grow sharper, louder. Eventually Asra comes back downstairs, and she seems devastated. Not knowing I am awake, she sits at the dining table and hides her face in her hands. The front door slams. Big tears filter through her delicate fingers and splatter the wooden table. He's left, she tells me. He doesn't want to see her anymore. He said he has to make a choice between her and his family, and he has chosen his family. She has too many troubles, he said.

"What?" I say.

"That's what he said."

Intelligence agents paid him a call during the day while he was at work. "We know all about your relationship with the Indian girl," they said. They had records of Asra and The Lover's weekend beach outings. They had started following Asra in December when she'd attended a rich kid's bash in the posh part of town. Little did they know, or care, that she was there as a reporter, working on a piece about sex, drugs, and rock 'n' roll in the port city.

"Stay with the girl," they directed The Lover, "and report back to us."

Though they never explicitly threatened him, the subtext was unmistakable. He was involved in an illegal relationship, and they could use that against him anytime they wanted.

This is a real threat. "Illegal" sex—*zina*—is punishable by one hundred lashes in Pakistan. Or worse. In parts of Pakistan—still, truly—women sentenced according to *sharia,* the court of Islamic law, are stoned to death for such behavior.

What is truly shocking is that the agents visiting Asra's lover seemed far more interested in investigating Asra than in searching for Danny. The fact is that she is a naturally suspicious character here. "I was born in India," she reminds me.

"President Musharraf also," I remind her. Musharraf was born in Delhi; his family emigrated to Pakistan during Partition four years later. Still, I'm not naive. I know that ISI suspects everything to be an Indian plot to destabilize Pakistan and endanger the county's relationship with America. It would not surprise me if Danny's abduction became the gist of new conspiracy speculations. But come on—to suspect Asra as somehow involved?

Under such circumstances, how can her lover leave her? Why does he not at least show her some kindness, some concern? He is proving to be even more of a coward than I expected, and I wasn't expecting much.

I take Asra in my arms, and we stay that way for a while, here in the deserted house, not saying a word.

Captain reappears, as I knew he would, by eleven P.M. The faithful Dost follows.

"Gilani is a third-class idiot," Captain proclaims, while Dost sits down and begins to type up his report. Picking away with his two index fingers, he writes, "MISSING JOURNALIST DANIEL PEARL."

Some of Captain's men have visited Gilani's house in Lahore. Gilani has three wives. Of all the people related to the cleric by marriage, they've managed to find only one, a sister-in-law, but she's been very communicative. She describes Gilani as "an idiot, arrogant with everyone and especially with the members of his own family, including his own father, who deceased approximately ten days ago. He loves to shroud himself in mystery but he is stupid." She thinks Gilani incapable of organizing a kidnapping.

Asra reveals the results of her latest Google search. "Okay, guys," she says, "here's what I've found. Gilani believes in invisible forces who inhabit the earth, damaging people, causing psychotic diseases, fits, epilepsies. He believes these forces are controlling human beings and are way more threatening than terrorists."

Dost is the first to burst out laughing, followed nervously by the rest of us. "We still have to find him," Captain says, removing a photo of Gilani from his briefcase. In the photo, Gilani looks square-headed and dull. Asra takes it from Captain and pastes it up on our chart. Dost approves with a nod. Asra apologizes for misspelling some of the names, but Dost tells her this doesn't matter because "all the terrorists work under pseudonyms." Some of them juggle more than a dozen identities.

"This Asif," says Dost. "What's the deal with the fixer?"

"He's been negligent. Behaved stupidly. But I'm not sure there's anything really wrong with the guy. He's got a wife and a little girl he loves a lot," I say.

Dost gestures with his chin in the direction of the living room. "He's here again, you know?"

I follow Dost's glance and see Asif-le-fixer sitting on the couch, anxious but quiet, sandwiched between two other men. Who are these guys? What are they doing here?

I shut the door to the dining room. I don't want them looking at our research. The two men turn out to be Saeed, the reporter with the poor sense of direction whom Danny used as a fixer in Karachi on the morning of January 23, the day he disappeared. The other man is Asif-le-fixer's brother-in-law. He is fat and wears a droopy mustache and an ill-fitting brown jacket. Dost knows the brother-in-law, who works at *Takbeer,* a jihadi newspaper. "It is very anti-U.S," Dost says.

That's daring, I think, bringing these men into this house. I explode at Asif, frightening him with my anger. I demand that the two leave.

Asif is here because Captain has ordered him to return to

Rawalpindi to help track down the Jihadi Spokesman. He will be accompanied by a police official, a man Asif says he knows by reputation. "This guy is a torturer. He will torture me." Asif looks piteous. I walk to the other room, where the dreaded police officer is waiting. He has a mustache, a gut, and a somber look. His hands are clasped behind his back. "Hello, what's your name?" I ask, extending my hand.

"My name is Butt. B-U-T-T." Asra almost fails to suppress an inappropriate laugh. Me, too. Dost is standing nearby. I take him aside to ask him to keep an eye on the guy's methods.

Dost tells me not to worry. Because of the high profile nature of this case, Butt has been notified by his superiors that he must behave. Still, to underscore that, Dost turns to Butt, pointing a finger straight at him. "*No torture, no bribes!*" he warns sternly.

Hands still locked behind his back, Butt nods and stares down at his feet.

Chapter Six

CAPTAIN AND I stand, as we so often do, before the chart. "What do we do now?" I ask him.

"Wait for a phone call. They are going to call you. They will call from a pay phone, or drop a letter, or contact the consulate or the press."

"Why don't they call now?"

Captain thinks for a while. "I am not sure. But they will."

"What can I do now?"

"Keep calling them."

There are three numbers I have dialed so often that my fingers can punch the buttons automatically: Danny's cell-phone number, Imtiaz Siddique's purported number, and Bashir's number. Considering that I've dialed Danny's number roughly four times an hour for the past sixty hours, I've punched it in about two hundred times, if you subtract the moments I've slept.

Yet there's nothing mechanical about the act. Each time I expect to hear Danny's voice break through the static, faintly, as if he's whispering from a hiding place, on a crossed wire, or reaching me from the middle of nowhere, from another country.

Hope is a remarkable muscle.

"If they want ransom money, how much will they ask for?" I ask Captain.

Because a higher percentage of Karachi kidnappers are being caught these days, the going ransom for a businessman has fallen from

$100,000 to $20,000. But whatever this is, it isn't your run-of-the-mill kidnapping. Someone suggests they may ask for $5 million, the same amount that the United States originally offered for Osama bin Laden after the 1998 embassy bombings.

Whatever the amount, I will get it somehow, and if they tell me, "You come alone," I will go alone. The police won't want me to; everyone—Captain, *The Wall Street Journal,* Asra, the FBI—will try to hold me back. So I will have to slip out of the house.

I station myself near the phone so I can be the one to snatch the receiver when the ransom call comes in.

In New York Danny's boss, John Bussey, is thinking similar thoughts. He's been on the phone with a "K&R" specialist—kidnapping and ransom. The K&R guy is a subcontractor to the *Journal*'s insurance carrier, because they, too, are readying themselves for a ransom situation, and Bussey wants to make sure money can be transferred quickly to Pakistan when needed. But the specialist is based in Hong Kong, and it dawns on Bussey that the guy doesn't seem to have a lot of experience in South Asia. "By the time I got off the phone Friday, I realized we weren't going to be calling on him," Bussey will tell me later.

Instead, Bussey calls us. He wants to come to Karachi, but he says he's worried that his appearance may disrupt the alchemy that has developed between Asra and me and the Pakistani authorities. Still, I suspect we could use him here. "Come," I tell him. "You be our public face. Meet with Musharraf and the interior minister, make the diplomatic rounds in Islamabad for us."

I continue to hover by Danny's phone.

Captain says, "You know, they may not want money for ransom. They may demand a prisoner exchange—Danny for Al Qaeda prisoners held in American jails or Guantánamo Bay."

A colleague in the *Journal*'s London bureau forwards an intriguing email from Andrea Gerlin of *The Philadelphia Inquirer*. She's attached an article from the January 24 *Independent,* a British newspaper, profiling a shadowy character suspected of having bankrolled the 9/11 attacks. The man's name is Omar Saeed Sheikh and he's a well-to-do Briton, a onetime student at the London School of Economics turned Islamic militant. Apparently Omar, from his base in Rawalpindi, wired $100,000 to Mohammed Atta, one of the 9/11 ring leaders, shortly before the World Trade Center attacks. But that is not why Andrea has passed along the article. What disturbs her is that Omar has a particular specialty: He kidnaps Westerners. The article contains diary excerpts in which he wrote of luring four students into one of his traps.

Omar Saeed Sheikh is a name that we will hear over and over again in the weeks to come. But for now we find nothing linking him to Danny's disappearance. Sheikh Mubarak Ali Shah Gilani, on the other hand, seems progressively more suspicious. His friend Khawaja has taken to calling us and ranting, each time more of a weirdo. During his most recent call, he claimed Gilani's father had passed away as a result of interrogations by the *Boston Globe* journalist investigating links between Gilani and Richard Reid. The old man supposedly died of shock upon reading a note from the journalist asking him about his son's connections to terrorists.

Khawaja has a supremely unpleasant voice, and he yells. But Asra and I are models of self-control, applying the first rule of intelligence-gathering as taught by Dost: Say little; let him do the talking.

"Where is Gilani?" we ask.

"I don't talk to him," says Khawaja, and rants some more.

After several of these calls, Captain decides to take over. He carries the telephone into the living room and, cupping a hand around the receiver, murmurs lowly, insistently. We don't know precisely what Captain is saying to Khawaja, but the tone doesn't sound like good tidings. Captain, with his soft voice, reveals how tough he can be.

Khawaja never calls back, and Gilani vanishes. Police have been searching mosques, airports, all his known residences (and there are many). They heard he was in Muzaffarabad, a city in Punjab on the border of Pakistan-controlled Kashmir. It made sense that he might be there—Muzaffarabad is on the travel route for jihadis heading to

Kashmir (where Gilani has yet another residence). But by the time the police reached the house, it had been cleaned out and the cleric had fled, along with his three wives (two American and one Pakistani).

Captain's cell phone rings constantly. Gilani's father has been located . . . his son is in custody . . . found in Rawalpindi . . . Gilani is in the air somewhere between Lahore and Islamabad . . .

There's hope.

And there is Captain. Wherever I am, he comes straight to me, his eyes almost plunging into mine, searching for doubts, hoping for trust. I try to give something back. I return his stare and I summon as much determination as I can. "You are the one who gives me strength," he tells me. Thus we take care of each other, bonded as we are in our defiance.

If hope is our most powerful weapon, fear is the greatest threat the terrorists wield against us. Fear paralyzes you, and I cannot afford that.

My father used to read Frank Herbert's sci-fi epic *Dune* repeatedly, as if it were a Bible. Herbert wrote: "I must not fear. Fear is the mind-killer. Fear is the little death that brings total obliteration. I will face my fear, I will allow it to pass over me and through me. When it is gone, I will turn the inner-eye to see its path. Where the fear once was, there will be nothing. Only I will remain."

I know that wherever they're holding him, Danny is doing precisely what I'm doing: refusing to allow fear to defeat him, letting it pass over him.

Little Embryo has been good so far, keeping quiet, not putting additional pressure on me. Every once in a while, I slip into my bedroom to check out *What to Expect When You're Expecting*. It's not like they have a chapter on what to do when your husband has been kidnapped, but they do advocate plenty of rest, avoiding stress, and eating lots of green vegetables. I'm striking out in all three departments, but I am keeping up my strength with a steady diet of chicken biryani and spiced chai. And I talk to the baby. I tell him, "You're going to be a warrior, baby, and we're going to be fine." I tell him that

I trust him. It never occurred to me before that one could trust a fetus.

It is Randall Bennett, who has finally decided to pay us a visit. "I've been busy, you know," he says somewhat pugnaciously. When I first saw him the day of the Pakistani-FBI conference call, I was expecting someone midway between a diplomat and a G.I. Not at all. For starters, Randall wears an earring, a tiny little gold stud in his left ear. His shoulder-length blond hair is slicked straight back, and he's dressed all in black—black jeans and black shirt, buttoned to the top as if he's on his way to a club. He may be in his fifties, but he's in impressive shape. As I later learn, he is a former tae kwon do instructor, works out regularly with a kick bag in his backyard, and also lifts weights in the marine gym. What's more, he is an expert knife thrower, an art he keeps up by teaching others. His wife, Carolina, whom Randall met and married when he was stationed in Colombia, has apparently become quite good at it, too.

We lead Randall upstairs to the private room off the veranda, where we can talk without being overheard. He pulls up a low wooden Indian chair and settles his large frame into it. He opens his legs wide, balances his elbows on his knees, and pats the fat file he holds in his big hands. "Tell me what you know," he says. It is clear he has ambivalent feelings about us, so Asra and I rise to the implicit challenge, delivering an authoritative and detailed report. Randall's eyes, bright blue and heavily lashed, travel between me and Asra, observing us carefully. He begins to take notes. We can tell we're winning his trust and, more, his respect. We watch him discover that he likes us. We like him back.

Later, he will tell us that he judged us to be "astute and highly capable investigators with aggressive and even adventurous spirits." He will say, "You reminded me of me," one of the most unexpected compliments Asra and I will probably ever get.

The file Randall has brought is labeled SENSITIVE BUT UNCLASSI-FIED. Opening it, he walks us through his discoveries of the past day and a half. Most have to do with Gilani and his jihadi group,

Jamaat al-Fuqra, and then there is an interview he has conducted with the Pakistani journalist Kamran Khan. Khan leads an interesting dual life as a star reporter for the English-language Pakistani paper, *The News,* and as a special correspondent in Pakistan for *The Washington Post*.

If the old adage is true that a journalist is only as good as his sources, then Khan is one of the greats. In order to maintain his relationship with the ISI, including those who remain ideologically sympathetic to the jihadi crowd, Khan sometimes appears to write as much to please them as about them. Most people turn a blind eye to this because they need to know the information he offers them. But to me he has made a Faustian bargain in order to burrow deep into the world of Pakistani politics and intelligence. When others rely on Khan, they strike a similar bargain.

That said, if Khan knows where Danny is, we want to hear it. He says he doesn't and that's probably true, but he posits that "the guys with beards" (i.e., jihadis) are, as Captain reckoned, holding Danny for a swap. The reason we haven't heard from them yet is that they're trying to reach a safe place, but the high visibility of this kidnapping has made movement in and around Karachi increasingly difficult. There are checkpoints and roadblocks everywhere, and it is impossible to fly. So the kidnappers will need time. Three days, Khan guesses, before they feel hidden enough to make contact.

One sentence from Khan sears itself into my brain: "They would consider him to be a high-value hostage; i.e., one they would want to keep alive."

I have never believed that Danny is not alive.

Randall starts packing up. "Okay, girls," he announces, "you've done a good job. I'm gonna take you to McDonald's!"

"Girls"—is he talking to us? I turn to Asra for a bit of sisterly indignation, but before I even look at her, I know it's a lost cause. Unwittingly, Randall has touched the very essence of Asra's Americanism. The prospect of a Big Mac is enough to make her forgive any potential insult to our dignity. Asra's relationship to those burgers is beyond my understanding. Whenever anything goes wrong, she heads for the Golden Arches. The only time I've ever gone to McDonald's was in India, where the franchise has outlawed the use of beef. Danny ordered a McAloo tikka burger made out of potatoes and cauliflower.

The thought of leaving the house is unbearable. What if Danny comes back? What if I'm not here to welcome him? What would I tell him, "Sorry, darling, I was at Mickey D's"?

Randall turns a deaf ear to my protests. He insists with such kindness ("You need a breath of fresh air," "Do it for your son") that I don't have the heart to decline. We climb into his 4X4, which is as black as his clothes, but the driver refuses to pull out until I buckle my seat belt. How absurd—we're beyond the backseat-belt problem, I want to say, but the guy is stubborn, and Randall takes the trouble of adjusting it to my swollen belly.

How strange to be riding again in the busy streets of Karachi. I have the feeling of being immaterial, as if I am suspended in time. With astonishment, I watch people going through the usual motions. I have a single thought: Go back, see Captain, resume the search.

The Karachi McDonald's is as uniform as all the others in the world, but the mall where it is located also boasts a shining cleanliness. The displays in the shopwindows dazzle. They look as if someone has tried to create the Western lifestyle in a laboratory.

Asra goes for the No. One Special meal, the complete McDonald's set—Big Mac, fries, and Coca-Cola spread out on her tray. Soon we are surrounded by the smell of fried oil, and thanks to Asra's overindulgence, I can settle for a small salad without being impolite. Randall eats little but feeds us tales from the front lines of life in Karachi. He shrouds them with mystery and alludes to important unnamed people, nasty terrorists, and uncovered plots. Randall has escaped death a hundred times. While all of his predecessors have been in a hurry to leave Pakistan, he has stayed for five years. I have never met a man with a higher level of testosterone; he sounds like a mercenary who has decided to be on the right side of the law. Here are some of the awards he's received in the last two years:

- 2000—Diplomatic Security Special Agent of the Year award, worldwide
- 2000—Diplomatic Security Special Employee of the Year award, worldwide
- 2000—U.S. Marine Corps Company B, RSO of the Year Award
- 2000—U.S. Secret Service Commendation Award
- 2001—Drug Enforcement Agency Outstanding Contribution Award
- 2001—FBI Director's Letter of Recognition (Director Louis Freeh)
- 2001—U.S. Marine Corps Commendation Award

This is one cool, international law-enforcing dude.

Randall's Pakistani sidekick, Zahoor, has come with us. Zahoor is a tall man, unusually tall for a Pakistani, and he is also the most handsome of all the men around us, though sophistication and charm are not lacking in our group of cops. His features are fine, his complexion is a beautiful copper, and his posture is impeccable. Randall introduces him as an elite policeman he has personally trained. When Zahoor goes off to do some shopping as we eat, Randall speaks of him as much with friendship as with professional kinship. I recall Randall's reference to Tariq Jamil as his brother, and the respect he showed Captain. It reassures me to see that all these men seem to consider him a real friend.

After Zahoor returns, we leave the shopping center, cramming into a glass-paneled elevator with a group of young foreigners, probably students.

"Where are you from?" Randall asks one.

"Australia," replies the young woman, "and you?"

"Me?" answers Randall without the slightest hesitation. "From Pakistan!"

On the discreet Zahoor's lips forms the shadow of a smile.

Later that night, Randall drops by to see us again. He's now wearing what looks like an Eastern Orthodox priest's frock, collar closed, fabric extending down below the knee. It takes me a moment to realize he's wearing a pure black *salwar kameez* without the *salwar* pants. He's got on his own black pants, and they look a bit goofy. It is not what one expects from the regional security officer, even if he's going to a Friday night party in a third-world country.

Patiently, persistently, Asra pokes around in Danny's computer and searches the Internet for more clues and information. She is the queen bee in this hive she has created as our headquarters. She makes neat folders, labeling and dating each and underlining the salient information. As he might instruct one of his children, Captain teaches her how to use a two-hole puncher so that the holes are consistently aligned. Over the next two weeks, she will fill more than sixty binders, and we will have to install extra bookcases to hold them all.

There's something very obvious that we've been unable to do: monitor the emails coming into Danny's *Journal* in-box. The New York office has refused to give us the necessary password to enter the company's secured messaging system. But they access Danny's mailbox and, sure enough, there is a new email from Bashir. They immediately forward it to us. This email was sent yesterday, Friday, January 25.

From: sima shabbir
Sent: Friday, January 25, 2002 4:56 A.M.
To: Pearl, Danny
Subject:

Dear Mr. Pearl, How did the meeting with the Shaikh go?
Do write and tell me what you discussed. I am away on business in Lahore right now but as soon as I get back I will go round to see the Shaikh and ask him what his impression of you was. Keep in touch. Adaab, Bashir

"That fucker," says Asra. "He knows Danny's missing. I wrote the night Danny disappeared and told him so."

"He wants to resurface because Gilani's name is out there and he tries to look blameless," says Dost. "He's covering his ass." Captain tells me to act as if I suspect nothing when I politely answer Bashir. Whom I hate with all my heart.

Date: Sat, 26 Jan 2002 22:24:23–0800 (PST)
From: "mariane pearl"
Subject: DANNY PEARL !
To: nobadmashi@yahoo.com

Dear M. Shabbir,
I am Danny Pearl's wife, Mariane. I have seen the email you just sent to Danny but I have to tell you that I am very concerned about him since he has disappeared since last Wednesday 23rd. I appreciate your concern for him so I wanted to ask you to help me. Please contact me as soon as you read this email. My landline: 021 586 20 76 and my mobile is 0300 856 80 13. I am waiting for your response. Thank you so much.

Mariane Pearl

Captain draws slowly on a cigarette. He turns to Zahoor. "Is there a way to find out where this was sent from?"

Zahoor thinks for a while. "Yes," he says, "but we will need the original header." It is only with the original header, he explains, that one can trace the telephone number where the computer was connected.

It's amazing, I think. You can trace the roots to almost anything— an international phone call, an email . . . I take Captain aside. "I need to tell you something: Danny is Jewish."

I explain that I've told no one else in Karachi, and that for the protection of Danny and the Pearl family, *The Wall Street Journal* has made it a priority to keep Judea and Ruth Pearl out of view and to convince the American media not to mention Danny's background.

This fear of revealing Danny's Jewishness is not new, and as his younger sister Michelle later puts it in an email, it's "not irrational paranoia, it is healthy paranoia, it is common sense." When Danny traveled to such countries as Iran, for example, he'd speak on the phone only with his mother, because his father's accent was too obviously Israeli. When Judea sent out an email about his views on Zionism a few days after the World Trade Center attacks, Michelle immediately returned an email castigating him for endangering Danny in Pakistan. "There are precautions people take, because we know how deep the hate runs. And it's all we can do in L.A., thousands of miles away from Pakistan," she wrote.

Captain knows, too, how deep the hate runs. Although he reveals little as he absorbs what I've just told him, I see that he doesn't underestimate its potential consequences. "Okay," he says, nodding. "Don't tell anybody."

Saturday night is like the nights before, dreamless and fitful. The next morning turns out unlike any morning imaginable.

It begins with Dost bringing in the morning edition of *Jang* clutched in his hand. Dost, usually so calm, is visibly shaken. Danny's photo is on the front page, surrounded by a thicket of Urdu calligraphy. The photo is achingly familiar. It is the one I entrusted to the young man when the police first swarmed through the house. How the hell did it wind up on the front page of *Jang*?

I ask Dost, "Who was that guy who asked me for a photo?"

"Military intelligence," he says. He studies the text, apparently uncertain what to say or do. "Do you want to know what it says?"

"Of course."

"It says that Danny is suspected of being a Mossad agent and of having 'relations' with RAW." The Research and Analysis Wing is India's intelligence agency.

I feel like I've been kicked in the stomach. In this part of the world, it's bad enough to publicly identify somebody as Jewish. To say he is a member of Israeli intelligence—of the hated Mossad—is tantamount to signing his death warrant. Not only does Arab-Israeli tension fuel the anger, but it is widely believed that Mossad has been supporting India against Pakistan in Kashmir.

And I have handed over Danny's photo to accompany this pack of lies. I erupt in unappeasable anger. I am sick of dirty souls, cops, intelligence agents, and so-called journalists. But who is to blame? The ISI? Who in the ISI? Of course, when it comes to intelligence agencies, lying is the coin of the realm. Sometimes they lie to protect you, sometimes to hurt you. Regardless, it's lying and it's what intelligence agencies do in order to do what they do. And this holds true in every country, under every regime, whether the agency is Pakistan's ISI, India's RAW, Russia's FSB, or the CIA. I just wish everyone would stop lying and tell me the truth. I storm to the phone and dial the only number I can think to dial. I call Lieutenant General (retired) Moinuddin Haider, the interior minister. The Ministry of Interior oversees the police and prisons and "regulation of entry and exit of foreigners." It also oversees the Federal Investigation Agency, which investigates bribery, corruption, and immigration. I am not sure that the Ministry of Interior is the right agency to call, but at least I can either ask for an explanation or raise hell. I have to do something. I'm about to implode.

Minister Haider gets on the phone, and I rip into him. He remains silent save for an occasional pandering mutter: "We're looking into it."

I end up drowning in my own powerlessness.

He gives me an appointment for later that day. When I put the receiver back in the cradle, Captain tugs at my arm and leads me aside. He seems relieved that, bad as the conversation with Haider was, it wasn't worse.

"Let me deal with it," he says. "I know you are right. But you must let me deal with it." When he is upset, his jaw tightens. It is very tight now. He makes me promise that I will not call anyone else about this, then leaves the house with a slam of the door.

I cling to Captain's indignation as I would to a raft.

Turning to look at Dost, I can tell he's searching for the right words. I know he wants to apologize for his country, and he wants me to know that not all Pakistanis are "like that." He would like to talk to me about traitors and cowards and the people who possess influence in this country, and why they have the power they do. I know he wants to ask me to trust him, and the truth is, I do. But he doesn't say any of this out loud; nor do I. We just stand next to each other, staring at the newspaper.

Where is Danny? Where's my boy?

Last year, Danny's mother found his fifth-grade diary and typed up all the entries. I read them as an introduction to my husband's heart. Danny hasn't changed much since he was ten years old. This was something I had sensed, and the diary confirmed it. As he and I read the entries on a flight back from Los Angeles, I watched Danny laugh at his younger self, and I hoped I'd managed to hold on to some of my younger self, too.

October 31, 1973—I think that for children love is hoping that the person you love loves you. . . .

November 2—I think Lisa Macey likes me. It may sound silly but it is nice thinking about it. I feel happy for that reason. . . .

April 13—I want to have a full life, and believe that I can. I would be a book critic but it doesn't sound very contributive to the world (I guess the only job that is is politics, which I wouldn't go into for anything).

May 10—Lisa Macey is pretty but she has a queer personality. Doreen Brand is pretty and has a good personality.

And then there is this, which I wish I weren't remembering right now:

November 3—All the time during my car pool I got scared that I was being kidnapped. I am going to compose a hopefully large piece about Nixon. We lost to the Apaches 2–0 but they were in first place.

Are all kids afraid of being kidnapped? Was I?

I slip back into my room to pray. I chant, *"Nam Myoho Renge*

Kyo." I urge Danny not to be afraid. I am with him, the baby is with him, and we will be okay.

The phone rings. It is *Wall Street Journal* deputy foreign editor Bill Spindle calling to say that Jonathan Friedland is sending me an email. It may be from Danny's kidnappers. Friedland is the *Journal*'s bureau chief in Los Angeles. Danny and I had lunch with him last year; he discussed his difficulty with readjusting to life in the U.S. after years as a foreign correspondent. Life was boring, he said. "Ah," we'd joked, "you miss the mess."

The email had made several stops before it was forwarded to us. It had originally been sent at one A.M. from someone calling himself "kidnapperguy@hotmail.com" to thirty-one assorted people at *Jang, The Washington Post, The New York Times,* and other international publications. Interestingly, no copies were sent to *The Wall Street Journal*. Among those to receive it first, *Washington Post* Southeast Asia bureau chief Rajiv Chandrasekaran has sent it to the *Journal*'s Anne Marie Squeo with an accompanying email saying: "have you seen this? is that him in the pics? this is just sick. i hope to god this is all a hoax and that he's released soon." Anne Marie then sent it to several executives at the *Journal:* "folks, i'm not sure if this is [a] hoax and i've only met danny twice, but this looks like what i remember of him."

With Asra and Captain and Dost clustered around me, I click on the attachment. I see the photos first, four of them. Danny is in front of a blue curtain, wearing something he would never wear—a strange jogging suit, shiny hot pink and baby blue. His wrists are in chains and his glasses are gone. In the initial image, a man in a white *salwar kameez* is gripping the back of Danny's head, shoving it forward, and, with the other hand, leveling a revolver an inch from my husband's head.

Tears spring to my eyes, but I have been preparing for this. I feel like a boxer who knows he is about to be hit, each muscle tightening so as not to crumble when the actual blow lands; ready to hit back, not to think but act. I force myself to study the next image, in which Danny holds a January 26 edition of the English-language newspaper *Dawn*.

"They put the picture with the gun first for a reason," Dost says softly. "They do it to shock you and get your attention."

I can feel everyone study me with alarm. Ah, I think, they expect me to go into labor right here and now. Instead, I start to smile, because in one of the next photos, Danny is smiling too. It is obvious, even though his head is down. And then I see it—in one photo, his fingers form a V for victory, in another, he's giving his captors the finger. You can sense his quiet triumph, the kind you feel when someone tries to silence you but your message gets through anyway. I was right: Danny *has* been fighting his fear. He's telling me he's not defeated and that I shouldn't be, either.

I study the accompanying text. It is bizarre.

Subject: American CIA officer in our custody
  The National movement for the restoration of Pakistani sovereignty has captured CIA officer Daniel Pearl who has posing as a journalist of the Wall Street Journal.

I look behind me at Captain, who stares at the screen over my shoulder. "What is this group? Who are these people?" I ask.

Captain shakes his head. "It's a group especially made up for this."

I look back at the screen.

Unfortunately, he is at present being kept in very inhuman circumstances quite similar infact to the way that Pakistanis and nationals of other sovereign countries are being kept in Cuba by the American Army. If the Americans keep our countrymen in better conditions we will better the conditions of Mr. Pearl and all the other Americans that we capture.

  If the America wants the release of Mr. Pearl, all Pakistanis being illegally detained by the FBI in side America merely on suspicion must be given access to lawyers and allowed seeing their family members.

The Pakistani prisoners in Cuba must be returned to Pakistan and they will be tried in a Pakistani court. After all Pakistan was a full member of the international coalition against terror and it deserves the right to try its own citizens. And Send Afghanistan's Embassador Mulla Zaeef back to Pakistan and if there is any accusition Pakistani Government should handle it.

Mullah Abdul Salam Zaeef is the former Taliban ambassador to Pakistan and one of the highest-ranking Taliban officials in U.S. custody.

Another message is attached. It is in Urdu, and the Urdu speakers among us lean forward to translate it. It is much the same as the English version, except for one additional demand: the release of a shipment of F-16 fighter jets that Pakistan bought from the United States in the 1980s, which was stopped after Congress cut off military sales to Pakistan in 1990. "These planes should be provided to Pakistan or money should be refunded with a 15% interest rate."

"These demands are impossible, they make no sense," I say. "These people don't want to negotiate with us. They're just trying to apply pressure on Washington and Islamabad."

"Yes," says Captain.

With our new printer, we make copies for everyone and pass them out. "I don't think it's Danny," adds Captain, studying his.

"Neither do I," says Asra.

I barely listen to them.

Randall has rushed over to the house with Zahoor and several Americans we haven't met before. Two FBI agents sit down and immediately get to work poring over the computer, looking for clues. They study the email addresses and search for the IP (International Protocol) address, the unique identifying number for the computer that sent the email. Every computer on the internet has one. One agent, Kevin, wears a fanny pack. He is not the most impressive presence, but it makes me think maybe he's a computer genius, like Bill Gates.

Randall studies our printouts. "That's a doctored photo," he says flatly. "It's not Danny. Check out the angle of the shoulder—that doesn't look right with the head. And the legs are too big. Look at the shoulders on this one. Now measure that against the other one here."

Every little detail—the type of camera used, the make of the weapon threatening Danny, the way words are used—is analyzed, and everyone has a theory. I let everybody play out his or her line because I want to get hooked by one. But through it all, I know this is my husband.

In the chatter, I hear Randall ask, "Do you recognize the wedding ring?"

"Yes," I say. "It's loose on his finger. It's always been loose."

The room falls silent.

Maureen gets down to business. "Well, let's send the images off to the forensics lab in Honolulu and see what they say." The Honolulu division is the FBI field office responsible for investigations in this part of the world.

"Yes," says Randall, "and to Washington, and . . ."

But that's silly. This is Danny. We don't have time to wait for "experts" in other time zones to authenticate what we can plainly see.

Captain tries to distract me. "Look, Danny's talking to you. He is smiling. With a gun to his head, Danny is smiling."

Yes, I see.

"He doesn't appear to be under too much stress or in agony."

I see that, too.

The printouts of the email are spread across the dining table, offered up to anyone's perusal. It's somewhat obscene. People slide the images around the tabletop, as if reorganizing them will reveal something more. They stroke their chins, murmur among themselves, mutter the usual clichés. The FBI team grows increasingly agitated; I hear them tossing around the names of various field offices and forensics experts and cyber-crime people and Quantico and God only knows what else.

I prefer to observe Captain and Dost. I can tell what they are thinking: It's time to outsmart the kidnappers by forecasting. What would we do in their place? Where would one hide a foreigner? In their imagination, they enter mosques, creep into *madrassas* and the labyrinth of the slums.

Danny's sister Michelle calls from California. "It's good news!" she says.

"What is?" I ask, startled by the happy lilt to her voice.

"Mariane, this means Danny's alive," she says, and she's exactly right. Because I've never allowed myself to admit he might be dead, the revelation hasn't sunk in that this is indeed positive confirmation that my husband is alive.

In the midst of everything—the shock of *Jang,* the blow of the email—Captain and Randall remind me that I have an appointment with General Haider, the interior minister. I have no desire to go, but the men assure me the meeting is important. At issue is the creation of a national task force to extend the investigation of Danny's kidnapping to the rest of Pakistan. For Randall and Captain to do their jobs, the task force is essential. Both men ask me, as a personal favor, to go.

As much as I may dread the meeting, Asra and I have an additional reason to attend. In order to demonstrate to the minister how seriously Danny's kidnapping is regarded in the United States, we have devised a plan with Paul Steiger, the *Journal*'s managing editor. Steiger, who has spoken with U.S. secretary of state Colin Powell, will just "happen" to call on my cell phone while I'm meeting with Haider. I will then "happen" to hand the phone to Haider so that Steiger can "happen" to pass along the gist of his conversation with the secretary of state.

The visit to the minister's office is turning into a delegation of senior officers, themselves accompanied by their subordinates. Plainclothes policemen arrive, one wave after another, all in their Sunday best, ready to join the caravan. Over my white shirt, I throw Danny's favorite scarf, a shawl-sized one from Kashmir; Asra grabs another. A distinguished-looking man with white hair waits for me outside the house. He is John Bauman, the U.S. consul general. He invites us to join him in his vehicle; he waves Randall in, too. Our convoy is set in motion. Several official cars follow, but at the end of our procession, I recognize the exhausted jeeps that have been keeping watch over our front door.

These are not happy times for Minister Haider. Forty days ago, three men on motorcycles assassinated his brother, Ehtishamuddin Haider, as he drove home from his job at a medical charity. The day before, Minister Haider had held a seminar in Karachi entitled "Terrorism—A New Challenge to the World of Islam." Danny covered the speech. " 'We can't place the reins of the country in the hands of illiterates who have read a few qaidas [Koranic chapters],' " Danny quoted Minister Haider as saying.

The minister wears a traditional silk mourning dress. I offer my condolences; he mumbles his thanks. He is in a bad mood. The policemen fill all the wall space, forming a living tapestry, until the entire room is covered. There are only three chairs in the room. I sit to the right of the minister, and to his left sits Kamal Shah, the general inspector.

Haider begins coolly but cordially. He offers an update of the investigations and agrees that a national task force is fully justified. He knows, he says, that while the abduction has taken place in Karachi, it was most likely conceived elsewhere. But he cannot contain his collegiality for long. "Three thousand journalists present during the war in Afghanistan and none of them got into trouble!" he snaps reproachfully. This phrase, it's like a mantra for him.

"What's your point?" I ask.

"What was your husband doing? What need did he have to meet these people? This is not the business of a journalist!"

"It all depends on what you call a journalist," I answer, ice cold. Maybe the thought of Danny's photograph in *Jang* prevents Haider from pursuing this direction, but he turns to another, just as shaky: India. He charges that India orchestrated the kidnapping of Danny in order to embarrass Pakistan.

The tension is such that our voices echo in the room in spite of the number of people present. It is as if everyone else has stopped breathing. Most men stand with their arms crossed or their hands clasped, fingers woven tightly. From where I'm sitting, I can watch rows of knuckles grow paler and paler.

My cell phone rings, and everyone exhales with relief. With dexterity, Asra grabs the phone and secludes herself in the corridor. She lets Steiger know what the interior minister is accusing, which is helpful, because, when the two men talk, Steiger appears able to cool Haider down.

I watch Haider closely. Here he is, one of the main players in the war against terrorism in this country, and one of its victims. How can he believe that Danny is a spy? Or that Danny's kidnapping is an Indian conspiracy? Who has been providing him with such "information"? Who has been briefing him? Above all else, how can an intelligent man believe such obvious lies?

As we prepare to leave, Asra cannot resist any longer. She turns her wide black eyes toward Haider, and with tremendous softness, she asks, "With all due respect, Mr. Minister, would you blame your brother for having been murdered just because he was driving the streets of Karachi?"

As we step outside, we hear Haider turn on the policemen who have remained in the room. "What's wrong with you people?" he yells in fury fueled by frustration and embarrassment. "Why haven't you found him yet? All of you: *Get me the journalist!*"

When he takes us home, Randall reprimands us for our lack of diplomacy and self-control. He is not pleased with our behavior, but he is also smart enough to feel the storm brewing in Asra and me, so he quickly changes tactics. "You need some rest," he says in a tone that has become pleasantly protective. He proceeds to explain at length why a person lacking sleep cannot remain rational. Then, expressly for my edification, he adds, "And you should know that you have many chemicals running loose in *your* body!"

I can't help smiling. But I face another sleepless night.

Asra tries to help. With expert hands, she massages my head. Though I do not relax sufficiently to cry (I ache to cry), I drift into a dreamless sleep with the strange feeling that I am tumbling into a pit. That night Asra stretches out beside me, and we begin from that moment a habit that will continue for weeks to come—we sleep side by side. Asra can watch over me, and I can watch over her.

Two women sharing a bed. The men around us find it intriguing at first. Then they find they are comforted by it, because by this point, everyone feels alone—and no one should be.

Chapter Seven

FOREIGN EDITOR John Bussey is over the Atlantic when the kidnappers' email comes. His Swissair flight out of New York has a stopover in Zurich, and Bussey is in the business-class lounge when he logs on for messages. He calls up the images of Danny in captivity, reboards, flies to Dubai, catches his connection to Karachi, and arrives at two A.M. on Monday morning, by which time all hell has broken loose.

The Wall Street Journal has leaned on U.S. secretary of state Colin Powell, who has leaned on Pakistani president Pervez Musharraf, who has assured Powell that the Pakistani government is committed to finding Danny.

Statements have been drafted and released. For example: "My name is Paul Steiger and I am Danny's boss at *The Wall Street Journal*. I would like to work with you to bring about Danny's safe release. . . . [Daniel Pearl] has never worked for the CIA or the U.S. Government in any capacity. Danny Pearl has no ability to change the policies of the U.S. Government or the Government of Pakistan. Nor do I. Therefore, I would ask that you release Danny so that he may return home safe to his wife and soon-to-be-born child."

The CIA, which traditionally refuses to comment on who does or does not work for the agency, has officially and categorically denied that Danny is a spy.

The international media, which has not paid particularly close attention to the story, is getting working itself into a lather. It has never occurred to me that the *Journal* even has a public relations department, but of course it does, and Steven Goldstein, chief spokesperson for the *Journal* and its parent company, Dow Jones, has plunged into the storm. Within twenty-four hours of the email with Danny's pictures, the media have made 600 phone calls and email requests to the *Journal;* the day after, 750 requests. Goldstein is doing his best to answer them all. "There's a moment in a crisis when you realize you are in a crisis. This was that moment," he will tell me when we meet later in Paris. He once worked on Capitol Hill, and he was with the head of NASA when the *Challenger* space shuttle exploded. He was a press officer in the Department of the Interior when the *Exxon Valdez* ran aground and spilled eleven million gallons of crude oil over the Alaskan coast. He was at *The Wall Street Journal* when the attacks of 9/11 nearly shut the paper down. "But I'd never seen a media frenzy like this in my entire career."

I don't want to talk to the press, I don't want to confer with Goldstein or Dow Jones execs or Danny's anxious colleagues. I want Bussey to handle it all. I cannot quite imagine how the editor, who they say can be picky, will adjust to our funky scene here on Zamzama Street, but I need him.

Captain looks out the window. "There is CNN fixing up the camera right on the lawn, and the Fox is there, and so is the Al Jazeera, all those media." He isn't pleased. I peer out over his shoulder. There's a phalanx of cops, then a phalanx of TV cameras, all pressing in on us, all separating us from the world outside.

The deputy inspector general is sending over a secure driver who can meet Bussey's plane. Dost opens the door. "I am here to pick up the American at the airport," the driver says, and Dost bursts out laughing.

"One minute, please," he says, shutting the door in the driver's face. "Captain, could you come here, please? Could you please take a look at the driver for John Bussey?"

The two investigators open the door and peer out at the bewildered driver. Skinny, with an unkempt beard and piercing black eyes, he looks like he's just made it back from the caves of Afghanistan. "If we send this guy, Bussey will turn around and take the next plane home," says Captain. A clean-shaven driver steps in as a replacement.

He's an intriguing character, John Bussey: quick-witted, preppy, sometimes imperious. He's fairly young, in his mid-forties, but used to giving directions—to a staff of roughly 25 reporters around the world, and to the waitstaffs of the five-star hotels he frequents. I call him Bussey the Boss. Danny respects him and also gets mad at him because Bussey, while brilliant, can be hard to pin down. But he is kind-hearted, and when my mother became sick with cancer and Danny and I needed to be with her in France, he was extremely supportive.

I first met Bussey when Danny enthusiastically introduced me to every single person at the New York bureau. Holding my hand, Danny took me from one cubicle to the next on three different floors. I forgot each name as soon as I learned the next, but it didn't matter, Danny said, "The point is that all my people see you." His pride made me happier than I ever thought I could be with a man. The next time I met Bussey, it was in India, during one of his tours of Asia. I helped Danny arrange for his boss to meet with a range of interesting Indian personalities—a young soap-opera queen, an epic novelist, a leftist unionist. Bussey was charming and articulate, and within two days, he talked as if he had figured out what India was all about, where its future lay, and what its position was in the globalization process. I was awed by how quick and assertive he was. After several months in India, I still could not figure out why, for example, some of our neighbors walked barefoot so as not to harm an ant, in a city where children were mutilated so they could be sent out to beg.

When Bussey walks into the house in Karachi in his wilted blue suit, he is ready to work, though it is the middle of the night, and he has been traveling for nineteen hours, and there is a ten-hour time difference. We brief him thoroughly. As he listens, I can see him taking it all in. Maybe this is even scarier than he'd expected.

*　　*　　*

Back in New York, Steve Goldstein is fending off the television net-works and wire services, all of which are demanding copies of the emails and photos. "No," he tells them. "To be honest, that wouldn't be seemly." They are agitating for an audience with Danny's parents and sisters, too. In Los Angeles, television and radio vans are pulling up outside the Pearl house. Michelle describes it to me: "They ring the doorbell; we pretend we aren't home. We close the curtains and hide out. Reporters come up to the front door and shine lights through the windows. One bangs on the doors and holds up a piece of paper, saying, 'I am with CBS. Please open the door, I only want to give you this note.' How about leaving it in the mailbox?"

Michelle doesn't let her parents answer the phone because of their accents, and she records a new message on the answering machine in her all-American voice. They don't even mention the family first names—Judea, Ruth, Tamara, Michelle—because those will be tip-offs, too. As Michelle puts it, "We do not exist—we are a liability."

Good Morning America, the *Today* show, *CBS Morning News*. Diane Sawyer, Katie Couric, Connie Chung, Larry King, and the BBC. They all want me, the wife. I hear the names of the shows and can see the news assistants at their desks, hounded by their anchors to get me on air. I know the pressure to "feed the beast"; I have felt it. I think about how easy it is to reduce this story to a simple tale: handsome hostage husband, pregnant despairing wife. There is no way for any of these shows to reflect the complexity of what is going on here, and while simplification of complex events may seem harmless, it isn't. I look from the chart to the cameras on Zamzama Street. I feel like telling them, "Yes, the world I am in right now is surreal, but in what world are you?" Then I think I'm being unfair. Or maybe I'm just on the wrong side of the camera.

In New York, Steve tries to slip away from the madness tem-porarily by going to the gym. He is trying to lose weight. One late night, in the middle of a workout, his personal trainer leans over the sweating Goldstein: "You know, Ann Curry from the *Today* show would really like to have Mariane on the show."

In Paris, people are finding their way to my brother, Satchi, the world's loveliest soul. He is not prepared for the attention. *People* magazine calls his house asking for family pictures in which we are all together and happy.

"Is there really any advantage for her to go on national television and cry?" Goldstein wonders on the phone with Bussey. "Or will it just look like she's begging?"

If I were to appear, I would tell interviewers that the kidnappers have the wrong man. That Danny is not a spy but a man committed to bridging a widening gap between civilizations. He is a citizen of the world, a lover of differences, a man capable of embracing them all. But I'm not sure that's how the hungry newscasters will want me to play it. Hell, I'm not even sure that's what my unofficial advisers want. When I do eventually sit for a few interviews, Steve Goldstein reassures me. "Remember, the best approach to take is that you're just two people trying to do a job. You're a professional, a journalist." At the same time, he directs John Bussey to make sure I come off as sympathetic. He says to make sure I'm obviously distressed and obviously pregnant.

"Right, dude. And how do I do that?" asks Bussey.

People obsess over my pregnancy. The baby is simultaneously another person to worry about, spiritual consolation, and a public relations tool. Asra showed me one of her favorite books, *The Muslim Marriage Guide* by Ruqaiyyah Waris Maqsood, a widely respected teacher of Islam who lives in England. In a chapter called "A Short A to Z of Marriage," I found an interesting discussion of abortion in which the author wrote that most Islamicists agree that a fetus does not have a soul until the sixteenth week of pregnancy, at which time it is "ensouled" (*nafh al-ruh*).

Nafh al-ruh. It can also be translated "the living soul." Or "a soul into which life has been breathed."

Maqsood continued: "This is backed up by the hadith [saying of the Prophet Mohammed]: . . .When forty nights pass after the semen gets into the womb, Allah sends the angel and gives him the shape. Then He creates his sense of hearing, sense of sight, his skin, his flesh, his bones . . ."

I am almost six months pregnant. To harm this baby inside me is a crime against Islam. And to harm his father is to harm the child.

When Goldstein talks to the Pakistani and Arab press, he makes sure to fit *nafh al-ruh* into the conversation as often as possible. "You know," he says, "she has an *angel* inside her."

As he rides around New York working his cell phone, working his BlackBerry, Steve Goldstein absorbs advice from wherever he can find it. "There are a lot of Pakistani cabdrivers in New York. I ask them, 'What do you think about this Danny Pearl case? If you were back there, would you watch Al Jazeera?' " Because Steve is reaching out to Al Jazeera. But the cabdrivers tell him that Al Jazeera is an Arab station and that Pakistanis don't consider themselves Arab. So that isn't going to help.

Judea tries to convince Colin Powell's office to issue a strong statement to the kidnappers, something along the lines of "The people currently holding Daniel Pearl captive should understand that killing an innocent journalist is considered a barbaric act that is inconsistent with the teaching of Islam," but the statement issued by the secretary of state is formal and lacking in heat.

Judea works feverishly to mobilize influential Muslims to appeal for Danny's release. Nation of Islam leader Louis Farrakhan steps up. So do several Muslim clerics overseas, and the emir of Qatar, who knows Danny and likes him very much. The heavyweight champion Muhammad Ali, a devout Muslim who is revered worldwide, agrees to issue a statement. Someone at the *Journal* suggests sending Ali to Guantánamo Bay. Why? So he can issue a statement declaring the treatment of the detainees humane. It is a horrible idea and blessedly dropped.

Basketball great Michael Jordan, not Muslim but also worshiped internationally, is asked to make an appeal. His agent says no.

When Ali's statement arrives, we gather around the dining table in Karachi to read it. It is beautiful:

WITH THE NAME OF ALLAH, THE MOST GRACIOUS, THE MOST COMPASSIONATE

I pray this message reaches those who are detaining Daniel Pearl. As a Muslim, I end each prayer with a plea for peace and compassion among all peoples of the world. During the most recent conflict too many people have suffered, too many have fallen victim to injustice and intolerance, many have lost hope that people can co-exist peacefully as nations without disrespecting the culture, traditions and rights of others. But by the mercy of Allah, I have not lost that hope. I believe Almighty Allah will guide all of us on the path of righteousness and mercy. I have not lost His hope in us to show compassion where none exists and to extend mercy in the most difficult of circumstances.

We as Muslims must lead by example. This same example that was given to us over 1400 years ago by the Prophet Mohammed (May the Peace and Blessing of Allah be upon Him). Daniel is a professional journalist. His job is to give a voice to those who wish to be heard by the world community. Daniel should not become another victim of the ongoing conflict. I appeal to you to show Daniel Pearl compassion and kindness. Treat him as you would wish all Muslims to be treated by others. Give hope and belief that Allah will guide us through these most difficult times. It is my most sincere prayer that Daniel Pearl be permitted to return safely to his family. May Allah have mercy on us all.

"That's great," says Asra. "But Cat Stevens would be even better." After his *Tea for the Tillerman* days in the 1970s, Cat Stevens became a high-profile convert to Islam. Now, having renamed himself Yusuf Islam, he has a major following as a Muslim educator and balladeer, with such albums as *A Is for Allah*. Asra recalls listening to Khalid Khawaja's wife sing along to Yusuf Islam's recordings when she visited Khawaja in Islamabad. Bussey dispatches an email to the *Journal* empire suggesting we enlist Mr. Islam.

Danny's parents get a phone message from *Yediot Achronot,* an

Israeli newspaper, which has decided that it's time to break the identity embargo. Judea calls the reporter back and tries to stress the importance of keeping the family's background secret for now. The reporter refuses to get it. "I can see my dad is getting frustrated," says Michelle. "I start to scream, loud enough to be heard on the other end, 'They will kill him! Doesn't he understand? They will kill him!' " For the moment the Israeli media keeps silent.

The British tabloids are dangling dollars before Steve Goldstein—finder's fees—if he arranges an interview with me. Highest offer thus far: $25,000. I'd get paid, too. Psychics are calling with visions, prisoners with tips. All over Pakistan, police are smashing down doors in waves of raids. Drivers are being pulled out of cars at roadblocks and searched.

I begin having contractions, and we send for a doctor from the Sheraton. When I open the medicine meant to stave off labor, I read the warning label: "No studies have been conducted on pregnant women." But of course.

Danny's older sister, Tamara, who trained as a homeopath in Canada, develops a strategy to keep me healthy until Danny can be found, and another to heal Danny when he comes home. She learns where in Karachi to buy the items, and emails us the name of a good local homeopath, Younus Billoo (which sounds to me like a very healing name).

Asra sends Imran out with the shopping list:

Aconite 1M (for fear)
Arnica 1M (for trauma, shock, and physical trauma)
Cocculus 200 (for loss of sleep)
Gelsemium 200 (for fear, with trembling or exhaustion)
Opium 200 (for fear, with seeing images over and over again)
Rescue Remedy, the Bach Flower Essence, to sip in water

Bussey slips into my room and carries off my copy of *What to Expect When You're Expecting*. He scans it from cover to cover, then quizzes me. He knows all about urine and blood tests, protein intake and fluid consumption. Someone has told him that pregnant women need to stay thoroughly hydrated, so he forces liters and liters and more liters of water on me. He will not go away until he sees me practically drowning in liquid.

Charles Fleming of the *Journal*'s French bureau finds the former Cat Stevens. Fleming has been helped by his nephew, Chris Martin, the ethereal-voiced lead singer for the cool British band Coldplay. Coldplay is at the Parr Street Studios in Liverpool, recording *A Rush of Blood to the Head,* and through music-world contacts, Martin tracks down Yusuf Islam's brother, David Gordon, who agrees to ask his famous sibling for help.

Speaking as "a Muslim from the West," Yusuf Islam writes:

> Now the time has come to show the world the Mercy of Islam. The Prophet Muhammad, peace be upon him . . . taught us that a man went to heaven because he gave water to a thirsty dog; and a woman went to hell because she tied up a cat, which starved to death.
>
> As a message to those who are holding the journalist Danny Pearl: If justice is your goal, then the cause of justice will not be served by killing an innocent man who has nothing but a pen in his hand.

They are wise and compassionate words. But we need to find where Danny has been hidden.

To that end, four distinct search teams operate at once. Like an orchestra conductor, Captain directs them all. There is a classic investigative team, tracking leads, coordinating raids across Pakistan. Then there is the cyber-crime team, trying to trace emails back to the computers from which they were originally sent. There's the FBI, which has set up a control room in Dow Jones's South Brunswick, New Jersey office, so it can monitor developments as they happen, around the clock and around the world. And then there is Jameel Yusuf's team.

When Citizen-Police Liaison Committee chief Jameel Yusuf walks into our house on the night of the emailed photos, it is with the air of a savior. Short and stout, in a three-piece suit, he glows with self-confidence. When it comes to solving kidnappings, Jameel Yusuf's track record is unparalleled.

He has been out of town—in Islamabad, on business—since Danny interviewed him on the 23rd of January, and by the time he appears, we know how much we need him. Without wasting any time, Captain hands him the kidnappers' email. Yusuf takes one look at it and shakes his head. "The demands are damn stupid," he says. If the casual, almost familylike atmosphere generated by our team surprises him, he doesn't show it. He surveys our chart and whipping out his Palm Pilot, records all the phone numbers on it.

"Can you help us?" we ask.

"We'll start working tomorrow," he promises.

Yusuf has been doing this for thirteen years. He was, and remains, a textile-industry tycoon. By 1990 Karachi had become the kidnapping capital of the world. Yusuf and his cohort were the targets—five million rupees to buy them back—yet the local police did little to help. So the business community complained to the Sindh province governor, and the governor turned the tables back on them: "Instead of complaining, take action!" he declared. Yusuf, who had spent four years in military intelligence, took up the challenge.

The rumor is that Yusuf is not exactly soft-handed when confronting thugs. In fact, it is said that he's inclined to use their methods, including kidnapping. He'll kidnap a kidnapper's family. He's unrepentant about any of his techniques. This, he will tell me, is because "I have seen the tears and the pain."

We have interrogated mr.D.Parl and we have come to the conclusion that contrary to what we thought earlier he is not working for the cia. in fact he is working for mossaad. therefore we will execute him within 24 hours unless amreeka flfils our demands.

It is the morning of January 30. Another email. This one with two photos attached, uncomfortably similar to those we received two days ago. Asra prints them out. In the first, a gun is pointed at Danny's head, but he looks as if he is laughing; in the second, he looks like he got caught midblink. The photo is supposed to seem depressing—and he does look more tired, more worn—but still, it just looks like a bad shot.

> we apologise to his family for the worry caused and we will send them food packages just as amreeka apologized for collateral damage and dropped food packets on the thousands of people whose mothers, fathers, sisters and brothers, wives, sons and daughters, grandparents and grandchildren it had killed. We hope Mr danny's family will be grateful for the food packets that we send them just as the amreekan public expected the afghans to be grateful for the food packets its airforce was dropping on them.

Sick bastards.

It rambles on about Pakistan's "slave-mentality" toward "amreeka." About the "vengeful amreekan war machine" and their earlier demands.

> We warn all amreekan journlist working in pakstan that there are many in their ranks spying on pakstan under the journlist cover. therefore we give all amreekan journalists 3 days to get out of pakstan. anyone remaining after that will be targetted.

How do we reach these people, stop them, talk to them?

Bussey holds a printout of the second email in his hands. It goes on and on, filled with impossible demands. It is probably the most meandering and seemingly incoherent text this brilliant editor has ever seen. But if you study it more closely, you realize it's written by someone who wants to cover his tracks, who wants us to think he's illiterate when he isn't. The syntax is clean, and the spelling isn't half bad: The writer has just dropped a letter here, a capital there. As for the words themselves, to those of us who have been in the field awhile, they are painfully familiar. The writer has clearly copied, syllable for syllable, the pseudo-political imprecations of a mullah—one of the increasing number who preach hatred rather than religion.

This is how we end up in a world where people talk not to communicate but to subjugate; where ignorance keeps people hostage; where those in power simplify complexity so as not to be questioned. This is why those same people hate journalists, at least those who reject black-and-white views of the world, because by exploring the gray zones, journalists can shed new light on issues like Arab-Israeli relations, American foreign relations, or Islamic fundamentalism. We have the tools and the language to reveal truths. We believe we can change the world by changing the way people think about one another. We can even create links, frail as they may be, between peoples. Thus, for those who promote hatred, we are the most hateable of all.

I flash back to New Year's Eve in Beirut four years ago. Danny and I spent a wonderful night with Lebanese friends, eating, dancing, laughing, and the next day one of those friends took us to a bar, where we started discussing politics. When he discovered that Danny was Jewish and that my father had been, too, our friend was dumbfounded. He'd never imagined that a Jewish person could be someone like Danny. For the rest of the evening he merely stared at Danny in disbelief. He was out with a Jew, and he had things in common with him, *and he liked him*. At the end of the evening he told us that he understood he'd been taught to reject a people he knew nothing about. It was as simple and as hideously complicated as that.

Now it has become evident to all of us that we must make as many people as possible—in Pakistan and around the world—aware of who Daniel Pearl truly is. So they might see for themselves what an objective reporter he is, we offer Pakistani papers some of his articles to republish. More are posted on websites. And Steve Goldstein, who has for the most part kept the media at bay, switches gears. His new philosophy is "Show me where people in Pakistan can see your show and I'll do it." In other words, it serves no purpose for a limited—say, strictly American—audience to hear our story; but if you're CNN or Fox or BBC, or any other network seen or heard in Pakistan, we will do your show. Paul Steiger is invited to do some broadcasts, and so is Helene Cooper, a *Journal* colleague and an old friend of Danny's. I am invited, too.

Throughout the ordeal, I haven't stopped taking baths. I have stopped doing almost everything else I typically consider essential for my survival—reading, listening to music—but not taking baths. It seems too basic, too obvious, to say that sinking into hot water makes you feel as if you're back in your mother's belly, safe and happy, but that is how it feels. Before leaving for the Sheraton for my first CNN interview, I lock myself in Asra's pink-tiled bathroom, pour children's bubble bath—reeking of synthetic strawberry fragrance—under the spout, and immerse myself for as long as Bussey can wait.

Bussey is my coach. Goldstein and Bussey have been working hard on this interview, making sure CNN agrees to its content, and Bussey is intent on making me rehearse the message I want to deliver to the kidnappers. Sitting in the living room, we have gone over it again and again, Bussey scribbling on a notepad, highlighting key words, underlining them, too. Is he that systematic in the rest of his life, or have his higher-ups instructed him to do this?

When the time comes, CNN's Ben Wedeman will open by saying, "Mrs. Pearl . . . the group holding your husband has given a twenty-four-hour deadline . . . or they say they kill your husband, Daniel. Do you have a message to that group?" Well trained, I will promptly reply, "Yes, I have a message, I have three different points I want to talk about. The first one is I want to remind them that my husband and I are both journalists. We are two people who met and fell in love because we have the same ideal . . . to try to create dialogue between civilizations."

I feel like I'm playing a mental game with an invisible enemy. They have terror to bargain with; my power is soft at best. If they are publicity-hungry, I could play this media waltz to our favor and force them to keep Danny alive.

Asra follows me around with motherly protectiveness. Her love is great, but her fashion sense is terrible. "No," she says, "you look wonderful. You don't need makeup, don't worry about your hair, bare arms are fine." I try to pull myself together anyway, and before Bussey and I leave the house, I grab Danny's Kashmiri shawl and toss it around my shoulders. I look like one of those Pashtoun guys you see in Peshawar, where the temperature is cold and men walk around wrapped in blankets. In Danny's shawl, I feel tucked inside a protective shell.

The car that the police have sent for us is waiting. This televised interview may be as close as we'll get to negotiating with the captors. Heavy with that awareness, Steve and Asra solemnly see us out the door. It is night, and I haven't checked my watch for what feels like days, so I have no idea what time it is, but the night is a brilliantly clear, and I can easily see the major constellations above. I look for Cassiopeia, and when I find her, I take a deep breath and climb inside the car.

Except it won't start. "Great," groans Bussey. "We got the one-eyed truck." Sure enough, our car has only one functional headlight, and when the driver turns the ignition, the car jerks forward a bit, then stops. A handful of guards push us, and the engine finally starts. Two vehicles follow us for protection; neither has headlights. Every car on the road seems more insane than the next. Bussey tries to laugh it off. "Can you believe this?" he whispers, then buries his head in his hands.

When the CNN camera finally rolls, I make the points that I rehearsed with Bussey, and I parrot the phrases suggested by Captain and Dost, whom I trust more than any communications expert. I describe Danny as someone whose "religion is Truth," and whose "mission" is to build "a better world" by "giving voice to those whose voices would not otherwise be heard."

I tell Ben Wedeman, "The reason we are in Pakistan today was because we wanted to know more about the people and write about their views." But now, I go on, "The dialogue has been broken. I ask them to have a dialogue because they're breaking the dialogue that existed."

I mention repeatedly that I am pregnant and that I am not American. "This is completely wrong, to hold us. It's just creating more misery, and that's it. Nothing can come out of [this]."

I talk to the kidnappers: "What can I do? Nobody has contacted me. . . . I have read the statement, I have tried to read it with, I think, an open heart to try to understand what they say—I think I do, I think I do—but it's a general statement and Danny is my life. So I need some indication what they want. What should I do? What exactly, precisely can I do? . . ."

"How are you coping with this?" Wedeman asks.

"I haven't slept in more than a week . . . but I hope. I'm not desperate, because if I stop believing in creating this dialogue, then I stop believing everything else. I can't do that. I'm pregnant."

Afterward I was asked: "Why didn't you cry?" American audiences want you to cry, they want to see your suffering. Why? Is it that displaying your grief on TV makes it true? I was angry. "Am I feeding some real-life drama-hungry viewer back home?" I ask Bussey. But the truth is, I was furious that nobody understood that a terrified reaction is exactly what terrorists want: They want to *terrorize* you. The more you show that, the happier they are. Win sympathy by being weepy? In reality, you can oppose them only with the strength they think they have taken away from you.

There is another thing: Danny might hear me; somewhere, he might be watching. I must show him that I'm okay, and that the baby is okay. I must feed him strength from my strength. I must give him hope.

Even after spending a full night before the computer screen, Zahoor remains totally composed, and this earns him the unspoken respect of the whole team. With a slight frown, he moves his hand across the computer keyboard as if he is Artur Rubinstein playing the Chopin scherzos. He looks for IP addresses, postmarks that should give him information on a message's origin and its trip through the World Wide Web before it landed in a mailbox.

In order to achieve that, Zahoor must have the original headers for the emails. Asra is trying to track them down. My head spins more than I want it to when they try to explain cyber crime to me. I try to stay calm when they walk me through how they can find Danny this way, but I find it freaky, as if I'm looking for my husband in a computer game.

I fear that Zahoor's chase will wind up in a cyber café in some non-descript district of Karachi, which is to say almost nowhere. In those cafés there is nothing to drink or eat. The only thing you're served is the ability to travel without ever moving. The customer settles into a little cubicle where he enjoys relative intimacy. For a couple more rupees, he can obtain a piece of cloth that gives the cubicle a hint of privacy. In a country with rampant illiteracy, the Internet has become the ironic dream of a better tomorrow. It appears as if some of Danny's captors belong to this crowd of uneducated yet computer-literate guys. They can barely read and write, but they speak Java, and they are adept at erasing their tracks.

Out of curiosity, Danny and I visited several of these cyber cafés. I had the impression that the people gathering there were those who dreamed of the West—and those who hated it. And then there's the primary group, those hungry for cyber sex. Near our house in Bombay, a snooker hall called Passionate has just invested in the Internet and changed its name to Passionet. It makes us laugh out loud every time we walk past.

There are eight more emails taped to our wall now, most of them hoaxes, we believe. They are of varying levels of ugliness. It's likely, says Dost, that the majority of the senders are under twenty-five years old.

—Original Message—
From: "al quida talaban"
To:
Sent: Thursday, January 31, 2002, 3:50 A.M.
Subject: kill

i will kill the english man today i am the leader of al quida and
we kidnaped english news writer.

and we shall crash many planes of usa

"Sick," says Bussey.

Asra writes in her notebook the comment of a Pakistani journalist who forwarded us one of those emails: "We have a lot of people trying to come out. We have a depressed society and all other avenues are closed. Only this avenue of violence is open."

Paul Steiger issues another statement aimed at the kidnappers: "The world now knows, and you seem to know, that Danny is a journalist, nothing more or less. Journalists are, by definition, trained messengers. Danny can be your messenger. A freed Danny can explain your cause, and your beliefs, to the world. . . . A captive or killed Danny cannot speak for you, cannot help you or your cause."

Bussey worries about us. He worries that our house isn't safe, in spite of the guards whose hovering presence makes us claustrophobic. At night, when we wait for Captain or Randall to return from their raids and tell us about them, Bussey will quit his computer and fling open the front door to inspect the number of guards present. Generally, after one A.M. the team has shrunk, and we rarely have more than two or three unfortunate soldiers spending the night next to a small coal *brasero*. One evening when our guards appeared particularly pathetic, Bussey woke Imran at three A.M. and asked him to use his Urdu to alert the security chief and demand reinforcements.

Every night before returning to the Sheraton, Bussey makes certain that all the doors of the house are locked. If he forgets to do it, he will make sure at the last moment to turn to me and Asra and sign the number three with his right hand. Translation: "Don't forget to secure all three locks."

Bussey has two daily arguments—with the security chief about the number of guards, and with Asra and me about moving to the Sheraton. "Oh, you're a security freak, Bussey," we tease him. He's already gotten Steve LeVine to change rooms at the hotel so they can be on the same floor. "I don't know," Steve jokes. "He *said* it was for security reasons."

Bussey gets a wicked look in his eye. "Well, when Steve learned that you and Asra were sharing a bed, he wanted to sleep in my bed, too—and I said, 'Absolutely not!'"

"Yeah, dude," he adds. "Rooms on the same floor of the same hotel. That's a guy's version of intimacy."

At the end of our long days, at two or three in the morning, Bussey and Steve repair to the Sheraton's eighth-floor lounge to have a cup of chamomile tea, and thoroughly review the day's events. While it's the last place I'd like to be, for the corporate American Bussey, the anonymity of the place is a source of comfort, and he relentlessly praises the hotel's advantages with the sugary rap of a sales rep: "Security, above all; swimming pool; sauna; hygiene."

Ah yes, hygiene. In addition to being a security freak, Bussey is a fanatic about germs. We call him our Minister of Security and Hygiene. One afternoon he almost has a heart attack when he spots little Kashva sitting on the counter with her bare bottom next to where her mother is slicing tomatoes, our own lunch tomatoes, I have to admit. His panicky admonitions terrify the kid and her mother. Neither has the faintest idea what his problem is. Nasrin is quickly sent back to her broom, and John orders chicken biryani to be delivered from the Sheraton for all our meals. Neither Asra nor I can bring ourselves to tell him what chickens feed on in Pakistan.

*　　*　　*

The analysis is beginning to yield results. Reluctant at first to show us his work, Jameel Yusuf now shares his discoveries and conclusions. Every night after midnight, his team prints out a chart that sums up the latest findings. It is a chart much like ours, though far more organized, and rather than names listed, there are telephone numbers, because this is the CPLC's process. They are taking the three phone numbers we know—those of Danny, Bashir, and the man called Imtiaz Siddique—and they are painstakingly analyzing every call made from each.

They look for patterns. If a number is called several times, especially in the course of one day, it becomes suspect. The duration and the hour the calls were made are factors, too. For each person called, the team tries to verify identity—name, gender, date of birth, address. It's not hard to determine addresses if the number called is a landline. But cell phones are hard to trace, and most are contracted under false names or simply the names of friends, because it is difficult to get phones here. Even Danny's phone was contracted by someone else.

At CPLC headquarters a few miles away, volunteers work like ants in an ant colony. Their work is tedious, but the payoff promises to be huge. Within a few days, of the seven thousand calls made by the three cell phones, the CPLC volunteers identify seventy-three numbers that might belong to Danny's kidnappers or their associates—or might be the first step in finding them.

For example, a house in Lahore, regularly called from Bashir's cellular, is determined to belong to a dealer of Sony TVs. By tapping his phone, the police are led to another phone number, this one in Karachi. Which leads them to a house in Multan where a man named Hashim has been living. Hashim, it turns out, is the man we have known under another name—Arif, the Jihadi Spokesman.

The police raid his house. Inside they find a family holding a "funeral ceremony." Oh, poor Hashim, they weep, he "died like a martyr in Afghanistan." Highly unlikely, given the fact that he was with Danny just a few weeks ago and on his way to Kashmir. So the presence of a body in the coffin is unlikely, but the police don't check. They do, however, keep looking for the Jihadi Spokesman. They go on to raid a Rawalpindi house that has been called frequently from Hashim's cell phone. It belongs to a friend, who says he doesn't know where the Jihadi Spokeman is, but to prove his willingness to help, he turns over a photo of the Jihadi Spokesman attending a wedding a few years ago, before he became a jihadi.

In the photo, Hashim stares straight out at the camera. He is a somber-looking young man of about twenty-five, with a mustache and short hair. A V-necked sweater is pulled over his *salwar kameez,* and his hands rest in his lap. His expression is chilling. He looks utterly unhappy, as if he's known all along that this picture will someday end up in hated police hands.

January 31, another email arrives. This one has been sent to CNN, the BBC, Fox News, and three Pakistani newspapers. These destinations break the earlier pattern; still, we believe it is from the same group. It declares:

> U CANNOT FOOL US AND FIND US. WE ARE INSIDE SEAS, OCEANS, HILLS, GRAVE YARDS EVERY WHERE. WE GIVE U 1 MORE DAY IF AMERICA WILL NOT MEET OUR DEMANDS WE WILL KILL DANIEL . . . DON'T THINK THIS WILL BE THE END. IT IS THE BEGINNING AND IT IS A REAL WAR ON AMRIKANS. AMRIKANS WILL GET THE TASTE OF DATH AND DESTRUCTIONS WHAT WE HAD GOT IN AFG AND PAK. INSHALLAH.

That same day, at a State Department press conference in Washington, D.C., Colin Powell, standing regally beside the diminutive King Abdullah of Jordan, is asked, "[The] kidnappers of Daniel Pearl have made demands of the United States. Do you think these demands are such that the United States would ever respond to them? And how concerned are you for his life?"

Powell responds, "With respect to Mr. Pearl, we are deeply concerned about his safety and our hearts go out to his family. . . . [But the] demands that the kidnappers have placed are not demands that we can meet or deal with or get into a negotiation about."

"That's what they always say," Bussey tells me. Maybe so, but it feels as if Powell has just tightened the cords around our necks. We have a twenty-four-hour postponement of the ultimatum—but in exchange for what?

We struggle with the lack of anything to hold on to. We are slowly sinking in quicksand.

Asra, John, and Steve seem hypnotized by their computer screens, but I know it's not because they have vital information to send out. Nothing they're writing is that important, but the nervous clicking of the keys, the speed of their movements, their silence, the way they don't look at one another—all of this is evidence of the sharpest anxiety we have experienced thus far.

There are some moments when I can tell that Bussey has been crying. He emerges with red eyes, but we do not speak of it. And we do not speak of what obviously eats at him. On the one hand, he has tremendous admiration for what he is finding in the house; for Danny; for the collective dedication to find Danny. At the same time, there is guilt, a huge pot of it, inside him—guilt because he wasn't always diligent about responding to reporters' phone calls; guilt because he sent us to Pakistan and authorized the Richard C. Reid–Gilani story. When he arrived in Karachi, I took him aside and said, "Listen. Whatever you feel, don't think about this now. We'll deal with it later."

Since Danny's disappearance, I've had the sense that I am an ambulatory pillar, ready to rush and support whoever shows signs of human weakness. It is my job, I believe, to prevent our crew from collapse. I am convinced that the mental energy of our household has the power to protect Danny's life.

But I can't seem to find the strength to break the silence that threatens to suffocate us. I prefer to retire. I need to be alone. My friends have never seen me like this. Under their sad, watchful looks, I head to the second floor to isolate myself, and as I slowly climb the stairs, I hear their worried whispers.

Upstairs, the soldier who paces back and forth on the veranda doesn't see me. I lie on the couch where I waited for Danny the night of his abduction. In the semidarkness, I do nothing but stare at the ceiling. In completely forbidding myself to express fear and anger, I feel like an Indian yogi who performs such impossible feats as holding his breath for hours or watching his fingernails grow for decades.

There is a knock at the door. I assume it is Bussey bringing me yet another glass of water, but when the door opens, it is Randall, asking politely if he can come in. He is wearing his black outfit (Bussey has nicknamed him "Black Hawk Down"). All I see is black cloth because I can't look up. Still, I move a little closer to the wall to make room for him on the couch beside me.

"It's not like they're going to have a good time once they're caught," he starts.

I say nothing.

He asks, "You wanna know how persuasive the authorities can be?"

I don't answer, but Randall goes on anyway. He describes how bad guys get beaten up and are hung upside down. He tells me how authorities use wooden sticks so they don't leave marks on the bodies. I ask Randall if he's ever been tortured, and he tells me about the time he was almost drowned. Someone held him by the hair underwater until he thought he was a goner. That was in Colombia. In Iraq he was beaten more than once. He describes how.

Suddenly I realize that Randall is giving me all these technical descriptions of torture for the sole purpose of making me feel better. They're the weirdest words of consolation I've ever heard, but he delivers them with such a good heart, and with such intimacy, that I can't help smiling. And this smile, faint as it is, seems to make Randall very happy.

"You can't collapse," he says. "Everybody else might, but not you. They won't get you. You're the strongest woman I have ever seen."

He says this hastily, seeming surprised by his own audacity. There must be a Perfect Cop manual somewhere that warns against emotional involvement with the "victims." Randall is transgressing all rules—for the first time, I'd wager—and he does it to "save" me.

"Well, I have work to do," he finally says, getting up. As he passes through the door, he turns and gives me a big wink. I know what it means: "I'm counting on you."

Me, I just pray that someday I will be able to tell Danny this story.

I have resumed lying flat like a mummy when, a few minutes later, Captain pushes open the door. This time I know for sure that Bussey has something to do with these visits. Captain grabs a chair and places it in front of the couch. I start to sit up, but he signals me not to bother. I wonder if he in turn will tell me tales from the torture chambers, but he begins to speak about the Qur'an. Or, more precisely, to offer his personal variation of the story of Moses.

"There is a man," he starts, "a man of pure faith who wishes to meet God. He goes to the mosque and asks a priest: 'What is the best way to approach God?'

"'Faith!' answers the religionist. 'Only through faith can you gain access to Him.'

"The believer in search of God goes to the riverbank and begins praying. And the purity of his heart is such that the waters open up in front of him and lead him to the eternal.

"When he comes back, his wish fulfilled, he meets the priest again and relates his experience. Jealous, the priest decides to go to the river also. He starts praying there, but nothing happens, for he is not really a man of sincere faith.

"Only absolute determination has the power to fulfill our wishes," concludes Captain. He pauses. "You and I can make the river open up."

When we go downstairs together and enter the dining room, there is such a palpable feeling of relief in the household that Bussey calls the Sheraton and orders enough chicken biryani to feed the whole street. No one makes any comment about what has just happened or about my conversations.

I sit down at the computer and borrow the words of the French writer Victor Hugo, one of my favorite authors. *"Quant au mode de prier, peu importe le nom, pourvu qu'il soit sincère. Tournez votre livre à l'envers et soyez à l'infini"*—"As for how you pray, the words do not matter if they are sincere. Turn your prayer book upside down and face the infinite." Someday I will translate the words for Captain.

I go back to Danny's notebooks, written in his Martian shorthand. I am looking for a single word, phone number, or email address that might help the river open up.

Chapter Eight

My in-laws have requested a conversation with Terry Anderson, the AP correspondent held hostage in Lebanon for seven years— *seven years!*—until he was released in 1991, when the Lebanese civil war finally came to an end.

The Pearls want to know everything: how Anderson managed to stay alive, how his family coped while he was in captivity, what shape he was in upon release. "What is our son thinking about?" they ask.

"Survival," Anderson says flatly. "That's what you think about— survival."

He talks about post-traumatic stress disorder and gives them the name of an expert in England. "I will not kid you," he says, "the situation is very serious." But he adds, "If Danny is likable and can engage even one of his captors, he will be better off."

If he is likable? "Everyone likes Danny," says Michelle. "Nobody would ever want to hurt him. Danny can charm anyone with an ounce of humanity in his bones." My in-laws keep themselves sane by imagining that Danny has won over his captors. They are sitting around playing backgammon. "Maybe soccer," says Judea.

Maybe he's composing music in his head. I once asked Danny what his dream achievement would be, expecting him to say writing an epic novel or winning two Pulitzers in a row. Instead he said, "I would love to write a hit song, one of those tunes people just can't stop singing when they're happy." The closest he's ever come is a song he wrote for a pregnant friend. She was overdue, heavy and miserable, and he pulled out his mandolin and composed a song on the spot that went, "Come out, come out / The world is not such a bad place." Okay, maybe it's not the song everyone will want to sing, but I like it. And it did work. The baby left the womb.

Before we came to Pakistan, Danny was on his way to becoming a local star in Bombay. We'd become friends with a singer named Joe Alvarez who has regular gigs at Indigo, one of the few Bombay bars that offer live Western music. Bollywood musicians gather there to jam when they tire of grinding out cheesy sound tracks for the massively successful Indian film industry. We'd show up, Danny with his electric violin, and settle in at a table. Danny would order a screwdriver, and a Bloody Mary for me, and from the stage we'd hear Joe let it rip: "And now, ladies and gentlemen, let me introduce you to the best violinist around . . . he comes from America . . . please applause Daniel *Peeeaaarl*."

The Bombay daily paper ran a photo of Danny wailing on James Brown's "Sex Machine." We've got that framed at home. I've lost track of most of the bands Danny has played with. I recall the Ottoman Empire, which he joined when he was at the Atlanta bureau of the *Journal,* because in our five-hundred-CD collection is an album they recorded. And I remember Clamp, which he played with in his Washington, D.C., years. I just found out someone has designed a "Wanted Back Home Safe" poster announcing a "Saving Daniel Pearl Bluegrass Show" for two nights at Madam's Organ, a blues bar in the Adams Morgan district of Washington, D.C., where Danny used to play. It reads: "Did you know that *Wall Street Journal* reporter Daniel Pearl is an accomplished Bluegrass fiddle player? . . . Well, his fellow musicians remember and they want to send a message to him and his captors. . . ."

When the FBI asks my in-laws to supply "proof of life" questions, which is to say those to which only Danny would know the answers, they offer this: What does Danny want for his fortieth birthday? (Danny's theory is that anyone facing a fortieth birthday desperately needs and deserves something truly wonderful to look forward to.) Answer: an upright bass.

Until he went off to college, Danny dreamed of becoming a classical violinist. He joined the Valley Youth Orchestra at the age of nine and always attended music camps. Two years ago I had the chance to hear him play with an orchestra. The Youth Orchestra was staging a reunion in L.A. They played Tchaikovsky, movements from *Swan Lake* and Symphony No. 4, Bizet's "Farandole" from *L'Arlesienne* and the "Hoedown" from Copland's *Rodeo*. Watching Danny absorbed in the music, I strained to see if I could hear his violin apart from all the instruments. I didn't think I could.

Since he's disappeared, I've left his stuff scattered throughout our bedroom the way he left it. When I glance around, what reassures me most is his mandolin. With stickers dancing all over its case, it says to me, "Don't worry—I haven't played my last tune yet." On one of the stickers, two sheep face each other over the line: "Fool's progress." Another says, "Ahlan Wasahlan Abu Dhabi." I must remember to ask Danny what that means.

Randall calls. "So how're the Pretty Thangs holding up?" he asks Bussey.

"You mean the highly intelligent, Ivy League–educated women?" Bussey replies. "They're hanging in there."

I like that expression, "hanging in there." In French we say *"tiens le coup."* I received my very first mailed card a few days ago. Sent to the American consulate in Karachi, it's a "hang in there" Hallmark card with a marsupial dangling by its tail from a tree. It makes me laugh out loud. The card comes from an old lady (you can tell from the nice neat loops in her handwriting) in Peoria, Illinois. Bussey says it's redundant to call Peoria the heartland of America.

Messages of support are beginning to arrive from everywhere—the States, Africa, Holland, Cuba, Japan, the Philippines, Colombia. I can't imagine how people are tracking down my email address, but many are. Sometimes I read the messages to the others; I figure we all need a little reassurance that a better world exists out there. "All of us here at People for the Ethical Treatment of Animals (PETA) are hoping for Daniel Pearl to return safely back." We like that one a lot.

I am hanging in despite the fact that the police have found Gilani and arrested him along with his entire family—men, women, children, old people, pregnant women, anyone remotely related to him—and, having interrogated him, are coming to the conclusion that Gilani doesn't know where Danny is. They're letting him go and shifting their focus elsewhere.

Just like that? Never mind the "mastermind"?

"Don't worry," Captain says, deeply inhaling a smoke. "We're getting much closer to the truth." I believe him, still and always. But I can also see that his face sags with fatigue, and his clothes, cut so stylishly, are beginning to hang a bit off his frame.

Now, a week and a half into the ordeal, everyone is worn to the bone. After being up seventy-two straight hours, Randall falls facedown on his keyboard while typing up a report for Washington. When he wakes, his monitor is filled with page after page of the letter "J."

Captain's wife comes by—to meet us and, I suppose, to see her husband. She is a young, beautiful lady with thick black hair tied in a knot and tucked under a *dupatta,* dark yet bright eyes, and a gentle, genuine smile. She is Captain's first cousin—like almost all of the marriages here, theirs was arranged—and when Captain speaks of her and their three children, you can tell he wishes he were with them more, and they him. This morning his youngest daughter refused to eat breakfast unless he fed her himself.

Asra and I try to be woman-friendly and honor our visitor. We make chai and sit down with our legs properly glued together. Captain's wife asks, point blank, "Do you think they are Muslims, the ones who took him?" Neither Asra nor I expected those words to be the first out of her mouth. We try to come up with the right answer, something like, "Well, you know, those are not the honorable Muslims.

They're not *real* Muslims." Recognizing our embarrassment, she quickly switches to safer ground: "What do you think of the weather in Pakistan?" This time we really don't know what to say. But we like her.

She is married to a man possessed. She would never complain, and I will always be grateful for that. Captain explains why he is so driven to find Danny: "I am a human being. Yes, I am a police officer, and most of us become immune to pain like a surgeon would after practicing his first incision. But I have never been like that. I can't do this, I have to remain a human being, first and foremost."

Captain rejoices in my pregnancy. I used to think it was funny and cute until late one night, when he told me about the daughter he lost in a car accident a number of years ago. She was seven years old and his only child at the time. It took him a long time to get over the incident, but it taught him the value of a single human life. Maybe that's why I trust him so much.

Captain is hurting at yet another level. "You cannot just kidnap an international correspondent and have him vanish! Daniel Pearl is not just an individual. He represents *The Wall Street Journal*. He represents America.

"People have asked, 'Why are you doing this thing?' You know why? It is for my national pride." He looks worried. "Do you understand what I mean?"

"Yes," I say. "Danny represents America, and you strive to represent the best of Pakistan."

Where is the ISI's national pride? Why has it shown such minimal interest in the kidnapping? The agency leaves its mark on every aspect of Pakistani politics; you would think that even for appearance's sake, it would want its presence known. We corner Jameel Yusuf and ask him why, in his opinion, the ISI hasn't shown up. Glowing in his ability to move mountains, Yusuf pulls out his cell phone and calls an ISI big shot. "So," he asks, "regarding the Daniel Pearl case, are you involved?" Yusuf's eyes twinkle as the other man natters on. Yusuf says, "If Danny is found, this will give a good image of our country." He's quiet again as the other man responds, and then we hear him say, "Well, I know him personally, he came to my office, *yar* . . ." (*"Yar"* is the Pakistani "dude.")

Off the phone, Yusuf tells us the ISI has in fact been here, even on the first day after Danny disappeared, though we didn't realize it. But, he says, someone is likely to see us officially. "Beware—they tap all the phones," he warns with amusement as he heads for the door.

Well, it's not like *we* have anything to hide.

The man sent to us is between thirty-five and forty, of medium build, and withdrawn. He wears a checked shirt, a brown and black jacket, and glasses that make him look like a junior clerk.

"What's your name?" Bussey asks with an air of professional respect.

"Major."

"And what is your rank?" Bussey continues.

"Major."

"I see," says Bussey, "Major Major."

Major Major sits on the edge of an armchair but doesn't utter a word. Determined to remain open all the same, Asra and I walk him through the findings on our chart while taking note of his minimal reactions. Major Major takes from his pocket the smallest notepad I've ever seen, so preposterously tiny that he has to hold it in the center of his palm to write anything down. He writes at most three words during our entire presentation.

When he visits again a few days later, Asra assigns him a task: Provide us with information regarding two people we keep finding intriguing—Khalid Khawaja and Mansur Ejaz, the businessman who put Danny in touch with Khawaja.

When he returns, Major Major still wears the same checked jacket. He retires to his armchair and, silent as a tombstone, pulls out his microscopic notepad, regarding us with a slightly annoyed expression.

"So what have you found?" asks Asra.

Major Major looks down at the pad but doesn't bother to open it. "Khawaja is a former air force officer. Mansur Ejaz is a Pakistani businessman living in the U.S.A."

Major Major must take us for absolute fools.

"Is that all you have?" snaps Asra.

"The rest of our reports haven't arrived yet."

"Why don't you pick up the phone, then, and call to find out?" Asra's voice is beginning to reach a dangerous level of intensity, but Major Major has survived worse storms, or so he thinks.

"We don't work that way," he answers, and his tone indicates it's useless for us to go further.

Asra doesn't see it that way. "With all due respect . . ." she leans in toward Major Major, stiff as ever. "With all due respect, you people suck."

My friend sweeps out of the room as if carried by the tornado of her own fury. Incredulous, Major Major turns to me. "She is angry!"

"You bet she is," I say.

Without another word, Major Major proceeds to the door, thus putting an end to our direct connection with ISI.

All right. If it's not Gilani, then who is it? Who's taken Danny and why?

Sitting alone at the dining room table, I stare up at the chart that occupies a full wall, twelve feet long and seven feet high. At its center, circled in blue, is Danny's name, and surrounding it are a sea of boxes—red for prime suspects, blue for sources and contacts, and black for . . . I'm not sure what the black represents. There are key dates and phone numbers, acronyms of terrorist organizations, and countless code names. Under several names, Asra has written the number of children attributed to them—Osama (21), Rabia (16), Mohammed (10)—and arrows shoot out from boxes to hook up one scary individual or group with another scary individual or group. It looks somewhat like a drawing from a children's book in which a fly must avoid the spider in a labyrinth and finds itself in a variety of increasingly dizzying entanglements.

Jaish-e-Mohammed. Harkat-ul-Mujahideen. Harkat-ul-Ansar. Lashkar-e-Jhangvi. Any could be involved; all could. As I study the interconnecting arrows, what has seemed a confusing mess becomes cohesive and coherent. Not long ago, I read a book on terrorism that warned we are facing the "first truly global insurgency." Here on my wall, I am looking at it and it has a name: Al Qaeda. I am acutely aware of the final truth that many seem to want to avoid—Al Qaeda is behind Danny's abduction. Casting a blind eye on the world, Al Qaeda goes after symbols: the World Trade Center and now an American Jewish journalist. They were three thousand, and he is but one man. The hatred, though, is one and the same.

How do you describe the worldwide network of clandestine cells that forms Al Qaeda? A monster with tentacles? A vast amorphous amoeba that assumes a temporary form to strike and terrorize, then dissolves until it can strike again? On the one hand, that definition feels accurate, but it doesn't credit the brutal efficiency of the operation; Al Qaeda is a totalitarian government that rules without national borders or a set address. In Arabic, "Al Qaeda" means "the base"; it can operate from anywhere, and it is methodical at many levels, ideological and military. It knows how to form alliances, how to make them work, and how to finance operations. But there is no real ideal or solution here, only a pitiful return to the "glory" of the Arab past . . . maybe. Al Qaeda destroys for the sake of destruction. It feeds on its militants' frustrations and thrives on the blood of innocents.

On the veranda, I sound out those I trust. But with the exception of the two reporters, Steve and Asra, no one wants to acknowledge that Al Qaeda is behind this.

In a country so adept at the conspiracy theory, hypotheses are plentiful. Blinded by their terrible obsession with India, many Pakistanis insist that India must have been behind the abduction. During the daily press briefing at the Foreign Office in Islamabad, the director general of the Inter Services Public Relations, Major-General

Rashid Qureshi, tells reporters that "all that I can say is that there is an Indian linkage" to Danny's disappearance. Peshawar's *Frontier Post* (January 30) similarly reports, "Investigators probing the abduction of an American reporter in Karachi are stumbling on leads that point to India's Research and Analysis Wing, RAW (Indian intelligence). . . . It is feared that RAW has staged the episode to defame Pakistan." February 2, on an official visit to Berlin, Abdul Sattar, the Pakistani foreign minister repeats rumors/reports of cell-phone tracings that prove six phone calls were made from one of the kidnappers' phones to high-level Indian government officials in New Delhi right after Danny was spirited away.

The morning of February 3, we open *The News* to a bizarre article about Asra. When Bussey arrives, he sits in his customary seat at the head of the table, takes one look at the headline, and bursts out laughing. "*Baffling* . . . yes, baffling," he sputters. "It took a Pakistani editor to finally find the perfect adjective to describe Asra."

BAFFLING QUESTIONS ABOUT INDIAN LADY IN PEARL CASE

ISLAMABAD—Security agencies are probing several baffling questions pertaining to the unauthorized stay of an American passport holder Indian Muslim lady, Asra Q. Nomani, with whom the kidnapped *Wall Street Journal* reporter Daniel Pearl had been living in Karachi. . . . It was discovered by security agencies during investigation of Pearl's kidnapping that Ms Nomani has got a house on rent in Karachi where she and Pearl have been living. . . . She was married to a Pakistani national but the marriage broke after three months.

The article goes on to publish the considerable (for this part of the world) rent that Asra pays for this house—"where she and Pearl have been living." It reprints her application for a visa almost in its entirety, and it goes so far as to list all of her addresses and phone numbers—in India and in Brooklyn, New York, which is where she was staying when she applied. Later published accounts will include her family's phone numbers and address in West Virginia.

An article in the daily *Dawn* reports that Asra has been arrested and is in the custody of a security agency for her "unauthorized" stay in Pakistan—and for a possible role in the kidnapping. When specifically asked about Asra at a press conference, all Major General Qureshi will tell journalists is "Several people are being interrogated, but I cannot give details on that."

What is he talking about?

Asra is like a cat. When she is sad or hurt, she looks for a corner and stays put. What pains her most is not that intelligence agencies slander her name in a country she somehow considers hers, or that most accounts imply she and Danny were lovers. What makes her curl up in the corner is that not a single voice has spoken up to defend her innocence. In an effort to cheer her, I quote what we say in France when confronted by school-yard bullies: "The toad's spit can't reach the wings of the white dove."

I'm afraid my words seem of little comfort to her. But Asra knows it could be worse. We've just gone through worse.

Four days ago, the bicameral reporter Kamran Khan raised questions about our friend—and much more—in the January 30 edition of *The News*. Continuing his practice of approaching the story in distinctly different ways for Pakistani and American audiences, he wrote:

> some Pakistan security officials . . . are privately searching for answers as to why a Jewish American reporter was exceeding "his limits" to investigate Pakistani religious group [*sic*]. These official [*sic*] are also guessing, rather loudly, as to why Pearl decided to bring in an Indian journalist as his full time assistant in Pakistan, Ansa [*sic*] Nomani, an American passport holder Indian-Muslim lady who had come from Mumbai to Karachi with Pearl, [and] was working as his full time assistant in the country.
>
> The same group of officials is also intrigued as to why an Amer-

ican newspaper reporter based in Mumbai would also establish a full time residence in Karachi by renting a resident. "An India based Jewish reporter serving a largely Jewish media organization should have known the hazards of exposing himself to radical Islamic groups, particularly those who recently got crushed under American military might," remarked a senior Pakistani official.

That same day Khan had a joint byline with Molly Moore on page A8 of *The Washington Post*: "U.S. Reporter Seen As Victim of Sophisticated Trap; Pakistani Police Describe Kidnapping Plot with Many False Fronts." There was no mention of Jews, Jewish media organizations, or mysterious Indian-Muslim ladies.

The following day Khan and Moore had another joint byline in *The Washington Post,* this one on page one: "Kidnapped U.S. Reporter Is Threatened with Death."

Hoaxes, hoaxes, hoaxes: "We have killed Mr. Danny. Now Mr. Bush can find his body in the graveyards of Karachi. We have thrown him there." Close to four hundred cemeteries later, after combing throughout the night, the police know there is no body to find. A call comes in to the U.S. consulate: "Two million dollars, we give you back Danny Pearl." Funny how you long for concrete demands . . . yes! dollars! serious dollars! No, just another hoax: "I am sorry. I sent the email in which the deadline of Daniel. Please pardon me! It was a fake mail. It also reveals the fact that the last mail is also a fake mail."

Which one? . . .

A storm of blackbirds swoops down on us like creatures possessed, mixing with other birds we can't identify. The symphony of squawks turns our eyes upward, a thunderous sound. I slip outside with Asra and Bussey to watch. The birds seem to refuse to fly over our house, but they all gather over the one next door, leaving the impression that the sky is otherwise empty. We don't know what to make of this. It feels like a bad omen or at least a warning, but we cannot bring ourselves to say so. Asra, sweet Asra, succumbs to a pitiful denial technique: "I bet it's a *good* sign," she declares bravely, but without conviction.

"I feel like I'm in an Alfred Hitchcock movie," Bussey says, and I can tell he is both fascinated and uneasy.

Things happen in the night without my knowing. Bussey and Steve LeVine are summoned from their beds to identify the body of a young man who's been shot and tossed from a moving car. Many millions of Americans are already under the impression that it is Danny's body, because ABC News reporter Jeffrey Kofman, trusting his Karachi police sources, has broken into a pre–Super Bowl basketball game to scoop the world and announce the news.

Steve Goldstein later tells me what it was like in the States when the story broke, or at least what it was like at his place: "Super Bowl Sunday. I thought, Finally it's going to be relatively calm. The whole country seemed to be taking the day off, and instead of getting seven hundred calls, by three o'clock we'd gotten a hundred."

Every year Goldstein's partner, Bill, throws a Super Bowl dinner for the same six people. Goldstein, who had not been home for almost two weeks, had promised to stay home and make it to the dinner. "Then Kofman goes on the air at three-ten P.M. In rapid succession, CNN, NBC, and CBS all call to verify the story, and within twenty minutes I've gotten over a hundred calls, and I'm thinking, Oh, no, this can't be! What the hell is going on? So I call Bussey at his hotel, and I wake him up, and I say, 'John, you've got to get up. I've got to know the truth.'

"He goes, 'No, no, Danny's not dead. I know he's not dead. I just spoke to Captain. It's not true, I'd know.'

"I say, 'I'm just telling you what they reported. I can't believe they would break in if it's not true.'

"So he goes, 'Just give me a few minutes.' I'm in a panic. Bill has a chef in the kitchen, she's helping him cook, and the phone starts ringing off the hook, and I say, 'Bill, I need you, get in here right now.'

"And he goes, 'We're doing the meringue.'

"I say, 'I don't give a fuck about the meringue! Get in here!'"

Together, the two men struggle against an avalanche of phone calls, and then John Bussey calls. "It's not Danny," he reports. "It's an Iranian student with braces who's about twenty-one years old."

"Okay. But I need a second source," says Goldstein.

"I'm telling you, Danny is alive," says Bussey.

Goldstein digs in his heels. "I am not going on national television saying that Danny is alive to later be found wrong. Now, give me another person!"

Bussey goes and gets Steve LeVine. "Danny is alive," Steve says, and Goldstein is satisfied. ABC retracts its story one hour after announcing it.

Randall is first to identify the body. Captain and Dost have asked him to because they sense there is a real possibility it is Danny's. "I was crushed," Randall will tell me later. He speeds to the clinic where they've taken the body. "As I'm moving around it, I begin to notice differences that do not match Danny. I see a slight bulge in the upper lip and I ask to have it raised. The man wore braces on his upper teeth. I've never been so glad to see a dead man, since it was not Danny. A strange conflict of joy with death."

Why would anybody want to kidnap Danny Pearl? Is it because of something he's written? Asra and I comb the articles Danny sent to Bashir as a sine qua non for setting up an interview with Gilani. These aren't benign topics—JEM's offices remain open; Pakistan's nuclear scientist has seen bin Laden with ISI's knowledge (and, some say, the CIA's). There are a variety of subjects likely to piss off a good number of people, among them the ISI chiefs who have been removed from the agency because of their close relationship with jihadi groups. Is there really such a thing, we wonder, as a "former" ISI chief? As

Musharraf strikes the Islamists with one hand, he pats them on the back with the other, to keep them fighting on the Kashmir front. Surely there are still officials in ISI who, because of their connection with the jihadi world, know who has kidnapped Danny and where to look for him. But no one wants to walk these lines with us, and we have stopped talking about ISI with Captain and others we care about in order to protect them.

After a lunch of chicken biryani, Asra and I meet on the first floor, where a guard has been posted by the veranda. We brought him a chair earlier, and now, knocked out by the heat, he has fallen asleep, his rifle leaning against the wall. This is fine; we like our privacy. We want to discuss President Musharraf, who is scheduled to visit the United States in less than a week, on February 12.

Asra sort of likes Musharraf. In an article for Salon.com, "My Crush on Musharraf," she described a dictatorial but nevertheless progressive president. The subtitle explains quite a bit: "With His Dogs, Drinking, Frameless Glasses and Armani Suits, He's Reviled by Modernists." (In Islam, touching a dog is considered impure and supposedly makes you too dirty for prayers.) Asra portrayed a man who is "reassuring, inclusive and strong," all positive stuff, but I'm not sure Musharraf is inclined to love Asra back these days.

This visit to Washington will be Musharraf's first as president. A theory is going around that Danny has been kidnapped to embarrass Musharraf before this meeting—either causing its cancellation, or at least seriously disrupting its agenda. As Bussey puts it, with Danny in captivity, "It's going to be hard for Musharraf to concentrate on the textile industry."

I don't doubt that whoever has kidnapped my husband wishes to humiliate Musharraf and to punish him for his collaboration with the Americans. But I have to assume there are other reasons, too. For example, I can't rule out that it has something to do with the computer *The Wall Street Journal* turned over to the CIA a few weeks ago.

Here is what happened. *Journal* reporter Alan Cullison was in Afghanistan for the paper when his computer was damaged. He set out to look for spare parts to fix it. He found a guy who offered to sell him a hard drive from a desktop computer and a Compaq laptop for four thousand dollars. Cullison talked him down to eleven hundred, and became the owner of an astonishing trove of information. As it turned out, the desktop had been used by Al Qaeda chieftains in Kabul for at least four years; as Cullison noted, it was "stuffed with Al Qaeda secrets." Both computers had been looted from an Al Qaeda office in November, after a bombing raid killed several operatives nearby and drove others from the area.

The desktop was used by one of the men killed in the raid, Muhammad Atef, who headed Al Qaeda's military wing—and by another top Al Qaeda figure, as well, Dr. Ayman Al-Zawahiri, considered Osama bin Laden's chief strategist. The two men were jointly responsible for the 1998 U.S. embassy bombings in Dar es Salaam, Tanzania, and Nairobi, Kenya. Inside the hard drive were roughly 1,750 documents—letters, reports, video and audio files—ranging "from the murderous to the mundane," as Cullison and his colleague Andrew Higgins wrote in a December 31, 2001, article for *The Wall Street Journal*. Using Arabic translators and computer experts to bypass encryption barriers, the two men sifted through the documents and, in two articles for the *Journal,* provided a taste of what they managed to retrieve.

There was a letter from two men purporting to be journalists, requesting "an interview" with the anti-Taliban leader Ahmed Shah Massoud—a request mistakenly agreed to by Massoud, because at that meeting, just two days before the attack on the World Trade Center, the "journalists" detonated a bomb and blew up Massoud and themselves.

There were chilling files outlining serious efforts to launch a program of chemical and biological weapons, "code-named *al Zabadi,* Arabic for curdled milk," and a video in which Osama bin Laden spoke for twenty-three minutes about, among other things, the 9/11 attacks. In another homemade video, "television footage of terrified Americans fleeing the flaming World Trade Center [is] overlain with a soundtrack of mocking chants and prayer in Arabic."

Most startling of all for me, there were records tracking the movements around Europe and the Middle East by an Al Qaeda operative scouting key locations to bomb. The terrorist's code name is Abdul Ra'uff, and over the course of several months, his reconnaissance trips took him to London, Amsterdam, Brussels, Tel Aviv, Egypt, Turkey, and Pakistan. When intelligence authorities looked at these documents, the terrorist's movements were already familiar to them. These were the very trips taken by a terrorist they already had in custody: Richard C. Reid, the shoe bomber.

Because the computer contained files that might reveal plans for future attacks or other "are lives at stake" issues, to use Bussey's words, the *Journal* took the unusual step of turning it over to U.S. intelligence. Paul Steiger told *The New York Times* that "In moral terms, we would have been devastated if we had withheld information that could have saved the lives of our servicemen or civilians," and such media watchdogs and ethicists as Bill Kovach, chairman of the Committee of Concerned Journalists, endorsed the decision, comparing it to the agreement by the *Times* and *The Washington Post* to publish the Unabomber's statement at the request of the U.S. government.

What was overlooked was the fact that turning the computer over to the government might protect some, but it endangered others, a risk intensified by the *Journal*'s trumpeting of what it had done. Danny and I were at the Chez Soi guest house in Islamabad when Danny read online what had happened. I was engrossed in Nelson Mandela's autobiography, stretched out on the bed, when Danny said, "Baby, we're in trouble." He was staring at his laptop, visibly upset. When Danny gets upset, he grows quiet and focused. When I get upset, I get more voluble. On this December day, I got good and noisy; I was furious.

When you are a journalist in a country like Pakistan, where you spend so much time trying to convince people you are not a spy, you aren't helped when the company you work for announces to the world that it is collaborating with the CIA.

*   *   *

February 5. At 8:57 in the morning, the landline rings in the bedroom, waking Asra and me up. We both jump for the phone, but I forget I am pregnant and get stuck on my left side. No one is there. Was it the kidnappers wanting to see who would answer, me or the police? We wait for the phone to ring again. Usually mornings are dreadful and I lie awake in bed, my mind filled with silly thoughts like, I won't move until Danny comes back. Today, while neither of us will admit it, we are convinced the kidnappers have just called, and we will lie here until they call again.

We are staring at the ceiling when the phone rings again. Nine-twenty-four A.M. It is Captain. He doesn't say hello, just, "I've got them, I've got their whole family."

I feel as if I will vomit, vomit *my heart,* but then he adds, "They will lead us to Danny," and I know we're not there yet. Still, this is extraordinary, the first good news since Danny left. Three men are in police custody, and all have something to do with the computer from which Danny's pictures have been sent. Captain, Dost, and Randall have interrogated the suspects all night long. "They are my guests," says Captain.

It began with Zahoor's efforts. Having painstakingly traced the route of the emails, he wound up with five connections that could lead to the senders of the scanned photos. Four led to cyber cafés around Karachi; the fifth, however, led to a landline. Ideally, Captain and his men could ask the phone company to name the line's subscriber, or at least the payer of the bills; but they were afraid to openly ask such questions, lest they tip someone off. Instead, they asked the phone company about phone boxes: In which box does this landline originate?

They got the box, which meant they got the line, and they followed it. They followed it through the twisted streets of Karachi, digging up the asphalt and poking through walls when they had to. They followed it to the end of the line—or rather, what was supposed to be the end. But the owner of a computer shop turned out to have been the original subscriber for that landline—no longer, though. By the time the police tracked him down—or more accurately, tracked down the plug for his phone—he had passed his phone connection on to someone else, who then shifted it to another, who shifted it again. In a poor country like Pakistan, this is common practice. And this is how complicated it can become: In its fourth shift, that one phone number that Zahoor found finally led to a server. And that server turned out to provide cable internet access to eighty different illegal subscribers.

Eighty! No wonder we've had trouble finding Danny. Any of these eighty subscribers could have been the one to send the email.

The subscribers all live in one dormitory-style building. Many are students, and all have computers hooked up to what the new owner of the line calls Speedy Network. Zahoor gives Asra and me a crash course on web navigation. A server, he explains, is basically a hub, a computer with a lot of memory, speed, and storage space. Think of it as a post office, with the computer being the mailbox. The mail is routed through the server. What the investigators had to determine was who in this building was online precisely when the first or second email was sent, and who used Hotmail or Yahoo! as an ISP, as the kidnappers do. Captain asked his best guy, Farrouq, to dig into the server and find this vital information. Problem is, while Farrouq "is very brave, he didn't know A, B, C about computers," in Captain's words. He didn't even know what a server was. Captain (who had just learned that tidbit himself) quickly trained Farrouq. On hand, too, were FBI computer experts, ready to provide more sophisticated assistance if needed.

For three nights police agents banged on the building's doors and demanded to check every computer. The tenants grew increasingly annoyed, and the outcome began to look doubtful. Then a nondescript young man, your regular, curious neighbor, approached Farrouq. "I might be of some help to you," he said. "I have a computer. There is nothing in my computer, but if you want, I can help you inspect other computers." He said his name was Fahad Naseem; he was connection number 66.

"He is voluntarily helping us, but I don't sort of trust him," Captain tells me. "So I tell Farrouq to bring him over to my office. I will bluff him. This is our own police way of dealing with suspects. I say to him, 'Okay, I put your computer to the test, and I have some software which can immediately, right here and now, retrieve deleted files. So don't bother to lie.'"

A nanosecond of panic flickering though Fahad's eyes is enough for Captain and Farrouq to know that Fahad is a suspect. "The bluff works! It works! So then I am jumping with excitement, you know? Because I know that I am going to get Danny alive today.

"Pray for me," Captain says to me. "I have told you this before, but one day soon I will be walking into your door, and Danny will be following me. And I'll just want to see that smile on your face when you see Danny for the first time. I won't be looking at Danny, but I will be looking at you."

He calls his boss and tells him, "The mystery is solved. I have the first person. Now I am going in for the second."

Meanwhile, the FBI has recovered two erased emails from Fahad's computer. One is in Urdu, the other is in English, and along with them are the attachments containing Danny's photos. Thirteen days have passed since Danny disappeared, and everyone is so tense that Fahad wisely doesn't try to play smart. Handcuffed, he leads them to the district where his cousin, Suleiman, hangs out.

Randall joins Captain, and they prepare for a raid. "I want to do it the perfect way. I want to catch this man in a surprise," Captain says. Suleiman soon comes strolling along a semblance of sidewalk. He is about to turn at the corner when an unmarked car pulls up beside him. Two men fly out, grab him, and throw him into the vehicle. Holding him by the hair, a policeman flattens Suleiman's face against the floor, and with a shriek of tires, the car backs up and speeds out of the neighborhood as quickly as possible. All it takes is a few seconds.

Captain is nervous. "We want, you know, quick answers," Captain will explain to me later. He wants to act before anyone notices the cousins are missing, and before any coded message or signal can endanger Danny's life. "But the men didn't want to speak, so . . . we made them speak."

It is past midnight. In two hours, the police have the name and address of a third accomplice. His name is Adil. "Call him," Captain orders Suleiman.

A sleepy, angry voice picks up the phone. It is not Adil but a member of his family. "He doesn't live here anymore," barks the man before hanging up. Captain can't tell—is the man speaking the truth or just irritated at having been woken in the middle of the night? If Adil isn't home, is he with Danny?

"Call Adil on his cell phone," Captain orders Suleiman. It works; this time the sleepy voice picking up is Adil's.

Suleiman repeats word for word what Captain has told him to say: "I've got something very urgent to tell you right now. It's very impor-tant."

"No way," says Adil. "I'm sleeping. Let's meet tomorrow morning, same hour, same place," and he turns off his phone.

Captain snatches the cell phone from Suleiman's hands and calls the cellular provider's headquarters, demanding to know which geographical section, or cell, Adil's phone was in. Their computers automatically monitor the weakness or strength of the signals, in order to switch a phone's signal from tower to tower as needed. If the cell provider can tell Captain which tower transmits to Adil's phone, we'll know what cell Adil is in. That's an area with a radius of roughly three kilometers. Not inconsiderable but small enough to establish whether or not Adil is staying at his family house.

But the phone company takes its time providing the information. One hour passes . . . another half hour . . . and Captain explodes. He orders his men to go to the phone company, break down the doors, and at gunpoint ask the questions again: *Which cell tower? Which cell?*

By the time Captain goes to the phone company, the representative is definitely not happy. "Why do you do this to me?" he asks Captain.

"This is our country. If I don't do this, the journalist dies. Do you want that?"

Captain gets what he wants.

When Adil is caught, he is home in bed. The same questions are asked, same methods used, when he refuses to talk. When he does reveal what Captain wants to know, it becomes clear that, like Fahad and Suleiman, Adil does not know where Danny is.

This is when Captain gets scared. The kidnapping has been much better planned than he'd suspected. Whoever is behind it is very good at what he does. The first man knows the existence of the second man, and the second one knows the third but not the fourth. Still, the third man has a fourth name to offer: Omar Saeed Sheikh.

Omar Sheikh. He's the onetime London School of Economics student turned Islamic militant featured in the *Independent* article. He's the man who wired $100,000 to Mohammed Atta; he's the militant who was jailed for kidnapping Westerners.

There is a house that has been wiretapped for days because the CPLC pinpointed it as one that Bashir frequently called before the January 23 abduction. Nothing has come out of eavesdropping on it, but Captain gets lucky for a second time tonight when one of his lieutenants mentions that the owner of the house may be related to Omar. The pieces suddenly snap together in Captain's head, and in a flash he understands something huge: Bashir, the man who lured Danny into the trap, is Omar Sheikh.

Furious not to have been better informed about the house's ownership, Captain rounds up a heavily armed special police unit. They scream up to the house, destroy the entrance, and storm the rooms. It is four in the morning. Roughly, they gather up the inhabitants, who, they are surprised to find, are a rather innocent-looking old man and a perfectly honorable-looking family, all devout Muslims. This is the house of Omar's aunt; this is her family. Under the glances— half frightened, half furious—of the family, the policemen search the rooms for clues proving Omar used this apartment to organize Danny's kidnapping.

Less than two hours remain before dawn and prayer time. Soon the news of the raids and arrests will be all over the streets. On an impulse, Captain calls an officer posted in Lahore, where Omar's father resides. "Go to his house," Captain tells the officer, "but do nothing until I tell you to."

As the policeman stations himself in front of Omar's father's house he can hear the phone ringing inside. From the home of Omar's aunt back in Karachi, Captain is calling Omar's father and calmly asking for his son's cell phone number. The father gives it to him. Then, under the watchful eyes of the aunt and her family, Captain dials Omar—who he assumes is with Danny. "My hand didn't tremble," he will tell me a little later that morning, "but it started sweating so much it was almost glued to the receiver."

Omar answers his cell phone. "I am the investigating officer," Captain says. "I know what you did, I exactly know. Your game is over. If you don't believe me, look at the caller ID." Captain has called from Adil's cell phone.

Captain holds the phone's receiver close to Omar's aunt, and she speaks briefly to her nephew. Then Captain puts Omar's cousin on the phone. One by one, the family members all have a chance to be heard by Omar. Then it is Captain's turn again. "You come from a respectable family," Captain says. "Do not humiliate them."

Omar is silent; then suddenly he says, "I don't know," and snaps his phone shut.

Captain doesn't worry. Why take in the whole family? (The aunt has confided that her nephew has "always frightened her.")"Bargaining chip," Dost explains laconically. "Thank God, we're the only twenty-four-hour pickup service in Pakistan!" He is confident that it won't be long before Omar is arrested.

Eagerly, Asra Googles Omar and prints out his photo. In early 2000, his picture was all over the papers, when Omar was freed from Indian jails with three other Pakistani militants in exchange for 178 people whose Indian Airlines jet was hijacked from Kathmandu, Nepal. Omar had been in prison since 1994 on kidnapping charges. One of the other militants freed in the prisoner exchange was Massood Azhar, the former leader of Harkat-ul-Mujahideen who went on to found Jaish-e-Mohammed. Danny wrote about him from Bahawalpur. Omar is said to be Azhar's disciple.

Asra pastes Omar's picture on the chart, next to the sketch the police drew of "Bashir" based on Asif-le-fixer's descriptions. Asif-le-fixer gave Omar a mustache and thinner lips, but there is no doubt the two are the same. Omar doesn't at all resemble the other jihadis. He looks more like the best student of the class than a soldier of terror. But if you look closely, the face staring back is devoid of recognizable human expression.

By the time the American consul, John Bauman, joins us, our excitement is at a peak. Sensing an imminent happy ending, we are indulging in silly speculation. Our adventure has turned into a Hollywood movie. The casting of Winona Ryder in the role of Asra is unanimously approved. Bussey will be played by James Woods, Randall by Steven Seagal. Bauman joins the game gracefully. "It will be a remake of *The Untouchables*," he says; and because he wears the same type of waistcoat, Dost will be our Elliot Ness.

Asra has begun gathering our documents. All of a sudden we feel a major urge to get out of here. To take Danny and run. Imran is sent to buy suitcases at the Chaowk bazaar. Steve LeVine rushes back to the Sheraton to pick up the bottle of Wild Turkey he's been saving for Danny. We hide it in the upstairs room so as not to offend our Muslim friends. I warn Bussey that, pregnant or not, I will have a sip when Danny gets home.

Randall and Captain stop by the house before returning to the cell where the three suspects are detained. "Cocky as they are," Randall says, clearing his throat, "under professional questioning, they'll undoubtedly provide the necessary information." Then he looks at me and stops playing tough. "I hate those bastards," he says.

"President Musharraf is calling Azhar." Though Captain's eyes are oddly wired from lack of sleep and he speaks in a sort of Morse code, we can easily fill in the blanks. Two months after the World Trade Center attacks, Massood Azhar, deemed potentially dangerous, was placed under house arrest. Now, Musharraf is calling Azhar so that Azhar can call his disciple Omar and tell him to let Danny go. It is brilliantly simple or totally surreal, depending on how you think about it. When Azhar was put under surveillance, the dangerous Omar remained free as a bird. Someone has been protecting him. Somewhere between corrupt politics and false preachers, Omar found a shelter.

Chapter Nine

WE ARE trying to kill time. Or rather, we are pretending time is not killing us. I have studied all the irregularities on the wall facing the rocking chair I am sitting in. The house has been recently repainted, but I can discern a few cracks and holes where pictures used to hang. I stay there much too long, hands crossed over what I presume is the head of our child. Seconds grind slowly into minutes, hours reluctantly become half days. You might think that the nightmares would come at night, but they don't. They come when consciousness washes over me and I say to myself, Am I going to make it? Can I do this another day without collapsing? I feel like a prisoner X-ing off the days on a homemade calendar. Each cross on the make-believe calendar is a victory in itself.

Omar Saeed Sheikh is on the run with his young wife and infant son. For all we know, he could be in the tribal areas by now, that is to say, in no-man's-land. This three-hundred-mile mountainous belt between Afghanistan and Pakistan is home to a tribal population that considers itself beyond the reach of the law. It is forbidden soil for most Pakistanis, and the military tends to keep out. As a result, the territory has always been a haven for smugglers and gunrunners, and these days it provides a natural shelter for Al Qaeda and the Taliban, whose members slip undetected between the two countries.

Danny and I once interviewed a tribal chief who had ventured out of his domain for the hunting season. At the time the Pakistani government was trying to convince tribal areas to quit harboring Taliban.

We went to a house that the clan used as a hunting pavilion. A dozen or so men, all in grayish robes and all carrying that essential accessory, an AK-47, sat in a circle on the floor of an empty room. The chief wore a white turban. When we asked if he had any intention of obeying Musharraf, he seemed amused by the question, as if we were passing along a joke. He summoned a servant and had him bring us a huge cake topped with creamy white frosting. With his own knife, the chief sliced the cake in half, and as if to prove that it wasn't poisoned, he cut a small piece for himself and, smiling, nodding, ate it. He divided what was left between me and Danny. The whole tribe studied us as we laboriously made our way through the giant pieces. Not a word was spoken until our plates were clean. Then the chief, who seemed to have become quite fond of us, invited us to visit him, under his "armed protection only," in the tribal area. Is this where Omar has fled?

Tonight Bussey and Steve aren't in a hurry to return to the Sheraton. Everybody has trouble accepting that each coming night brings no more news of Danny than the one before. When Bussey isn't riveted to his computer, he is immersed in the administrative tasks he likes so much, and he has begun to resume contact with the foreign correspondents. More and more, he slips out to the side alley to make phone calls. He thinks he's being discreet, but he has to talk loudly to be heard, so we can follow his conversations as the sound filters into the kitchen through the fan.

Our collective ability to laugh is wearing thin. We avoid speaking for fear some words might sound out of place. Then again, we sense that if we speak too little, the silence created by all these doubts will become too heavy. Asra wanders in her own mental space, attending to business. Our headquarters are impressive. The files are labeled, with all the events registered in chronological order. We have notes on everything—what has been discussed, how the investigation has gone, who has been involved and to what degree. Everything has been recorded in these books—every meal we've had, every sound we've heard, every hope we've borne.

The raids have been intensifying. The police and the FBI are jointly going after any fundamentalist militant group linked to Omar, hoping someone might know where Danny is detained. Captain conducts the most important raids himself, using private cars and dressed in undercover clothes, mostly jeans. ("God," says Bussey, his admiration mixed with disbelief. "Captain's elegant even going on a two A.M. raid.") Randall, dressed ninja-style, all in black, rides shotgun with Captain, but Captain makes sure Randall stays at a safe distance from the action. "I am not looking for more trouble for Pakistan," Captain tells him. "If there's a shootout and you are hit, it will be splashed all over the press. So come sit in my vehicle, watch, but that's it."

Forty-five people are being held in custody, including all of Omar's family, with the exception of an aunt whom police hope will convince Omar to turn himself in. They're detaining the family as bargaining chips—turn yourself in, Omar, and we'll give you an uncle, two cousins, and your grandfather. Bring us Danny, and you can all go.

"They kidnap, we kidnap," Dost sums up, only half jokingly. "It's cultural—as a Muslim man, you don't want to bring shame to your family." Oh, the code of honor! Dost assures us that Omar's family is not being mistreated. But, Steve points out, it's a different story for Omar's associates. As a journalist, Steve is wrestling with an ethical dilemma. "If there is physical abuse, I cannot know about it," he says. "And if I do know, then I have to write about it."

"So ignore it," Dost advises him, as if the issue is a no-brainer.

Me? Uncharacteristically, I worry little about the ethics of the situation. I feel we are the ones being tortured here.

In Danny's ThinkPad, I discover a bit about Omar Saeed Sheikh. When it was uncovered that Omar had allegedly funneled $100,000 to Mohammed Atta, Danny had his assistant in India pull together and email him more information on Omar. The resulting files are sketchy. As I read them, Omar strikes me as a loser. I mention this to Randall. "He's not," Randall responds. "He's a psychopath."

*   *   *

I have freaked people out. I have gone to the Sheraton Hotel for a BBC interview and told the terrorists, told the *world,* "Don't harm an innocent man, because you're just going to create one more misery. Using Daniel as a symbol and all of this is completely wrong, completely wrong. . . . If anyone's going to give his life to save him, it's me. Please make contact with me. I'm ready."

Bussey didn't like that but knew better than to confront me directly, so he let the FBI deal with me. They flipped. Bob Dinsmore called; he is part of the FBI negotiating team. "I'd like to, uh, make some observations from what we've been observing," he told Asra. "We might want to minimize the communication from Mariane and you. Apparently Mariane made a statement and solicited the kidnappers to contact her. Sometimes nasty people will take advantage of this. It's just a suggestion, but you might consider holding back a bit. We want to make Paul Steiger the person they should call."

Steiger tries to replace my hot message with a cooler one. In a letter that *The Wall Street Journal* sends to news organizations around the world, he writes:

I know that the National Movement for the Restoration of Pakistani Sovereignty is very serious and wants others to know about its movement. To assure that this happens it is important for you to respond to this message. I have not heard from you for several days and want to begin a dialogue that will address your concerns and bring about Danny's safe release. Since your last email I have received numerous emails from people who claim that they are holding Danny. Because of these claims, it has become difficult for me to know that I am communicating with the people holding Danny. . . . Also, these numerous messages, which have been made public, detract from your serious concerns. . . . I suggest that we use an email account or a private telephone number of one of two friends of Danny, both best men at his wedding. This line of communication would show me that Danny is with you and would allow us one-to-one contact. We are eager to hear from you soon.

Everyone behaves as if my BBC appearance was a suicidal impulse. Everyone except for Steve Goldstein. After all the restraint of my earlier televised appearances, he is relieved by this outburst of emotion. "Oh, no doubt the FBI freaked, but I think it played really well."

Truly, I am not suicidal. It's just that the thoughts popping into my head are probably much too intimate, dramatic, radical to share. I should keep them to myself for now and stay at my shrine upstairs and pray. Praying, I can connect to Danny instantly. I know what he's feeling. Yes, something is happening to him that isn't happening to me, but we are both in captivity.

On the night of Saturday, February 9, we receive a new email. It says Danny has been killed and his body placed in a canvas sack near the Karachi industrial zone. Everyone is pretty sure it's just another hoax. At least that's what we tell each other—oh, absolutely, no question, got to be. Still, the police search the vast area and find a bag containing a corpse. It isn't Danny's—this murder apparently stemmed from a local family fight over money—but the coincidence feels amazing and creepy. Then one of Tariq Jamil's investigators casually tells us they always find bodies in sacks in the industrial zone—on average, two or three a week.

Captain comes over carrying a worn-out dark green canvas school bag, with Magic Marker traces and two zippers. "We have seized this," he says, throwing the bag on the couch. Inside, there are no schoolbooks or pads, but there are a few sheets of paper folded in four, a photo of a young man too young to grow the beard he's clearly trying to grow, a Pakistani passport, and a letter with a poorly drawn heart on the envelope. The bag's owner is at the police station for "suspicious behavior." I open up the passport: no visa or stamps. One of the folded sheets happens to be a letter from the American consulate refusing the young man entry to American territory. The other is a document attesting that he has studied computer engineering at a private institute in Karachi.

It takes me a few seconds to grasp what the last two sheets represent. They are detailed drawings of commercial planes. The first offers a lateral view indicating the position of the engines and the fuel reserves. The second details the inside of the plane, the cockpit, and the precise dimensions of the aisles. The envelope with the heart contains a love letter addressed to a young girl whose name is not disclosed. In his best English, the bearded young man promises her eternal faithfulness.

Captain says he intends to keep the terrorist wanna-be in custody for a few days. "Just long enough for his passion to cool out a bit."

Captain visits every day, and every day it is the same: Before he greets anybody, he walks up to me and looks me deep in the eyes. He wants to see how I'm holding up; he wants to make sure I still trust him. His leitmotiv is "If I believed Danny was dead, I wouldn't be working so hard for him." It makes sense and I believe him.

Dost is having mother-related anxiety attacks. She does not trust him. She came to visit a few days ago to hook him up with one of his first cousins. She has come to believe that her handsome son is never home because he is secretly in the arms of some woman. This is not the case—Dost really is busy around the clock with police work. But it is true that this gorgeous, brave, and poetic man is trapped in a classic and emotional imbroglio: He is secretly in love with someone else, someone his mother will never approve of.

He is surrounded by men who, like Captain, find genuine contentment and happiness in their arranged marriages. But he has seen other marriages turn out miserably, and he wonders how one can ignore the passionate song of the heart. Asra and I counsel him in our rare relaxed moments. We advocate free choice and rally behind marriage-for-love. Asra, *La Pasionara,* pleads for liberation with such vehemence that it's a wonder Dost doesn't run away. But as we sit around the dining room table, analyzing his life and loves and future, we glow with genuine friendship. It is as if we've known one another a very long time, or perhaps it just doesn't matter how long we've known one another. We are friends, and we would never intentionally let one another down.

We now have two photos of Omar Saeed Sheikh on our chart. One shows him lying bearded, skinny, and wounded on a hospital bed in India, recovering from a 1994 gunfight with the Indian army. In the other picture he is emerging from a car on his wedding day. Dressed in white and wearing flowers around his neck, he isn't smiling. When I got married, I couldn't stop smiling. I smiled for the three days our party lasted. My cheeks ached, but my smile wouldn't fade. I study the photo of Omar some more. I keep looking for features that would define him as a terrorist. But in truth, he looks like the kids I grew up with, only he has a beard. That's all we need, I think: terrorists who don't look like terrorists.

With articles and bits of information sent by fellow journalists, I do my best to assemble a portrait of this man. At age twenty-seven, Omar is already a sort of living legend. In 2001, an Indian daily newspaper proclaimed him "Osama's Top Aide," which is undoubtedly an exaggeration, but it offers an indication of the aura surrounding him.

His background—he was raised mostly in England—contributes greatly to his reputation. The son of a well-to-do Pakistani-born garment-business owner, he attended elite schools in both England and Pakistan, a combination—wealth and education—which make Omar the model of a new generation of worldwide terrorists with ties to both the fundamentalist Muslim world and to the West.

His commitment to the Muslim jihad dates to 1993, when he signed up to go to Bosnia on a mission organized by the Convoy of Mercy, an Islamic charitable association, registered in the U.K. Omar fell ill in Croatia and didn't make it to Bosnia, but that trip provided the road map to his future. In an April 1993 diary entry, he wrote:

"Meet mujahideen going into Bosnia who recommend training in Afghanistan first. Back for England with recommendation letter from Abdur Rauf for Harkat-ul-Mujahideen. Try to get back into academics to prepare for exams. . . . Can't settle down. Leave for Pakistan. Go to Lahore office of Harkat-ul-Mujahideen."

The young rebel had found his cause. Those who knew him as a boy say they do not understand where or when he went wrong. His true nature seems to baffle everybody—strong willed-but unstable, craving recognition. Good in mathematics, expert chess player, and, inspired by a Sylvester Stallone movie called "Over the Top," crazy about arm wrestling. He is described alternately as soft-spoken, smart, restless, prickly, temperamental, and manipulative. An Indian official who interrogated him told *The New York Times,* "He studied people's minds. . . . He studied your mind and thought how he could manipulate you."

He joined Harkat-ul-Ansar, spent a year training in Afghanistan, and officially entered the holy war. Omar was twenty-one and had chosen his specialty: kidnapping foreigners—Westerners—which could benefit the jihad either by raising money through ransom demands, or by supplying kidnap victims for hostage trades. With his British accent and elite-school manners, Omar was well suited to it.

The journal Omar later kept in prison has been posted on the Internet. The handwriting is tidy, rather childish in its evident desire to be correct. Some words are carefully crossed out, as in a ten-year-old's letter. About his first mission, Omar wrote:

> Shah-Saab gave me my next instructions. I was to go to places of tourist interest inside Delhi and see if I could start establishing friendship with tourists. Our next meeting was arranged for Jamia mosque. On the outset, I found the friendship task next to impossible. How on earth do you go up to a foreigner and suddenly become friends? Especially when he has a female partner with him or a dozen salesmen calling out to him. In our meeting at Jamia

mosque, I told Shah-Saab that the only way was the stick 'em up and snatch style. But he urged me to keep trying.

Eventually Omar found a target—a six-foot-three Israeli tourist. An Israeli! Omar was so excited he woke up his Shah-Saab in the middle of the night to tell him. "You fool!" was his only answer. "You'll get us all killed. Take him back to his hotel at once and come back in the morning!"

In 1994 Omar abducted four backpackers, three Britons and one American, to exchange them with Islamist militants detained in Indian prisons. He chained his victims to the ground and threatened to decapitate them if the government refused to collaborate. One victim later recalled Omar laughing while telling him this. Before an exchange could be made, Indian police were tipped off, the unharmed hostages were freed, and after a shootout and a trial, Omar was tossed into an Indian jail.

On Christmas Eve 1999, in Omar's fifth year of captivity, hijackers seized Indian Airlines flight IC-814, taking off from Kathmandu, Nepal, bound for New Delhi. Using horrifying intimidation techniques similar to those that would be used in the planes on 9/11, the hijackers slit the throat of a passenger—a young man on his honeymoon—and made his fellow passengers—including his bride—watch as he bled to death. They rerouted the plane to Kandahar, Afghanistan, and it was there, eight days later, that they exchanged the 178 people on board for three militants in Indian prisons—among them, Omar Saeed Sheikh and Massood Azhar, the founder of Jaish-e-Mohammed.

Azhar watched his tongue in jail. "It is against the tenet of our religion to bargain over the lives of innocents," he reportedly said to one of his guardians. But back in Karachi, his fiefdom, Azhar recovered his warrior's rhetoric. "Don't hail me," he told fired-up crowds. "Don't congratulate me over my release. Don't raise slogans for me. Instead present me with a garland of shoes, blacken my face, because India is yet to be destroyed." This is the same man we now pray can convince Omar to let Danny go.

As for Omar, he simply disappeared, evaporated. Pakistani files do not have the slightest indication of his return to Pakistan after liberation in Afghanistan. Indian intelligence agents spotted him several times in Pakistan, notably in a bookstore in Islamabad.

I keep wanting to know how the kidnappers got Danny into the car. He is such a cautious man. Did they pull a gun on him? Hit him? Captain doesn't worry about this aspect quite as much as I do. "Mariane," he says patiently, "Omar Sheikh is an expert. It is Danny who is being kidnapped for the first time. It is Omar Sheikh who has done it ten times. There is a difference. Omar Sheikh has had a chance to learn from his mistakes. He is expert at this. After this, do you think Danny will ever be kidnapped again? No. No, he will not."

"It is only with the heart that one can see rightly. The essential is invisible to the eye." So says the fox to the Little Prince in Antoine de Saint-Exupéry's classic tale. Asra bought the book not long ago at Paramount Books in downtown Karachi, and she has it opened on her lap when I find her curled in a corner of the couch, wrapped almost entirely in her gray shawl. Though the book is open, she isn't reading. "She's missing that no-good lover," I think. Asra just gazes strangely at a meaningless spot on the wall in front of her. My friend, usually so animated, has become a rag doll—limp, staring out from big black button eyes.

It hits me: Asra is melting down. That look in her eyes—that's the look of someone who's losing it. We can't afford a breakdown right now, and I tell her so: "I know it's unfair, and you have the right to be depressed, but not now! Are you scared?" I ask. "Are you exhausted? Do you have your period?"

"No," says Asra.

"No, what?" I snap.

"No, I don't have my period. I'm three weeks late."

I guess this is crazy enough to be true. As is supposed to happen before you die, everything unfolds like a film in front of my eyes: Danny, the *Journal,* The Lover, Merve and Blink, the accusations against Asra, Morgantown, single motherhood.

I say, "If you are pregnant, you must keep it." I don't know why I say that. I have absolutely no right to be so assertive when the consequences of such a decision won't be mine to bear, and when any discussion of the future seems inappropriate. I mean it, though.

Asra and I concoct a semblance of a calendar, trying to diagram the dates of her relationship with The Lover, her last period, her ovulation dates, when her due date might be. But our minds are swampy with fatigue and anxiety, and we can't figure it out.

Still, now that the possibility has been said out loud, we need to know the truth. It is past midnight, but in Karachi there is one all-night pharmacy, so Asra tells our guard we have to go there right away. He is, to put it mildly, reluctant, but when Asra begins chattering in Urdu about hormones and other similar issues, he nervously relents. I haven't been out of the house in what seems like a lifetime, and part of me is desperate to taste the air beyond these gates. But I can't leave. So off Asra sails, accompanied by two armed soldiers, in a broken jeep that seems transformed into a magical coach.

At the pharmacy, the soldiers deny Asra privacy, but they avert their eyes as she studies the home-test kits. She picks one, brings it back to Zamzama Street, and we have our answer.

This is how weird our lives have become: It seems almost, *almost* logical. Almost remarkable, sweet. Asra Q. Nomani, putative Indian spy has gone and gotten herself impregnated by a man to whom she no longer speaks, in a land where illegal sex is punishable by lashes or stoning to death. Now every woman in this house, including Nasrin, is expecting a baby. "Asra is such a good friend," I tell Bussey, "that she even thought of making a buddy for my baby." We don't need to convince Bussey the pregnancy is lovely news. He genuinely rejoices for Asra and shows up the next morning with brownies. The truth is, I'm pleased our son will have someone with whom to swap tales of an eventful life in utero.

We are learning a great deal about the early days of the kidnapping. For example, that the three men arrested on February 5 were drafted into action by Omar just days before Danny was kidnapped on January 23. Suleiman was roped in on January 21; his cousin, Fahad, the computer guy, came aboard the twenty-second. Omar Sheikh had been setting traps for Danny for weeks; he just needed local mules to make it all work.

Jihadi militants keep lists of potential candidates for jihadi work. The *madrassas* of Pakistan, an estimated forty thousand, overflow with these available young men—men who may not be able to write their own names but can recite whole chapters of the holy book in their sleep, and know that America is "the nexus of evil."

I once accompanied Danny on a visit to a Jaish-e-Mohammed *madrassa* on the outskirts of Karachi. Even though my head was covered, I had to stay hidden in the car. The walls of the *madrassa* were scrawled with slogans; debris was strewn everywhere. As I peered out, I watched young men—kids, really, barefoot and dressed in dirty *salwar kameez*—enter the *madrassa*. It was like watching them enter a brainwashing factory. I scribbled observations in my reporter's notebook, but the one word I wrote and underlined repeatedly was: *SCARY*.

When the Taliban-supported training camps still existed in Afghanistan, a few "students" were singled out for forty-day basic training programs in which they learned how to terrify, torture, kill. It cost only about twenty dollars to train a person, fifty if you factored in weapons. While they learned the terrorist technique, they also learned never to question the organization that would take complete control of their lives. When they were not on the battlefields of Kashmir or Afghanistan, they were sent home to behave as "gentlemen" and gain the respect of their communities by being "good Muslims"—shelter one another, forge new bonds, and look out for new recruits.

This is the world of the three men arrested February 5.

Syed Suleiman Saquib joined the jihad in October 1998. "I wanted to go to Kashmir but Harkat-ul-Mujahideen bearers sent me to Afghanistan," he said in his deposition, translated into English by court transcribers. There, after several months on the front lines of Bagram, he was shot by a machine gun in the abdomen and repatriated to Pakistan. He sustained thirty operations in a variety of hospitals and still walks with a bad limp. He had met Omar only twice over the past two years, both times in Jaish-e-Mohammed offices, but all the jihadis knew who Omar Sheikh was. As it was explained in the deposition of Adil: Omar "is a great mujahid, he had come after his release from India, I had great respect for him."

One day in January, Suleiman received a surprise phone call from Omar. "I am coming to Karachi, can I meet you there?" Omar said.

"I replied [to] him 'You should come I will meet you tomorrow.' Next day, he informed me on the telephone that 'I am arriving from Islamabad from aeroplane, can you visit [the] airport to receive me and whether you have some conveyance?' I replied I do not have any conveyance, but on your insistence I can arrive by taxi."

Omar landed at the Karachi domestic airport the next day, January 21. He was standing in the lounge with a man he introduced as Naeem when Suleiman arrived. "We have some work to do," Omar told Suleiman. First Omar and Naeem needed to "fresh" themselves, so Suleiman took them to his uncle's house. Then they headed for the Student Biryani House, a popular restaurant, where Omar talked "secretly" to a new individual. Omar led his growing group, including this secret individual, to a residential compound called the Muhammad Ali Society, where they searched for bungalow N-D 17. A two-story house with a lawn in front, it turned out to be the home of Omar's paternal aunt.

The next morning, January 22—around the time Danny and I

were leaving Islamabad for Karachi and bidding farewell to the Chez Soi gang—Omar again called Suleiman, who was getting ready to go to market with his cousin Fahad. Omar asked them to meet him at his paternal aunt's house on their way. When they arrived, Omar told the two of them, "I had some work for you at this time but I have asked it to someone else. If I get some other work I will call you, now you may go to the market."

In two hours, Omar called Suleiman on his cell phone. "Buy me a Polaroid camera," he said. Suleiman protested that he had no experience with such things. They are simple, Omar replied; one buys them at the electronics market. So that was what Suleiman and Fahad did. After interrogating the men, Captain learned more. Suleiman "allured Fahad with good sweet talk—'God has chosen you to do some service to Islam,' and Fahad fell for it. And since he was an expert, teaching in the institute about computers, he thought he would get away with it. He almost did."

Suleiman testified: "After getting free from my work, I accompanied by Fahad went to Sadder [a district in Karachi] where I purchased a Polaroid camera against 1,500 Rps [rupees] along with two cartridges of this camera, then we went to D/17 [the bungalow of Omar's aunt] to deliver the camera to Omar Sheikh. At that time two more persons were present there, out of whom one was Quasim and second one Adil whom I already met once."

Omar, Adil, Suleiman, Fahad, and this newly-identified man, Quasim, prayed together, after which Omar handed Suleiman and Fahad texts in two languages. He told them that he would soon have the cousins email them domestically and internationally, but they were first to wait for another "thing" that they would send with the emails. The cousins were also asked to wait for two "friends" and to instruct them on how to use the Polaroid. It took two hours for the friends to show up. Suleiman recognized one as the boy he had met at the Student Biryani House.

Fahad Naseem's deposition added more details to Suleiman's account. When introduced to Omar by his cousin, Fahad was told,

"This is the man who was released from India alongside Maulana Massood Azhar and arrived in an airplane." When Fahad informed Omar that he was a computer programmer, Omar replied, "God has helped me! I was looking for the right person and I found it." Omar quizzed Fahad: Could he send a movie by email? No? Too large? What about photographs? Negatives—no? But Polaroids were okay?

"Meanwhile," Fahad said in his deposition, "a man with a big beard joined us in the room where we were meeting. [This was Adil.] He sat down. Four or five minutes later, another man came in. He was called Quasim. Then Adil made 'Imamat' [the call for prayer] and all we offered 'Zuhar' [early afternoon] prayer behind him. Thereafter Omar Sheikh said, 'Now you should go and bring me a camera.'"

Fahad was taken to the Stock Exchange Building in Karachi, where some foreign currency was changed—he doesn't know which kind—into Pakistani rupees, and that is when they purchased the Polaroid. Fahad was told to study the booklet and learn how the camera worked.

When Fahad was given the email texts, he asked Omar what they were about. "Basically, Daniel Pearl is [a] Jewish and American agent who works against Muslims," Omar replied. "If you assist me in this task, God Almighty will reward you, for it is a very big task. And even you can participate in this great task just by sending an email." When Fahad asked what Danny's fate would be, Omar answered: "Do whatever I tell you to do, and nothing else. And do not ask any more questions. It could only create problems for you."

Omar left Karachi for Lahore on the evening of the 23rd, as Danny was heading over to his meeting at the Village Restaurant. The next day, Fahad was summoned to a hotel called Nau Bahar. He was asked to buy a scanner and bring it along. While handing over the scanner, Fahad witnessed yet another layer of this endlessly layered process: Another man he'd never seen before entered the hotel, handed an envelope to yet another man, who then took the envelope into a washroom, apparently to check the contents.

On January 26, Fahad was taken to a cyber café, handed a floppy disk, and ordered to send the messages and their attachments to a list of recipients. The computer at the Internet café turned out to be too slow, so they tried another café. This time, it worked.

(The more I learn about the kidnapping process, the more my anger grows. So many people could have stopped it, derailed it, let slip a key piece of information. This secret man, that secret man . . . the man at the airport . . . the man in the hotel washroom . . .)

After a few days, the whole emailing process was repeated with two new photographs. But before Fahad and Suleiman sent the second email, Omar called and directed them to make a change in the text following this key sentence: "We have interrogated mr.D.Parl and we have come to the conclusion that contrary to what we thought earlier he is not working for the cia." Originally, what came next was "therefore we shall release him." But Omar wanted this: "in fact he is working for mossaad. therefor we will execute him within 24 hours unless amreeka flfils our demands."

The cousins abided by Omar's request, but Fahad cut corners, and "though I had been instructed not to," he sent the email from his home in the student building where Captain later arrested him.

The second emailing ended the participation of Fahad, the kidnappers' computer expert. When the time came for Fahad to sign his statement in court, he apparently did not know how to write his name, so he signed it with a thumbprint.

Another deposition. "Name of the accused: Sheikh Mohammad Adil."

Not only is Adil a cop, but he also belongs to the same branch of intelligence as Dost. There the similarities end, and while Adil served as a policeman for ten years, he didn't make it far up the ladder. In 1999 he took a two-year leave without salary to become a mujahideen. Harkat-ul-Mujahideen sent him to Kandahar, in Afghanistan, and then to Kashmir. It was during Adil's training as a terrorist in Afghanistan that he met Omar on the front lines of Bagram.

Adil's experience in Karachi was similar to that of Suleiman—met

Omar here, he was with an unknown bearded man; saw him there with a few more unknown bearded men. On January 22, Omar brought Adil to a meeting under the Baloch Bridge. Two men were waiting in a white Corolla for Omar to appear. The man sitting in the passenger seat got out so Omar could sit. At this point Adil was instructed to pray at the Sabeel Wali Mosque in the Grumandar area. "We will meet there," one of the men told him.

So off Adil went and offered his prayers, and then he was handed an envelope by the two men in the white Corolla, now parked outside the mosque. He met with Suleiman and Fahad, and he delivered the envelope to Suleiman. In a couple of days, he made a second delivery, but by now, he insisted in his deposition, he was having grave reservations. "I open[ed] both the envelopes and found [them] containing the photographs of American journalist. Prior to this I was not aware to the fact that I had been involved in the offence of American journalist Daniel Pearl by the clever techniques of Omar Saeed Sheikh. Actually Omar Saeed Sheikh remained me unaware and used me for his aim wrongfully without coming into my knowledge, while I had the respect about him in my heart. I am not happy with the act of Omar Sheikh. I think it is not fair and my conscience is opposing me, and Omar Sheikh has used me wrongfully for his bad aims."

The Qur'an is very clear: It is wrong to harm the innocent. I dare to wonder if Adil could save Danny in the name of the Qur'an.

"Hmmpph," sneers Captain. "Adil was trained in Afghanistan. He is a fundamentalist terrorist."

"Is there any chance at all that his faith will lead him to repent?" I ask. Captain shrugs and lights another cigarette.

A plump and jovial-looking man appears at the door bearing a bag of spices, an apron, and a book of international recipes. This is Yussuf, John Bauman's star cook. The exceptionally attentive U.S. consul has decided it is time for us to move beyond Sheraton Hotel chicken biryani, so he is lending us Yussuf for the rest of our stay. With his Einstein-style mustache, the cook looks like an ideal grandfather, a misleading assumption. Coming here represents a major sacrifice for Yussuf, and he's not entirely thrilled by the assignment. Nevertheless, he introduces himself with pride. He has studied gastronomy in London and Paris; this is a man who cooks only for the greats of this world, or at least of his world.

Failing to fully appreciate who and what we have been given, Asra and I vaguely point Yussuf in the direction of the kitchen when he arrives. After close examination of the premises, opening cupboards and drawers with consternation, Yussuf-le-cook proceeds to refurbish the kitchen, buying an assortment of pans, knives for bread, knives for fish, still more knives for desserts.

With heavy sighs, he prepares princely food amid general indifference. Then the hour to eat comes, and our team, exhausted, finds a dining table fully dressed. The silverware is presented European-style, fork on the left, knife on the right. Napkins of an immaculate white are folded like accordions within our glasses. We dine on cucumber soup with mint, stuffed turkey, lemon and cardamom pie. Licking the wounds of his dignity, Yussuf accepts our praises with grace and a pinch of hauteur.

One day we almost lose our chef. He has chosen to astonish us with crab in a white sauce, but the dish is so strange-looking that no one dares touch it except Steve. I have a good excuse: I'm pregnant. Asra is too, and Bussey is too concerned about hygiene issues to go near the things. Close to tears and revolted by such ingratitude, Yussuf comes close to bolting. Trying to mollify him, Steve accepts seconds. Bussey soothes Yussuf by pointing out how remarkably successful he has been in satisfying two Jews (Bussey and Steve), one Muslim (Asra), one Buddhist (me), and a Christian (Yussuf himself). This seems to smooth the cook's feathers.

Yussuf is a very devout Christian, one of the 13 percent minority in Pakistan. As he cooks, he speaks about God obsessively and prays to Him constantly. He prays to Him that we find Danny.

*　　*　　*

Suddenly it happens. Omar Sheikh turns himself in near the Punjabi village where his father was born. Returning to Karachi handcuffed and with a bag over his head, he tells Captain, "Danny is alive," but he will not or cannot say where my husband is.

To alleviate my frustrations, Captain does his best to keep me informed on what is happening in the interrogation center. Even in a prison cell with walls gnarled by moisture, dirt, and rats, Omar seems to maintain his authority. The prison guards won't go near him, terrified he will accuse them of mistreatment and target them for retaliation. Although not much of a preacher, Omar has called on Allah and threatened them. Captain refuses to be scared off. "This person is my enemy," he tells me. "I say, 'Let's see if you or your organization can do something. To me, you are a normal criminal and so you will be treated like one.' No difference. No special facilities. No respect."

Omar claims he kidnapped Danny to "teach a lesson to America. Right or wrong," he says, "I did it because I don't think Pakistan should be catering to America's need."

I propose to talk to Omar, but Captain says quickly, "Leave it to us, we'll take care of him. We're ready."

Just as quickly, I respond, "Me, too," and I am grateful when Captain nods as if to tell me, "I know you are."

According to Captain, there are several stages to any investigation. In the beginning, "when you are looking for a criminal, you are generating hate against him. And every day the hate—or, more accurately, the *angerness*—is increasing, and it is growing more personal."

Captain well knows that "it's not worthy of a police officer to behave out of a revengeful attitude, or angerness, or hate." He knows that it is important "to overcome the hate and resist it." But he also knows that police officers are human beings. "In movies, on TV, sometimes the police are chasing a criminal in a speeding car—they're chasing, chasing, ten, fifteen miles, and he is crossing one-ten, one-twenty, and suddenly they make him stop. And you know what they do then? All they do is take him out and beat him.

"But," Captain adds, "after the police officer has taken him in custody and booked him, and two or three days have passed, is the police officer that angry still? No. He is calmed down. And he knows that he has caught the criminal and that the criminal is going to remain his guest for maybe as long as he lives.

"Now comes the stage when you start really probing the criminal."

How fortuitous it is that Omar has surfaced in time for Musharraf's long-awaited meeting at the White House. It would have been awkward for the Pakistani president to have no good news for Bush or the American press. He tells reporters that, based on what Omar Sheikh has said, he is "reasonably sure" Danny is alive, and "We are as close as possible to getting him released," as if that means anything. Still, Musharraf cannot quite contain himself, and reveals suspicions. Danny had been "overintrusive in whatever he was doing and getting into the thick of these extremists," he says. He also says that "such things can be expected." Oh my God, I think; we're collateral damage.

It will be tough to break Omar. John Bauman calls him a "cold, hard young man"; he is "one of those terrorists who can lead others to commit suicide," Captain says. American and Pakistani teams take turns spending nights with him, keeping him awake with buckets of cold water.

I'm riding an emotional roller coaster, and it's making me sick, but Captain is sanguine. "There is no gauge to go into the human heart and know if what he tells you is the truth or not. But when you are an experienced police officer, you develop an ability to read minds and expressions and body language. Unwittingly, police officers become psychologists. They don't learn it from books but from their experiences. And they learn how, over three or four days, you can come to know a person's weaknesses—and exploit them."

A faint smile of pride softens the troubled lines on Captain's face. "This guy has, for example, a weakness for his son. So that is something I'll exploit. I'll talk about his son, how old is he, how he resembles the father or the mother, that kind of thing. Foolish talk, nothing to do with the case. But as I am easing him off, I am driving him where I want him to go. And maybe he starts crying, he misses his child . . . That is the point when most of the people don't tell lies. Or let's talk about his religion. This you can exploit, too. When you are in front of God, you are praying and you are promising that you will be a good person, and instantly you can't tell a lie. When you are before God, you are sort of scared that He knows what I am doing, you know?"

For days Captain talked to Omar about his son, about family, about religion, and interspersed into that the kidnapping, and kidnappings of the past, and jihadi activity. All the while he took careful notes. Omar was good, which is to say consistent in his stories and the information he was willing to divulge. Periodically they brought in a polygraph expert, and Omar, cool psychopath that he is, again and again, passed those tests, too. But after three or four days, exhausted, Omar slipped up, and Captain caught him in a lie. A small one, having to do with a phone call he did, or did not make. Still, he gave Captain the ammunition he needed.

Captain acted shocked. "I said, 'I considered you a Muslim, and I thought you were a very good Muslim—but you are a liar. How should I believe what you are telling me? I don't believe you. You are a liar.' "

Omar kept quiet for a few minutes, and then he asked if he could offer his prayers. Captain said, " 'Why not?' He said, 'I need the Qur'an.' I gave him the Qur'an. And I took off his handcuffs and the shackles he was in, I even allowed him to have a bath and change his clothes. He offered his prayers. He recited Qur'an. And then he shouted for me. He was in the cell. He shouted, 'Tell Captain that I want to see him now!' "

Captain said, no, that Omar Sheikh would come to his office. "I made him comfortable, made him sit in a chair, offered him a cup of tea. I said, 'Do you want to tell me something?' "

Omar told Captain that he had indeed lied in the past, but from now on he would tell the truth. He provided Captain with small but vital pieces of information, a few nicknames, some dates. And he told Captain this: He had been in custody since February 5.

February 5. The night Captain arrested Fahad, who led him to Suleiman, who led him to Adil. The night Captain tracked down Omar and called him on Adil's cell phone from the home of Omar's aunt. The night we thought Omar had eluded the law and escaped, untraceable, untouchable, into tribal lands.

But he hadn't. He had turned himself in to retired Brigadier Ejaz Shah, home secretary of Punjab, the district from which Omar's wealthy textile manufacturing father hails. Brigadier Shah, a former ISI officer, showed absolute disdain for the law, for justice, for President Musharraf, for the United States, for me. He kept Omar's detention a secret. From February 5 to February 12.

Captain didn't know. Nor did the FBI—did they?

Did the ISI know? They had to. But did they allow Omar to be detained because there was information they wanted from him? Was there information they *didn't* want revealed? Were they making some kind of deal with him—"go to jail for a bit and we'll make sure you're set free"? Or are they just taking their time to erase the clues leading back to them?

Captain tries to disguise how profoundly angry and sad he is, but he can't. He mourns for me, for his compromised ability to pursue the truth, and for his country. Above all, Captain is a Pakistani patriot. Still, there is only so much he can openly discuss, and I have come to understand and respect that he cannot talk about the ISI with me. "Mariane," he says, "if you ask who kept Omar or what was the reason he was kept, I don't know. I am very, very honest about it. I exactly don't know."

Here on the veranda, with lousy Internet lines stolen from the neighbors, I struggle to snap the pieces of the puzzle that we *do* know into place. I have had to face—we have all had to face—that while Omar may have been our original target, in truth he's just one link in a massively complicated chain. Yes, he's good at his evil craft, but ultimately he is a tool. But whose? It's become clear that Omar doesn't know where Danny is. That's never been his role. He was the lure; others are the captors. Who's in that group? Omar has served up the name of a go-between, the man who's had contact both with Omar's cell and the kidnapping team. That's a start. But who is overseeing it all? Who pulls all the strings?

I think about things like this: Who told Omar that Danny is Jewish? Who had that information to give?

Information flies out of the Internet. I am amazed to find how much is circulating out there about Omar and his apparent links to both Al Qaeda and the ISI. I read that the U.S. embassy in Islamabad asked the Pakistani government to hand over Omar on January 21—two days *before* Danny was kidnapped. The reason given for the U.S. request was that the 1994 kidnapping included an American citizen. But it seems clear to me that the U.S. authorities wanted to follow up on a much more disturbing trail. In October 2001, the FBI were looking for a link between Omar Saeed Sheikh and the then director of the ISI, Lieutenant General Mahmood Ahmed. They wanted to know who instructed Omar to wire the $100,000 to Mohammed Atta. I read too that Ahmed had been dismissed as head of the ISI by President Musharraf on October 7, 2001.

So, it appeared Omar may have associated with the head of ISI *and* Al Qaeda. He surrendered to another former ISI officer who held him in custody for a week until just one day before Musharraf met with President Bush. Just in time for Musharraf to go before Bush and the American press and, pointing to the "arrest" of Omar Sheikh, declare, "We are as close as possible to getting [Danny] released."

Questions bounce back and forth in my brain like a Ping-Pong ball gone wild. The distinctions between good and bad, government organizations and terrorist organizations, are not simply fading; they seem to be faces of the same coin.

Did Musharraf know Omar was in custody? Could he not know? The CIA (God only knows what their position is here) didn't know?

Which of Omar's ex-ISI friends are involved and to what degree? What about Brigadier Abdullah, responsible for the Kashmir cell of ISI before his dismissal by Musharraf during the recent purges of the organization: Is he involved, too? Does he work for Osama bin Laden? What was Omar promised in exchange for his arrest?

After several days of interrogation, Omar is handed over to the court, where he brags that he carried out the kidnapping "on my own free will." But he startles everyone by changing a part of his story. When Captain first encountered Omar, the terrorist said, "Danny is alive, he is okay." Now he says, "As far as I understand, he is dead."

When asked why he believes this to be true, Omar talks about code phrases that the kidnappers used among themselves. He says that on February 5 he called his associates to tell them to release Danny: "Shift the patient to the doctor." But it was too late: "Dad has expired," he claims he was told. "We have done the scan and completed the X rays and postmortem."

What a psycho, we tell one another. What a liar. They're all psychos and liars. There is no more reason to believe this statement than the earlier one.

Still, I can't breathe.

Chapter Ten

IT FEELS as if a thick fog has swept into the house and taken it over. We tiptoe through the rooms, lost in our own thoughts. No one knows which way to go, let alone what to do or how to think. Nightly raids continue, but where this house was once flooded with people day and night, there are now long hours of screaming silence. John Bauman gives Bussey and Steve daily reports, Captain comes regularly to check on me, but if there is action, it is happening elsewhere. Mostly I sit at my shrine and pray. This house is the last place Danny and I were together. It is almost unimaginable to me that I might ever leave it.

Which is what Bussey wants me to do. He is desperate for me to focus on the pregnancy instead of on Danny. "For the health of the baby, you need exercise," he decides, so he arranges for Asra and me to walk in Zamzama Park, a couple of blocks away from our gated community. There is no sidewalk, so we have to walk in single file along the roadside with two armed guards ahead of us and two behind; we look like prisoners being moved to a new location. On our way, we walk by a *madrassa,* in front of which an old man yells at students who are taunting him. One of our police officers stops to intervene, but something holds him back and we all keep walking. When we reach Zamzama Park, our guards aren't allowed inside with their weapons, and the park—nicely designed by Musharraf's daughter—reeks of sewage from nearby streets.

I get dizzy. They take me home.

Bussey and Steve think Asra and I would be well served by massages at the Sheraton. As we enter, the director of security hurries over and blurts, "My gut tells me he's alive."

As if I care what his gut tells him. I climb right back into the car, and here I am back home again.

Inconceivably, the hours grow even longer. I still won't let myself cry, but I feel like a dam about to be overwhelmed by the flood of tears I have been holding back. To steel myself, I dredge my mind for helpful memories. I think about hardships Danny and I have faced, of his pragmatic approach to problems. I flash back on a book I loved as a teenager, *The Loneliness of the Long-Distance Runner,* about a race of endurance and the endless interior monologue that keeps the runner going.

Asra and I are lying on the couch in her office when my cell phone rings. We used that phone a week ago to send a text message to Danny's phone: "We love you Danny."

Asra looks down at the cell phone's bright little screen. "Danny," it says. She snaps the phone open. "Hello?"

"Give me the wife of Daniel Pearl," a voice rasps in Urdu. In Urdu people tend to speak in one of two tones, either obsequious or bullying. This is the latter. "I want to speak to her."

"Okay," says Asra carefully, recognizing that the caller is related to the kidnappers. "I am going to put you through to her, but you should know she doesn't speak Urdu."

The man on the line apparently turns to someone else. "She doesn't speak Urdu," he says. Then he hangs up.

"Oh my God! What have I done? They hung up!" Asra cries, hysteria in her voice.

"Shut up," I tell her, "let me think."

"No, no, it's okay, it's fine. They were making some contact," says Randall when we tell him, as if our news offers a little bit of light in this ever darkening darkness. It is hard to see his point. Nothing makes sense. If Danny is still alive, why haven't there been more emails, more demands? And if Danny is dead, why aren't his killers boasting about it?

Captain comes over to tell me that his assistant also received a call from Danny's phone. The caller swore the kidnappers would kill the assistant and his wife and their three children. Then he hung up. Now the mysterious phone call seems less of a mystery. The Urdu speakers weren't calling to make contact. They were calling to make a threat.

February 21. I sit at my shrine. Asra sits beside me, distraught that The ex-Lover hasn't come by for one of their periodic discussions, even though he said he would be here by nine P.M. Dejected, she goes downstairs and is telling Steve about her disillusionment with men when Bussey enters the room, frenzied, yanking out his cell-phone earpiece and stuffing the phone in his pocket.

"We have to go," Bussey tells Steve. He is speaking way too fast.

Steve tries to argue that Asra needs attention, but Bussey just says, "It can wait," and they are gone.

Something is wrong. I can sense it. When I come downstairs, Asra describes their rush out the door. This is bad—why did they leave without us? "Call them, call all of them," I say, and Asra tries all the cell-phone numbers she knows, but nobody answers. Finally she tracks down Randall. She's aggressive with him: "Hey, what's happening? You can't leave us out of the loop."

He yells at her, "You want me to tell her this on the phone?" Then he hangs up. Tell me what? My hands shake so fiercely I can't tie the laces on my jihadi boots.

"Let's get out of here," I say. I don't know where to go—the consulate?—but I need to get out and find the men. As Asra dials Eurocar to send over transportation, the men appear at the door, Bussey first, then Captain, Dost, John Bauman, Steve, Randall, and a man I do not know. It is late, and against the black night, they look spectral. Bussey's face is dead white, waxen.

They file into the living room. Bussey speaks. "He didn't make it," he says. "They have proof."

I push him aside; I need to get to Captain, whose face has turned a horrible yellow-brown. There's a strange film over his eyes, deadening eyes once bright in their darkness. "Mariane, I'm sorry," he says. "I didn't bring your Danny home."

I rest my head on his shoulder, and we stay that way for a while. When I look up, he is crying. "I am a human being," he will tell me later. "I couldn't control my pain. I knew what you were expecting from me. I had promised this thing to you. And I was unable to keep my word."

I let go of Captain, and as I pass the frozen crowd, I tell them, "Leave me alone," and head for my bedroom. I slam the door, and with all my might, I cry out. I have never screamed like this before. I can feel that I'm screaming, but the sound that rips up out of me is alien, as if everything is coming out of me. I sound like an animal caught in a bone-crushing trap.

Asra crouches outside my door, chanting a Muslim prayer for protection.

I go into the bathroom and bang my head on the wall. I can hear voices in the hallway, frantic murmurs, trying to figure out what to do. God, they suffocate me. I throw open the door. *"Stop that crap!"*

It comes to me: Why should I believe them? I don't think this is true. It's not possible. I pull Captain to the couch and sit beside him. "How do you know he's dead?" I ask, out of hope or maybe despair.

"There's a video."

Now, this is something I know about. I'm a filmmaker. So I say, "Oh, Captain, that's what it is? Don't worry. It's really easy to fake a murder on film. Anyone can do that. It's a montage—"

"Mariane," he says, "Danny is dead." His voice is grief-stricken and coarse, as if every syllable has been drawn painfully from deep inside. "Now it's you, your duty is to pursue his mission." What is this sudden sternness in his tone? I stare at him, unable to understand what he's talking about.

"Mariane, you have to accept that he's dead."

I resist, so Captain repeats it over and over. "Accept it, he's dead. Accept it, he's dead. Accept it. He's dead." He needs me to break down.

"What makes you so sure he's dead?" This time I direct my question at John Bauman.

"They had a knife, and they used it in such a way there is no doubt—"

I challenge him: "What do you mean 'there's no doubt'?"

"He was beheaded."

They are all crying, every single one of them, the whole goddamn team. They cry like men. No sobs, no streaks down the face. But their eyes swim in their stricken faces. I am not sure whether they cry for me—because I refuse to acknowledge that I have lost my husband in a way none can bring himself to describe—or for Danny and what he went through.

"You all watched this video?" I study their faces and know the answer without being told.

Asra flares up. "Show it to me. I want to see it!"

"Stop it," I snap. I don't want to watch it, and I'm not going to let her see it, either.

Captain puts his arm tight around my shoulders. Both of us shake. Very slowly he starts describing to me what happened to Danny.

"Who's this new guy?" Asra asks Randall about the strange man sitting in the living room.

"A doctor for Mariane."

"Make him leave. No strangers now," she says.

Later, I sit on the edge of the couch, head high, straight up, as if ready to get into the starting blocks for a race. Bussey sits next to me. He is still as pale as a white tablecloth, but I am glad he is here.

"I don't know what I am going to do," I tell him.

"You shouldn't rush anything. Take it step by step, little by little," Bussey says.

But that's not what I mean. I mean I am deciding whether I want to go wherever Danny is. How can you explain something like that to a John Bussey?

"It's like Romeo and Juliet," I say. "You can't separate them. Otherwise, there would be no Shakespeare."

Silence.

I decide to be more straightforward. I tell him, "Nothing frightens me anymore. I am not even afraid to die."

Bussey's eyes, already wide open, grow even wider. My death is the last thing he needs.

I have the strange feeling that there are two of me. One observes the conversation while the other does the talking. Everything is abnormal, especially this extreme calm that has taken me over. I try to explain to Bussey that if I decide to die, it will be without bitterness. I know I did everything I possibly could, so it will be a respectful farewell. I will bow to life like an actor, who, having delivered his lines, bends deeply to his audience and retires. I tell Bussey that this decision has nothing to do with him, that it is entirely mine. I will choose either to live or to die, but I cannot allow myself to live in the in-between. I do not want to go through life like a ghost.

"Do you think you'll find Danny this way?" Bussey asks.

My mind sifts through all available theories on the afterlife. It is as if this metaphysical question has become as real as the air we breathe. Buddhism teaches that life is an eternal cycle without beginning or end. I recall the metaphor: "Our individual lives are like waves produced from the great ocean that is the universe. The emergence of a wave is life, and its abatement is death. This rhythm repeats eternally."

Finally I answer Bussey, "No, I don't think so."

Bussey seems relieved, but I'm more panicky, because I had never thought that I could wind up alone. In my mind, whatever the odds, Danny and I were and would be together forever.

*   *   *

Randall and the others head out to find the killers. I run after them. I grab an AK-47 out of the arms of a guard and declare to Randall, "I'm going with you!"

"You can't," says Randall. "It's too dangerous."

"Fuck you! I don't fucking care about danger!"

Randall's eyes fill with tears again. "Mariane, please."

I hand the guard his gun and return to my room.

Captain stays with me. He holds my hand and tells me about his little girl who died. "It's going to be very hard for you," he says. "It will be a terrible hardship. But you will get through it because you are brave, you are a warrior, you can do it.

"I will tell you something else," Captain says. "I will always be here for you."

I don't know when or how I fall asleep. I just collapse. When I wake the next dawn, I am alone in our bed. My body curls forward, ready to be spooned. Then I hear the rain. It hasn't rained once since we've been here. But it is pouring now, as if a heavenly cistern has overflowed. It will continue all day, even when the sun comes creeping out.

I call my older brother, Satchi, in Paris. "It's over," I say. Satchi reacts as I did: "No, we can't give up, it's not true. We just need the whole world to chant with us." All over the world, Buddhists have been chanting for us. Most belong to the lay Buddhist organization Soka Gakkai International. SGI is a network of people at once remarkable and ordinary, headed by Daisaku Ikeda, a fighter for peace. Members spontaneously started chanting for us some weeks ago, and soon—as in a relay race where you hand the baton over to the next runner—they ensured that twenty-four hours a day, through all the time zones, people were chanting for us.

For a moment I see the world through Satchi's eyes, and I type out a message: "Keep going; keep chanting for Danny." But as soon as I hit the send button, I know it is over. It is time to tell the rest of the world that Danny is dead.

My beloved mother was terrified of dying. As we came to understand that the cancer would kill her, I knew I had to help her overcome her fears. But I knew, too, as she faced this crossing one can only make alone, I could not defuse her fears until I had overcome my own.

She died exactly one month after Danny's and my wedding. We were by her side, Danny, Satchi, and I, when life left her body. She let out a last short sigh, almost like an expression of relief, and I felt my own energy rise upward with her. I looked at her, astonished to still be alive. I glanced up at the ceiling, imagining my mother floating somewhere above our heads, and her great surprise at finding all of us gathered around her empty body. I smiled under the worried glance of the nurses who had rushed into the room. I kissed my mother's lips, still warm.

A few weeks after Marita's passing, I discovered that my mother hadn't left any material goods. No furniture, no will, no possessions, only a wish. I found it in a school notebook in which she had written why she destroyed her previous diaries: "My monologue has lasted long enough." The rest of the notebook was blank except for one page, written in Spanish, which I immediately translated for Danny: "I have to go to Santiago [de Cuba]. I have to go see somebody there. Who? I don't know . . . It could be a woman or a man. Possibly a child or a landscape. A street? A tree or a mountain. Anyway, today I had the conviction that I am going to find there what I am missing to be happy. Maybe it is a song, or maybe it will only be 'la casa de la nueva trova' with my little black musician friends who have started taking so much interest in the dollar bill."

A month later, we were due to leave for the airport—Danny, my mother in her urn, and me. My mother was in a metallic blue box that had an elegant lid sealed with an iron ring. Initially, Danny and I were scared, not knowing how to relate to this new version of Marita. Danny broke the ice. He placed the box on top of my desk and began explaining to it that the three of us would soon arrive in Santiago de Cuba, where we would scatter her ashes on the first morning of the new millennium. He spoke to her as one does to a child, with a smile in his voice. I knew she adored that. Because I didn't know what else to do, I decided to write her a letter.

Mami,

We had to turn you into ashes. Satchi liked that better. You know how much he hates worms. Those nasty little creatures waiting to feed on you. So I want you to know that there is no way you are going to stay in the Père-Lachaise cemetery where your soul would wander between heavy stones and sad lights. Danny, my angel-husband, and I are taking you back to Cuba where you belong. I haven't decided where exactly. I would like you to appear in my dreams and direct me, you're also welcome to visit me during days.

The Cuban customs officer was a bitter woman who vociferously demanded a burial authorization before she would let us in the country. She was probably convinced that my mother was a repentant traitor who, having abandoned Cuba, longed to repose there forever. I didn't have the strength to explain how legitimate it was for my apolitical mother to rest in this land. She *is* Cuba, I thought without saying anything out loud. Using his cartoonlike Spanish, Danny handled the situation. He described, mainly by gesture, that his mother-in-law would not go underground. Waving his arms wildly, he tried to imitate ashes flying away. The customs officer lady gave up and waved us onto the island.

The next two days we took my mother everywhere. We bought her a Cuban cocktail at La Casa de la Trova, where we found the musicians mentioned in Marita's note. (And they did show interest in the few dollars we bequeathed them.) We celebrated New Year's Eve with some other musician friends of Mami's. Whenever they told us how much they missed Marita, Danny pointed to the box and said, "Well, in fact, she's right here . . ."

On January 1, 2000, Danny put on his favorite shorts and one of his silly T-shirts, featuring Mr. Bubble. I put on a purple beach dress. We were so used to carrying our box around that we didn't even think of dressing up for the big day. In our rental car, we roamed the outskirts of Santiago until we settled on a glorious tree high atop a hill. A lone carob in a sea of royal palms, it dominated the landscape.

Danny tried to remove Marita's urn, but the box was sealed shut. Danny was battling to liberate my mother from her metallic prison when Providence, in this magnificent and deserted environment, sent a peasant our way. There he was, barefoot, with a hat and a big smile and a machete. The sickle-shaped blade he used to cut sugarcane was, finally, stronger than the urn's lid.

Danny lifted his violin out of its case and began to play my mother's favorite song, "Chan-Chan," a traditional country tune, while I fed her body to the wind. Her flesh had become ashes and her bones burned into small stones, light as gravel. Once Danny had finished the song and the urn was empty, I sat beside the trunk of the tree and cried.

Satchi arrives in Karachi accompanied by two consuls, one French, the other American, both kind enough to pick him up at the airport in the middle of the night. He drops his suitcase, takes me in his arms, and we cry and sleep next to each other for the first time since our early childhood.

When we wake the next morning, Zamzama Street vibrates with the bleating of sheep. It is Eid-ul-Adha, commemorating Prophet Abraham's willingness to sacrifice all for God, including his son, Ishmael. Because God spared Ishmael and substituted a sheep in his stead, the celebrants do likewise, and while I believe in feasts and I confess I love lamb, the cries are distressing. It is very much to our dismay that we realize that our neighbors have their future dinner tied up in the alley behind our house. Satchi is getting a crash course on life in Karachi. After visiting Kashva and her parents out in the cubbyhole meant to be their home, he has to be persuaded from moving them inside the house, along with the neighbor's sheep.

Satchi is a concentrate of human warmth, and although he is still in a stupor of exhaustion, barely capable of distinguishing reality from nightmare, he doesn't forget to hug Bussey, Captain, Dost, and all those "who have taken such good care of my sister."

Oh, the sheep. From the veranda where we're having lunch, we hear fewer and fewer bleats. Shabir radiantly concludes, "Our neighbors are already cutting off the ears of the animal!" Bussey attempts a personal definition of the tradition: a Muslim feast that consists of buying a sheep, taming him, and showing him affection—before sacrificing him.

When I enter the kitchen for some coffee, Bussey grabs Satchi by the arm. "You must absolutely speak to her." Bussey is afraid I'll sacrifice myself.

My brother and I have a conversation deeper than I ever thought an exchange with words could be. I still haven't touched Danny's belongings in the bedroom. It is there, lying on the bed, surrounded by all these small things that make Danny so painfully alive, that Satchi and I go to the essential. We define what is worth living for and what is worth fighting for. We talk about death at length, about winning battles and the price one must pay to get there. We talk about missions and fears. We talk about our mother, our father, Satchi's two children, my son.

We talk about Danny. About what he said when he played the violin at our mother's funeral: "The only way I can make Marita happy is by making her daughter happy." And about the only way I can confirm Danny's victory of the spirit—by pursuing life and striving to become happy again.

No matter what happens, Danny used to joke, "Don't lose your smile, okay? We're going to get bald and fat and old, but you can't lose that smile."

That sentence keeps coming back to me. What an unbelievable challenge. I don't know if I can become happy again. It seems like a mountain too high for me to climb. To give up would be so much easier. Which is precisely why I should go on, I know.

I also know that if the terrorists have killed in me the desire to live, then Danny will have lost. And that's wrong. At no point did he bow his head to these men. They had his body, but they did not have his spirit. I cannot let them destroy mine. In that defiance, Danny and I will remain together forever.

And our son lives.

"If you kill yourself, you kill the baby," Bussey says as if he's experienced a major revelation. His words help me see that I might have no choice, because if I live, the baby lives. And if we both live, Danny wins.

Maybe the choice isn't between living and dying. Maybe it is between victory or defeat. When it comes to going on, to living, there is nothing in between. Talking to Satchi, I understand this. Thanks to my brother, I stand up again. I take my first step in this battle to defeat the absolute darkness that breeds terrorists: I call Musharraf's office. The president and I should meet, I tell his assistant.

Danny tried to escape.

I will learn in the coming months that the kidnappers held him in an isolated shack at a compound on the northern outskirts of Karachi, far from a road, far from people passing by. While unshackled to use the toilet, he tried to escape by shimmying through a vent. When he was caught and brought back, he was chained to the engine of a car, too heavy to drag. Another time he tried to break loose when walking with his captors in the compound. Once he heard a vendor going door-to-door selling vegetables, so he shouted for help; they hushed him up, either threatening him with a gun or covering his mouth with their hands. When he became suspicious that his food might be drugged, he didn't eat for two days. It was only after one of the guards sampled a sandwich brought to Danny that he agreed to eat.

Sometimes when I think about how scared Danny must have been, I become physically ill. But they didn't torture him. They didn't beat him badly. They fed him, though not a lot. His meals were brought to him by Naeem Bukhari, the go-between of the two cells—Omar's cell and the cell that held Danny captive. Naeem has been a powerful force in Karachi. Leader of the local branch of Lashkar-e-Jhangvi, Naeem was being sought by the police even before Danny's kidnapping. He was wanted for the murders of dozens of Shiite Muslims. Naeem was with Omar at the Karachi airport on January 21, and one of the men who met with Omar under the Baloch Bridge on the following day. The day after that, on January 23, when Danny got into the car at the Hotel Metropole, it was Naeem, astride his motorcycle, who led the way to this merciless compound.

The men guarding Danny spoke very limited English. He couldn't communicate with them or they with him. I suppose that's why they didn't notice what he was doing with his fingers when they took Polaroids of him—flashing a victory sign to us with one hand, shooting the bird to them with the other. And they couldn't control the spirit and defiance he showed in his face.

To the end, he fought back. In the video, my friends tell me, Danny says, "My father is Jewish, my mother is Jewish, I am Jewish." Yes, I'm sure they made him say that, just as they made him denounce American foreign policy and even perhaps include the fact that his father comes from a family of Zionists. The family did, after all, move to Israel in 1924.

But here is how I know Danny was undefeated to the end: He says on the video, "In the town of Benei Beraq in Israel there's a street called Chaim Pearl Street, which is named after my great-grandfather, who was one of the founders of the town."

This was not a piece of information his captors could have known or forced Danny to utter before the cameras for their propaganda purposes. The choice of those words and the decision to say them was pure Danny Pearl, his own act of defiance, essentially saying, "If you are going to kill me for who I am, then do it—but you won't *have* me." Danny said this for me, and for our son, and for his parents. He said it so we'd know. So we would be proud, so we would go on. His words about the past created a future.

He did not know until the end that he was going to die. According to authorities, around February 1, a garment manufacturer named Saud Memon, who owned the compound, drove three new men—Arab-speaking, probably Yemenis—to the compound. I later learn what they believe happened in an article Steve writes for the *Journal*:

> [Naeem] Bukhari directed all the guards but one to go outside and leave the Arabic-speaking men alone with Mr. Pearl. . . . The guard who stayed . . . was an employee of Mr. Memon's named Fazal Karim. Mr. Karim, who knew a little English, later told police that at least one of the visitors communicated with Mr. Pearl in a language the guard didn't understand. Mr. Pearl, who could speak French and Hebrew, responded with an angry outburst, his first conversation of any length since his capture.
>
> After the interaction calmed, one of the visitors turned on a video camera, and another asked Mr. Pearl questions about his religious background. At least one major Pakistani newspaper had by then reported that Mr. Pearl was Jewish. After the videotaped statement by Mr. Pearl, in which he described where he was raised in the U.S., his family's religious heritage and his sympathy for individuals captured by the U.S. in Afghanistan and held in Guantànamo Bay, Mr. Pearl was blindfolded and killed.

We waited in vain for three weeks before we knew of his death; it took them that long to put together a video of the event. To anyone who has seen Osama bin Laden's tapes, particularly the gloating one released not long after 9/11, the style of the videos will seem remarkably similar. Behind the primary speaker—in this case, Danny—plays a montage of images from various conflicts: shots of wounded children, explosive noises. Unlike Osama's video, this one concludes with the very graphic and barbaric slaughter of my husband.

The first thing the kidnappers did was deprive Danny of a voice. No phone, no pen, no computer. Even so, hundreds of thousands of people all over the world not only embraced him as one of their own but understood precisely who he was, what he was doing, and why. His murderers tried to reduce him to a symbol—a Jew, an American. But people knew, in a miraculous way, how charmingly goofy he could be and how great a journalist he was. They were grateful to him. They could tell he was a wonderful friend with a generous spirit. Through what he woke in people's lives and in their hearts, Danny's life shines brighter, while his killers' lives wither in darkness.

Here is another reason I can say he won: Though badly wounded, I was able to stand up again. Danny lost his life, yet he won a bitter but final victory.

There is no reason to stay in Karachi anymore. In fact, it is dangerous for me, but the idea of leaving Pakistan without Danny is torture. I have no desire to stay but no desire to leave.

Bussey tries to put pressure on Asra. "If she delivers her baby here, you'll be held responsible for it."

"What is the problem?" answers Asra. "A hundred and forty million people have been born here."

Her point eludes Bussey. They are getting me out of Pakistan whether I'm ready or not. But before I go, I want to address the people of the country. I want to make it clear that I do not blame them for what has happened. I want to share what I have learned about a threat that concerns us all—terrorism in its most desperate manifestation. And I want to explain why I am convinced that Danny's spirit lives on.

For my first public appearance since learning about Danny's murder, I agree to go with CNN, because it can be seen all over this country. Chris Burns, who has covered the kidnapping for the network, will interview me. I have prepared thoroughly; I know the message I must deliver. Later, remembering this scene, Satchi will write that while he was listening to me being interviewed, "I finally understood what she meant by 'Danny isn't dead.' It was obvious that Danny had transmitted to her his strength, his courage, his heart, and a son. In spite of this enormous pain, by totally refusing to give up, she could shout at his kidnappers: 'You have lost! You killed his body but not for an instant did you kill his soul because now it runs through me.'

"My sister is one of these people who are devoted body and soul to changing the world as much as they can."

When Bussey, Satchi, and I get out of the elevator on the eleventh floor of the Sheraton Hotel, another CNN newscaster grabs me, throws her arms around my neck, and pulls me as close as she can, given the barrier my belly presents. It is Connie Chung, who has flown from the States to convince me to be on her show. Disengaging herself, she hands me a letter she's written to me and asks if she can sit in on my interview with Chris Burns.

As I prepare, Chung asks around and manages to find out my brother's name. She finds it difficult to digest that my vaguely Arabic-looking brother's family name is van Neyenhoff and that he is a Dutch citizen.

Bussey's attention is divided. He doesn't know where to look—at Connie Chung or at what's happening in the studio.

Burns and CNN and I have agreed on the parameters of the interview. I've warned that I cannot handle discussing the specifics of Danny's death, and they've said they understand. Yet at the end of our talk, Burns leans toward me with avidity. "Did you see the video?" he asks.

What words are there to explain how I felt? *"Vous n'avez donc aucune décence?"*—Don't you have any decency?—I shot back in French, because I knew he spoke it. "After all I have just explained to you, you still ask me this kind of question? Have you even listened to what I said?"

Chris Burns mumbles excuses. But it's my turn not to listen.

"He looked as if he had been punched by Muhammad Ali and Mike Tyson together," says Satchi as we leave the room.

Connie Chung follows us into the corridor and wraps her arms around my brother's neck. "I'm so sorry," she says, "so sorry." Pulling him even tighter, she whispers in his ear: "Do you have a middle name?" Satchi is stunned and wrests away from her grasp. He cannot believe his eyes when our elevator arrives on the ground floor, the doors part, and we're faced by a herd of jostling journalists and photographers. Bussey swiftly shuts the doors and takes us up to the second floor, where the hotel manager, dressed in black, leads us through the kitchens to a service elevator. Which gets stuck. Once freed, we cut through a laundry room, into another basement room of indeterminate function, and finally to the parking area, where our car awaits us.

"All right, dude!" Bussey tells the driver. "Ever seen those films on TV when the cops chase the bad guys, and the tires squeal, and they go really fast? That's us! Go for it!"

The driver is only too happy to oblige. He takes off at such speed that he almost runs over the journalists gathered at the hotel exit.

"Yesssss!" says Satchi.

Steve has been appointed our leader in matters related to shopping and errands in Karachi. He has a list of stops as long as his arm—pick up plane tickets, buy locks for the suitcases, and reward the guards outside with money—and in his haste, he has committed a serious blunder. He has refused to swing by McDonald's for Asra.

"No time," he shouted back to her when she called out her request.

As he heads out the door, Asra lets loose a wail. "Seeeeeeeee? Nobody likes me!"

Such a heartbreaking scream would move even the coldest man in the world. Asra charges up the stairs as the men below stare at her in pain and utter bafflement.

"Don't you understand?" I say to them. "She is pregnant!"

Bussey rushes to the kitchen and, in a brave and bold act, enters the room where Asra is lying on the floor in tears. He holds a banana out to her at arm's length. Asra smiles. Steve dashes in the door with a McDonald's No. One Special meal just as President Musharraf calls on the landline, the one we reserved for Danny. Musharraf is warm, and inquires about my well-being, our well-being.

"We should meet," I say.

"Do you want to come to me?" he asks and I say yes. The world seems completely insane.

Asra has been packing. Just for herself, she has six enormous third-world-looking suitcases. She also packs up Danny's stuff—the silly T-shirts and funky ties, the comic books, a sole tennis shoe since Danny managed to lose one, and the mandolin bedecked with stickers.

On our last night I invite over all the men who helped me look for Danny. Randall snags beer and bad wine for the non-Muslim and the nonpregnant from the U.S. consulate commissary. Yussuf-le-cook makes canapés nobody eats. There's Captain, of course, and Dost. Jameel Yusuf and Randall Bennett. Tariq Jamil and John Bauman. FBI agent John M. and John Bussey, Asra and Steve. Zahoor. We all seem older, gray-complected with unerasable rings around our eyes, and rage and grief in our hearts. But everyone has dressed finely, as befits a ceremony.

We gather in a circle, and for a while we sit in silence. Nobody is bothered since we are sharing something none of us can express. Dost presses his hands together as if in prayer, and it does feel like we're about to take an oath together. Our silence is thick with sorrow and love—and defiance.

Finally I find my voice. "You are the bravest men I have ever met. You went straight to hell, where darkness is the deepest, because you hate injustice, and racism, and tyranny. You did it for Danny and for me and for our child. But you also did it on behalf of the rest of the world. You are on the front lines of the fight against terrorism, and still, nobody knows you and how brave you are. Nobody sees how your willingness to fight the darkest threat for humanity actually makes each one of you shine as an individual."

Captain has stopped looking at me. I know he is struggling not to show his tears. I think he is proud of me. I want him to know—I want them all to know—how proud I am of them. "I have gathered you to say thank you for having shed tears with me and also to inform you that I am going to tell the world about you. First I will tell the presidents, and then I will tell all the people.

"People need to know the truth," I go on. "If we want to put an end to terrorism, terrorists will have to face opponents as determined as they are themselves. You all are. We all are."

I stare intently at their handsome faces, lined and puffy with fatigue and anguish, and I try to carve them into my memory for the rest of my life. "I have gathered you here," I say, "to let you know that without amazing people like you around me, I couldn't have any hope left by this point. And how can anyone live without hope?"

There's a crash in the corridor, and our circle freezes. Then we discern the source: Kashva—who regularly lets herself in and roams our rooms—has dropped one of her treasures. She stares boldly up at the big men, then scampers away. Captain smiles first at the little girl, then at the rest of us. In his gaze, I can see this odd mix of pain, pride, and solemn dignity we all share.

Chapter Eleven

LIKE SHADOWS sneaking out in the dark of the night, we are leaving Karachi. Since Danny left, Nasrin has carefully avoided arranging his belongings in our room. But now everything that lay strewn about—the comic books . . . the random wires to plug into this, to plug into that . . . the solitary sock—has been respectfully packed away. Nasrin turns down our bed as if to deny that no one will sleep in it tonight.

Shock has blasted out, blanched, my ability to see clearly. Struggling to focus, I am almost surprised to find they are all still here, the props of my tragedy. The golfer clock on which the swing of the golf club hammered each passing second of Danny's absence. The carved chair where I rocked endlessly, soothing the baby while waiting for Danny. The wall chart that Asra ceremoniously folded as one would a flag for a fallen hero.

I call on the romantic French poet Alphonse de Lamartine to find words of farewell to this house that I wish never to see again, and which I cannot bear to leave.

> Objets inanimés, avez-vous donc une âme
> Qui s'attache à notre âme et la force d'aimer?
> Inanimate objects, do you possess a soul
> That comes to our soul, and demands to be loved?

Ours is the only house on Zamzama Street with lights on. All the suitcases, Danny's included, are neatly lined up in the hallway. Asra has six suitcases all to herself, but in truth, beside her few pairs of Nike pants, they contain mostly research and evidence—sixty files, a waist-high stack of newspaper clips, notebooks, and a few key books.

Satchi has disappeared, but we find him walking up and down the darkened sidewalk, shaking the hands of all the guards. He offers an abundance of thanks, sandwiching a hand of each policeman between both his own as if to warm it. Bussey spots him and bursts out laughing. "Look at Satchi! He should run for mayor!"

A few minutes later, our convoy moves out, accompanied by the flashing red lights of our considerable police escort. John Bauman leads the way in his black diplomatic four-by-four. In an uncommon move, Bauman failed to appear when he'd promised to; he had over-slept. But not even ten minutes after we called him, Bauman showed up at the house—a bit dazed with fatigue but neat in a pressed suit, white shirt, and tie. Our sadness makes us feel exposed and shy, and to avoid real conversation, our mourning team takes bets on whether or not the consul slept with his clothes on.

When I look out the car's windows, I am relieved to see that before the break of dawn, the streets of Karachi, silent and empty, don't even look familiar.

First stop: Islamabad.

At the presidential palace of President General Pervez Musharraf, the ceremonial guards wear *kolas,* turban-style caps with towering domes, and they stare straight ahead as Bussey, Asra, Steve, Satchi, and I climb the red-carpeted stairs. We are ushered into a vast room with high ceilings and ornate, gilded Victorian furniture. There are red velvet chairs for us to sit in, but they are positioned so far apart we cannot gossip among ourselves. Instead, I study a huge portrait of Quaid-e-Azam Muhammad Ali Jinnah, the founder of the Pak-istani nation who was once known as the ambassador of the Hindu-Muslim unity. After a few minutes, we are led to a reception room where President Musharraf is waiting for us. Small yet wearing an unmistakable air of authority, Musharraf has on a *chirwani,* the traditional Pakistani suit. On each seat someone has placed a cardboard tag with one of our names on it. Asra's is misspelled with a "Z" instead of an "S".

So much for intelligence, I can hear Asra thinking.

Wrapped in Danny's shawl, in my green pants and combat boots, I feel like a pregnant guerrillera on a diplomatic tour.

"I trust you have met moderate Pakistanis while here," President Musharraf says to me. Yes, I assure him, I know that all Pakistanis aren't kidnapping murderers.

The president serves us honey-roasted almonds, the best I have ever had. I observe him more than I listen to him. He's obviously conflicted: sincerely sorry for me while still furious at Danny, choosing to believe my husband brought this all on himself. I try to ask Musharraf about ISI and Omar's disappearance in the week of February 5. Instead, he steers the discussion toward the enormous problems confronting Pakistan: Kashmir, India, jihadis, Afghanistan, poverty, illiteracy.

When Musharraf finishes, I tell him about Captain. "You have wonderful men," I say. "It is important that their efforts not be in vain." As I talk, a thought keeps running through my head: They executed Danny, but somehow you are the one they wanted to kill.

As if reading my mind, Musharraf blurts out, "They're also after me."

I nod.

"We will find the killers," Musharraf says, as we rise to go.

I nod again.

We're flying out of the country that evening to Paris, and I still don't know where Danny is. I am a wandering soul in search of its own body.

Bussey has worked hard on our travel arrangements. He intends this trip to be the safest any of us has ever taken. There's just one leg that's beyond Bussey's control—the stretch between Islamabad and Dubai. For that we must take Shaheen Air, the only airline on this route that suits our schedule. For the most part, Shaheen shuttles Pakistani workers by the bunch to the United Arab Emirates, where they feed the incessant demand for cheap immigrant labor.

A bus ferries us to the plane's steps. As we board, Bussey rears back with obvious alarm. The three pilots, all from the former Soviet Union, have either not slept for two straight weeks or are so seriously hungover that they have moved into another dimension of being. We get on anyway.

We are "first class" travelers, which turns out to mean the first row of the plane has been reserved for us. Bussey twists around to survey "coach." The cabin is entirely filled with jihadi-looking bearded men, stares fixed, silent as tombs.

"Oh, this is great—great," Bussey says. He turns to Satchi. "What is it you Buddhists say—*Nam Myo* . . .what?"

In Montmartre I hide in Danny's and my little Parisian shelter. It is a good place to go underground; the neighbors are notoriously indifferent to anything other than tax cuts and weather reports. I am waiting for some sense of reality to sink in. Both Danny's and my bags remain in the middle of the room, unopened, untouched.

I have no desire to speak to anyone, except perhaps President Jacques Chirac. I do have things to say to him. I feel a driving need to remind him that it is time for Europe to stop regarding terrorism as a bilateral issue between America and the Muslim world. To reinforce that terrorism is as rooted in Europe as it is in the rest of the world.

We make a date, the president and me.

In his filthy old car, Satchi drives Bussey, Asra, Steve, and me to the Palais de l'Élysées. We are late, and by the time we reach the palace, all of the presidential staff has left for the day, save for the president's spokesperson and Jacques Chirac himself.

President Chirac is supremely tall and handsome and warm. He wants to know everything: what kind of man Danny was; who Gilani represented; how the Pakistani intelligence agencies behaved. He is worried about me—how I'm holding up, whether I can support my baby boy. He makes Satchi promise to alert the president should I ever need anything.

As our meeting comes to an end, Jacques Chirac decides it needs to be memorialized with an official photo shoot. But no photographer is available. *Pas de problème.* He runs out of the room, fetches his own point-and-shoot, and expertly choreographs us in a series of official government portraits: the widow and the president. The widow, her brother, the president. The *Wall Street Journal* gang and le president. Bussey, Asra, and Steve speak little if any French, and none of us is particularly fond of posing, but we are all highly entertained by the president's spirited direction.

Asra is on the phone offering directions to First Lady Laura Bush's chief of staff. "We're in the eighteenth arrondissement of Paris, almost all the way up on the Montmartre Hill. I gotta warn you, though, it's really a pain to find a place to park here."

"Thanks, we'll keep that in mind," says the man.

We found out yesterday that Laura Bush wants to visit. I still don't feel like having visitors, but it seemed absurd to turn down a first lady. What do you a feed a first lady? we wonder. Bread and cheese? Olives and wine? *Une tarte aux pommes?*

We decide to hold our meeting with Laura Bush at the little apartment, two blocks away, that I've rented as an office. It's less messy than my place.

"How do you talk to a woman like her?" I ask Asra. I amend that thought. "How do you talk to any woman?" In spite of our pregnancies (I am roughly the size of a baby elephant now), we haven't been around other women for what feels like a really long time. We shifted continents two months ago, but we haven't really been able to leave Pakistan; our world remains as insular and intense as before. Omar Sheikh and his three accomplices are being tried in the antiterrorism court in Pakistan. Our days are spent following up on the latest developments in both the search for those at large and the trial.

The defense has tried every trick in the book. They have tried to finger Asra as the mastermind behind Danny's kidnapping. They have tried to claim that I wasn't actually Danny's wife, and that maybe I was a spy. (A freelance journalist? Who ever heard of such a thing?) Certainly, they've insisted, Danny was a spy. And they've forced the court to view the video to decide whether it can be used as proof that Danny has indeed been murdered.

Upset, we email Randall for advice on how to handle the lawyers. "Hey, kiddo, remember," he answers, "I know and beat the defense fucking lawyers. They are like children and of no significance. They seek stupid directions because they have no others. It is strictly a diversion tactic and no one takes it seriously or cares."

My sense of time has gone wild. I feel like turning back to look at the future; the present is too fractured for me to grasp. When Asra and I speak of what lies ahead, we go no further than the births of our children.

We can't ask the first lady for advice on becoming single mothers, and we won't necessarily tell her about the front lines in Karachi, but it seems we've forgotten all the topics in between. I've already met with her husband, George W. Bush. I visited the White House in mid-March, two weeks after leaving Pakistan, one week after meeting with President Chirac. Bush was my third president in under a month.

Washington, D.C., was exhausting, a nonstop round of interviews beginning with the president and ending with Larry King. Danny had introduced me to the Larry King phenomenon when we were at a bar in India. He pointed up at a TV hanging from the ceiling. "See that little fellow with the glasses, suspenders, and rocky voice? He'll tell you something about America."

Bussey, Asra, Steve, and I stayed at the Mayflower Hotel in downtown D.C. An American flag flapped against my window. At three o'clock one morning, the fire alarm rang out. It took me only thirty seconds to get out of bed and my room, but in the hallway, all my routes out looked blocked off. I started to panic, but then I saw an

Indian man open a door leading to the stairwell. I followed him. "I'm so sorry," I said to him. "Really, I'm sorry. So sorry."

The man looked at me, a pregnant woman in her nightgown, and he was baffled but said nothing as he led me to a safe spot to wait out the alarm. It wasn't until the all clear sounded and we were heading back to our rooms that he turned and asked, "Please, what were you sorry about?" I realized that up until that moment, I'd been convinced the hotel was on fire because of me.

To George W. Bush, I told tales from the streets of Karachi. I described to Bush and Attorney General John Ashcroft and Secretary of State Colin Powell and National Security Adviser Condoleezza Rice how the men I had met who are fighting the real war on terrorism have next to nothing—barely-functioning transportation or printers, no cell phones. I told them what America looks like seen from abroad. I pressed them to use their vast resources to find Danny's killers, and to bring them to justice, no matter how difficult the task. I warned them that the political difficulties might far outweigh the law-enforcement issues. I suspect they already knew that. Just for the hell of it, I told them how my mother was born in Havana and my mother-in-law in Baghdad. I was glad to see that Bush found this funny.

But what he really wanted to understand from me was "How come you're not bitter?" I told him that if I let bitterness overcome me, I would lose my soul, and if I lost my soul, I also would lose Danny's. "This," I told the President of the United States, "is my biggest battle."

On May 9 a suicide bomber in a red Toyota pulls up alongside a bus in front of the Sheraton Hotel in Karachi and detonates, killing eleven French engineers and two Pakistanis. The French engineers had been working with the Pakistani navy on a submarine project. So much for Bussey's insistence that the Sheraton Hotel is the safest spot in the city.

President Musharraf calls it "an act of international terrorism." President Chirac calls it a "murderous, cowardly, odious terrorist attack."

I still haven't unpacked Danny's suitcase. I am lonely, trying to take care of the two men in my life, though one is dead and the other hasn't been born. He should come sometime before June.

The baby's heartbeats rocked me to sleep yesterday as I went for my last sonogram before the big day. I am trying to keep him inside.

They have just found Danny's body. It was cut into ten pieces. Nobody told me this. I learned it in an email that had been attached by accident to another email being sent to me. Danny was found in a four-foot-deep grave in the compound on the outskirts of Karachi where he was held the whole time. The authorities were led there by three members of Lashkar-e-Jhangvi who had been swept up in a raid by the police after the car bombing at the Sheraton Hotel.

The email refers to "the remains." For me, what actually remains of Danny is in my belly.

Danny will be buried in Los Angeles, close to where he grew up. I don't want to attend the service. I can't, not with the baby coming any day. Besides, in a way that it is difficult to articulate, I am too concentrated on Danny's future to dwell on what is gone. His parents have courageously dealt with the painful details of Danny's return. They have found a beautiful hill on which to bury their son. Danny would love to see the headstone of the grave next to his. It reads: "I told you I was sick!"

Lately, every email I open, every phone call I answer, feels like a missile blowing up a little more of my life. People call to ask for DNA samples, they want a comb or a toothbrush, they insist on telling me about autopsies or crime evidence. A total stranger calls to ask about Danny's toes: Is one of them slightly bent over the other? I feel like I'm watching a horror movie, except I can't cover my face to avoid the bad scenes. When the phone rings, I instinctively place my hands on either side of my belly, as if to cover the baby's ears. Ever since I stumbled across the news of Danny's body, Asra has assiduously done her best to screen all emails. I can tell when she reads a particularly offensive one, because her eyes widen in a peculiar way that I have witnessed countless times over the last few months.

We spend our days exchanging instant messages with Captain, who has decided this is our safest channel of communication. We call Washington, Islamabad, and Los Angeles regularly. We are two little pregnant warriors fighting to keep the momentum going.

The Pakistanis are pressuring me to return to Pakistan and testify in the trial of Omar Saeed Sheikh and his three accomplices. The trial has already been plagued by problems and challenges—the judge has been removed, the starting date has been put off, and since the prosecution has concluded it is dangerous to continue in Karachi, it has been moved to Hyderabad.

Two of our FBI agents have gathered the courage to testify. One is a man who became particularly dear to all of us in Karachi. John M. just appeared one day, sitting on the couch in the dining room. A mountain of muscles, still and silent, in a dark green shirt. Randall had introduced him to us the way you display a winning card: "John M., FBI, nineteen kidnappings, zero failures." He turned out to be as nice as he was impressive. This was his first overseas assignment; previously, he fought street gangs in New Jersey. After testifying, he called me to describe the experience—the trial is being held in a cell so tiny the witnesses can't sit; John stood for six hours of cross-examination, as inches away from him the defendants shrieked at him, hurling venom from the cages in which they were held. After this experience, he returned to battling the Jersey gangs—"a piece of cake," he said, after his stint in Pakistan.

The Wall Street Journal, which hates the idea of my going back to Pakistan, is pressuring me not to testify. I am frustrated because they won't send a representative from the newspaper, and I feel one of us should be there. I want Danny represented in court. I end up talking to a lawyer for the *Journal* who tells me, "This is your case, not ours." A friend suggests I hire a lawyer to talk to the lawyer.

"You must relax," says my obstetrician.

"Think about the baby," say my in-laws.

The video of Danny's murder is on the Internet for anybody to see. "We've tried to get it off," warns Bussey, "but there's nothing that really can be done." I cannot believe that is the case. I call Attorney General Ashcroft, forgetting that it's night in the United States. "Call in the morning," says the guy at the other end of the line.

Asra plunges into the problem, putting all of her well-honed crisis-management skills to work. The Web host turns out to be Lycos.uk. Assuming such a video runs afoul of any number of United States statutes, we call the FBI. "I'm so sorry," says the agent. "Unfortunately, there's no law that can be used to stop this. First Amendment . . . freedom of expression . . . you know?"

"But this is obscene," protests Asra.

"Yes," he says, "but it's not *technically* an obscenity."

We call Scotland Yard. Better. In the United Kingdom it is a crime to post such a video. "Violates the obscenity law, you know?" With Scotland Yard's help, we track down the Lycos officer responsible for Web content. His assistant is so nice, she makes us want to cry. She is horrified by what we tell her, and she gets her boss on the phone right away. From them we discover where the video is coming from: Saudi Arabia, posted in Riyadh. In roughly ten minutes, the video is off the Internet.

For now.

Asra is having a boy. I take pictures of the sonogram, and we go out to a café and split a nonalcoholic beer to celebrate.

My baby doesn't kick me. He moves gently, as if to say, "I'm here.

When you have a chance, let's get me out." I keep telling him, "Hold on just a bit, this is not such a good day to be born."

I write him a letter.

May 16, 2002

Dear Adam,

This is the first time I am writing to you. So far, we have communicated in a different way and I have asked you to just be with us. And you have done exactly that.

In a few days, I will merge both, life and death.

There will be joy and pain as you come to the world. But please always remember how your birth granted me a future and granted your dad eternity. Together, we will be able to give Danny the most beautiful present one could ever think of, you, Adam, a son, the promise that his legacy will go on. The burden of our struggle, however, won't be on your tiny little shoulders.

We are lovers of life and you are the best of us.

I might be sad at times, even when looking at you, but I will do everything humanly possible not only to make you happy but also to help you grow as a man of value. Eventually we will all be together. I already love you,

                                                              Mammy

Bussey calls again. "More bad news?" I joke.

"Yes," he says, not joking.

Fifty minutes from now, CBS will broadcast part of the video. *The Wall Street Journal* says it has spent the day trying to stop CBS, but without success. Danny's parents have asked the State Department to stop the network, and the State Department has tried, as has the Justice Department, but to no avail. Dan Rather and Jim Murphy, anchor and executive producer of *The CBS Evening News,* are intent on airing excerpts.

A heat wave sweeps over my body; I literally see red. I am transformed into a fire-breathing Taurus. I appeal to Andrew Hayward, the president of CBS News. Oh, he sounds empathetic. "I am so sorry. I know what you feel."

I answer, "You have no idea how I feel unless *you* are about to give birth to a son whose father has been murdered on tape—and *you* are talking to the gentleman who is about to air it."

He mumbles something.

"Forget about me," I say. "Give me one journalistic reason to air it."

"It has news value," Hayward answers in a tone that makes me think he is trying to convince himself.

"You sleep with your conscience," I tell him. "But I'm going to tell you what really makes me sad. It is that those fuckers knew all along they should make a video, because they knew all along you'd be ratings-hungry enough to broadcast it. They appealed to your weakness, and *you gave in*."

Asra and I are heading over to my office to meet Laura Bush. As we hit the streets of Montmartre, we can see why the first lady's chief of staff didn't seem particularly concerned about parking availability: The Americans have taken over the entire neighborhood. The narrow and curved little streets of the hill are barricaded, and every fifteen meters or so stands a giant man dressed in black and murmuring into a headset. The men form protective walls on either side of the avenue, and we two round-bellied women waddle our way down the street alone. We are like marbles rolling down a chute. Nosy neighbors poke their heads out of windows and watch us. *"C'est qui?"* they demand. Who is it?

Yes, indeed. Who are we?

We carry boxes of petits fours and bags of fruit juices, forgetting that the first lady probably won't be allowed to have any of it for security reasons.

"Remember," Asra says as we climb the stairs to the office, "every night she lays her head next to the president's."

When Laura Bush arrives, her serene though cool beauty startles me. She hands me a fragrant bouquet of pink and white roses, then she sits next to me on the edge of my raggedy couch, back straight, a bit shy, and very dignified. She is not here for small talk or to score political points; the press hasn't been alerted to the visit. She is here because she has things she wants to say to me. She knows that the video of Danny's murder has been posted on the Internet, and that CBS has aired parts. To me, this feels like the rape of a murdered man, and Laura Bush is similarly outraged.

She is not reluctant to articulate faults she finds with her countrymen. She talks about how unprepared America is for the kind of war it faces. "Sometimes in our culture," she says, "it seems as if we've digested so much, we can't seem to absorb something that is complex anymore." I tell her that my impression is that the terrorists know much more about America than America knows about them, which is why the West needs to embrace the world better. She and I discuss ignorance and poverty, the two pillars of global misery. We come from completely different walks of life, but as we sit here, we are simply two women sharing a struggle.

She talks to me about the difficult path I have ahead of me. She tells me my son is lucky to have me as his mother. She says, "You have a mission. It is crucial that you speak up and share what you understand with the people in America."

At this point the door flies open and a gorgeous blond girl in her early twenties joins us. It is Jenna, one of the Bushes' twin daughters. She grabs a chair and sits across from us, and the conversation turns to the political apathy of American youth and the U.S. military strikes in Afghanistan. "I have always been against the bombings," Jenna says. Laura Bush casts a quick, motherly look at her daughter, watchful yet protective.

When I agreed to meet the first lady, I wasn't expecting to be moved by the visit. But Laura Bush strikes me as an intense, compassionate person, and I feel her seriousness of purpose having a real impact on me. When she leaves, I am surprised to feel stronger than I have in a while.

During our visit, a crowd has gathered downstairs, and when the first lady and Jenna climb into the car, the spectators burst into warm applause. Laura Bush waves to them in the way that first ladies do. I lean my forehead against the windowpane and, with the crowd, wave back as I watch her go.

I have almost stopped talking altogether. For the last twenty-four hours, I haven't uttered a word. I am reminded of my maternal grandfather in Cuba who one day decided to become mute because he could no longer tolerate the fights he had with his wife. My grandfather was a tall, handsome man with very fine hands. When I was nine years old, I went to visit him. One morning I woke at dawn, as he did, and I asked him to talk to me. He took me for a walk along a deserted railway line and talked for three hours straight. He fed me mangoes and then talked some more. He told me how he had driven buses around Havana all his life; how much he had loved women; how he played card games for money. He told me I was good at making people talk, that I should become a journalist.

On our way back home, my *abuelito* and I found that my grandmother had sold the mosquito netting I had brought him from Paris. She sold it to a young woman in the neighborhood who planned to turn it into a wedding veil. My grandfather didn't argue. But he stopped talking again, and he remained silent until the day he died. And I became a journalist.

There is something I must do before the baby is born. I have to face what Danny faced. I have to confront the truth, because it is like an enemy: If you turn your face from it, then you are crushed by it.

On May 25, two days before the baby is due, I take the phone off the hook, lie down alone, and imagine everything that happened to Danny. That doesn't take a great act of imagination; by this point I have a lot of details. But I force myself to see it all—when they blindfolded him, when they took out the knife, how long they interviewed him before they started killing him. And I make myself think about what Danny thought, and to know when he was most afraid.

For two days I live through this. They are the craziest days of my life, but I have to do this, and I have to do it alone. When it is over, I know nothing can happen anymore that I don't have the courage to fight within.

Around eight P.M., I call Asra. I know she's been worried. I tell her I'm okay, but I don't tell her that labor has begun, because I don't want to think about it too much. I want to husband my strength for when I next truly need it, so I sit in front of the TV all night and watch five films on HBO. I must look like a lunatic, lying in my beach chair staring at the screen, but I suppose that doesn't matter. The whole time I am in my head, talking to Danny and to our son. I tell them, "We're going to be fine. It's going to be all right."

By ten o'clock in the morning, the contractions are growing serious, so I call my dear childhood friend Ben, who drives me to Maternité des Lilas, a joyfully cosmopolitan maternity clinic. Ben helps me stretch out in the backseat of his car, asking no questions, respecting my intense need for unspoken communication. He turns on the radio, and a playful Brazilian song comes on, which makes me smile and recall the first time Danny and I went to the Maternité. We were there for a party. The mother of Satchi's wife worked there, and someone was retiring. Kids were running all over the place, and Danny chased them. When salsa music started playing, I danced with Dr. Strouk, who was to become my Ob-Gyn. A very cool doctor—certainly the only one in the Maternité who came to work on a black and chrome Harley. In a few months, that man knew a good deal more about me than my dancing technique.

Throughout my pregnancy, I've flown back to Paris for regular prenatal checkups, regardless of where I've been in the world—India, Qatar, Bangladesh, Canada, Pakistan. When I was about four months along and having a sonogram, I could finally distinguish the baby's features. I was so excited that I called Danny on his cell phone. He was in Yemen. "I see his face," I tell Danny, "I can see his eyes, his nose . . ."

"His nose?" Danny asked. "Does he have a Jewish nose?"

I laughed so hard Dr. Strouk made me turn off the phone.

What is most painful to me is that I know how happy Danny would have been to be with me here. How he would exercise his genius in preparing for the birth of our son. He would have cried when I had pain and brought all my stuffed animals over to the maternity room. When my mother was sick and I spent the days at her bedside, I came home one night to find that Danny had drawn a bath for me and filled it with rose petals. When times were difficult, he would sing my favorite American ballad, a silly one about misery in Arkansas. He would cook pumpkin soup and rub my feet. He would call the entire planet to announce the birth of Adam, a name he chose as if we were creating the first man.

I have decided to give birth alone. Without my mother and Danny, it will be just me and a midwife. But as they wheel me into the elevator en route to the delivery room, I am terrified. God, I think, he really is not here! I am wearing a long white shirt Danny and I bought in Dacca, Bangladesh. An African woman nods at me in a gesture of silent complicity. For a split second I want to ask her to come hold my hand.

I begin to chant. I pull myself together. I am ready.

I am also in terrible pain, contractions coming like tidal waves, and when the most violent wave tears me apart from inside, I howl a bestial cry for the second time in four months. I am like a she-wolf wailing to the heavens.

But when the epidural takes away the pain, I finally have a taste of victory. An odd joy takes me over, as I continue my monologue with the father of my child so he can share my euphoric sense of absolute defiance. "Here I am," I tell him, "lying on the delivery bed, confronting the reality of your absence, embracing the pain it induces and finally giving birth to our son." I feel like the hand opening the cage so the bird can fly again. We won't be prisoners of our own fate. And somehow, beyond life and death, Danny is with me.

For seven hours this goes on. Then suddenly the midwife starts fussing and a nurse appears. "We will have to do a C-section," the midwife says. "The baby's heartbeat is falling."

I can hear Adam's heart on the monitor. The beats are slowing down and the women around me are moving faster. I start to chant like I have never chanted before. The midwife thinks I have lost it, but I chant out loud, as fiercely and with as much focus as I can. I pour all of my life into my prayers. As I recite the mantra, I hear the sound of the baby's heart picking up, picking up, picking up, picking up.

Twenty minutes later, Adam's head emerges from my body, and I manage to bend over and grasp the tiny little man, still halfway in. I pull him out and lay him on my chest. Only when I see his eyes open wide, searching for my face, do I cry.

It has never occurred to me until this moment that the baby might not make it. But we won, and I can feel Danny's relief wrap itself around me. I want to cry out my victory, but I pass out from exhaustion.

His full name is Adam D. Pearl. Danny chose the name in honor of all the different bloods that run in his veins. He called him "the universal baby." From his earliest moments, Adam has looked at me with his dad's expression. There's a rare purity to it. It makes me feel that life is just like a book that never ends. And it reminds me of a wish his father and I made early on: that in our son's lifetime there would be more people ready to give their lives for peace than for the hatred in their hearts.

I stay a week in the maternity clinic. I have asked the doctors to keep me even if health reasons do not require it. I do not want to talk to anyone. Or, to be more precise, not to anyone still belonging to the world of the living. I need to cry, a lot.

The woman at the desk downstairs has the mission of holding all calls. But she pokes her head in my room the day after Adam is born. *"C'est Georges double v Bouche,"* she announces, a hint of terror in her voice. When the president of the United States asks me how I'm feeling, I bravely hold my tongue and resist mentioning stitches, milk, or anything too graphic. He is truly and sweetly happy about Adam's birth. We have exchanged several letters since we met in March, and I believe his concern for me and my son is very real.

A little later, the woman from the front desk appears again. She is short of breath with excitement. *"C'est Jacques Chirac!"* she announces triumphantly.

Adam, my wonder, sucks quietly at my breast, placidly ignoring the excitement. He is a triumphant little concentrate of life.

Asra brings an instant message from Captain:

captain1pk (21:40:47 PM): "about 5 mins ago i got long awaited news of ADAMS arrival. CONGRATULATION_ i hope mariane is fine. i am so excited , it is a very sad time as well, tell her that i will always be there for her and her son. lots of love to three of you . . . capt."

When he found out I was pregnant, Danny said, "Our child is going to change the world!"

I argued: What if he does not want to? What if he wants to own a flock of sheep or make flutes? No, Danny insisted. "He'll do something big . . . I don't know what, but I can feel it!"

We left it there at the time. But last night, Adam's first night, I snuck into the nursery where they had taken the baby so I could get some sleep. I bent over the crib and watched Adam's chest rise and fall, and I stroked his downy cheek. *"Mon amour,"* I told him very softly, "it is fine by me if you want to change the world."

Epilogue

May 20, 2002

> asra (08:17:46 P.M.): i'm here are you there?
> captain1pk (08:18:01 P.M.): yes very much
> asra (08:22:09 P.M.): how are you?
> captain1pk (08:30:55 P.M.): GOOD NEWS i now exactly know
> who the killers are i'll tell you in a day or two, dont tell mariane yet
> we will give this to her as a surprise

Some days it was as if Asra and I had never left Pakistan, as if Captain were about to walk through our front door at any moment. We shared information via a steady stream of instant messages, and it sometimes felt as if our friends in Karachi needed to hear from us as much as we needed to hear from them. None of the investigators had ever gotten so emotionally invested in a case. They had set out to save the life of an innocent man, and when they couldn't, that fueled their desire to march even further into hell to avenge Danny.

To this day the Pakistan police and the FBI continue to pursue his kidnappers and killers. But the toll of "the Pearl case" on all involved has been huge. Here's a summary of what has happened since we left Karachi on February 27, 2002.

RANDALL BENNETT

Left Karachi a wanted man.

After we left Pakistan, Randall became a lead investigator of the bombing at the Sheraton on May 9; he was one of the first on the scene. "I found a hand," he wrote us. They caught the bomber, "with the Captain's folks of course and the FBI." Less than a month later, on June 14, Al Qaeda staged another suicide-bombing attack, this time slamming an explosives-filled vehicle into the concrete barriers surrounding the U.S. consulate—right outside Randall's office window. Fourteen people were killed, all Pakistanis. At least fifty more were injured. "We caught all of them [the terrorists behind the bombing] over the following weeks, but it took forever to fix the building and it has never been the same again there."

Randall had planned to leave the city permanently in July 2002, but in June Pakistan Intelligence advised him that Al Qaeda was planning to ambush and kill him as he left for the airport. "The agents recommended I leave immediately. I concurred and was already packed, so . . . adios."

This wasn't the first time Randall had been threatened. He told us of other threats in an email a few weeks before Adam was born. He was hiding out in Bangkok, Thailand, enjoying reflexology massages, when he learned that I'd had my son. He rushed to a nearby cyber café to send a congratulatory reply:

> I have taken a week to get away from the scourge that is Karachi. I am tired of looking over my shoulder and need a short break. I am in Bangkok for 8 days enjoying a happy and peaceful culture where terrorism has not struck, yet. Thailand is just what I needed. Not only do I get a week's rest and joy but the Lashkar-e-Jhangvi guys who were hunting me are probably running in circles wondering where I went. I will invite them to meet me when I return.

Well, time to go walk casually down the street like a normal person and not have to carry a gun, radio and cell phone.

Lots of baby talk to Adam,
Uncle Randall

When Randall left, thirty of his closest police friends came to bid him farewell. "We were crying, hugging, and pledging our friendship and loyalty. I have never been so touched. My life had been changed by meeting some of the finest people on earth over the previous years," said Randall afterward.

Randall is now regional security officer in Madrid, "responsible for the safety of all Americans in Spain."

JAMEEL YUSUF

His career suffered, although there is some dispute as to whether it was a direct result of the Pearl case, or simply classic Karachi politics.

What cannot be disputed is that, after fourteen supremely effective years as the head of the Citizen-Police Liaison Committee, the charismatic Yusuf was dismissed. As he put it in an email to Asra and me, "The order disassociating me from my honorary and voluntary work in assisting victims of crime irrespective of their caste, creed, status or wealth was issued on the night of 22nd March 2003."

Because he had gained the trust of the FBI and had worked closely with them, he found himself caught in a web of jealousy and intrigue within the police and intelligence forces, and ugly rumors arose that he was a CIA agent. In April 2002, when Omar Sheikh and his three accomplices were tried, most of the witnesses for the prosecution were treated with discretion and, to a certain degree, protected. Not Yusuf. He was made a prime witness in court, exposed before the defendants, and had to weather threats hurled at him and his family.

In his fourteen years at CPLC, he had apprehended four to five hundred hard-core criminals and/or terrorists, but he'd never felt the need to protect himself. Now he was being overwhelmed by threats, and was forced to hire guards to protect him around the clock.

Yusuf remains a highly successful businessman and has turned his energies to humanitarian causes.

DOST

Shortly after we left Karachi, Dost did too. "Bosses were not happy with anyone after the case. In the spirit of deference in the subcontinent to superiors, I couldn't defend myself," Dost wrote to me in his uniquely poetic fashion. "There was no ground to say anything."

Dost left military intelligence, moved to Islamabad, and entered a police training program. With this career change, he lost all the benefits of his seniority in his own branch. "Enjoying low profile life and good weather in Islamabad," he wrote. "World is not nice place, but one has to find happiness on their own."

Dost's love life hasn't benefited from his new posting. He ended up with neither his girlfriend nor the woman his mother had picked out for him. "My love life needs a double-click. Somewhere in the process called life, my document titled 'love life' has been lost. And, like a cyber-crime investigator, I am trying to recover the lost file from the formatted hard disk of my heart."

JOHN BUSSEY

John Bussey remained our Minister of Security and Hygiene as long as we traveled together. He accompanied me to the Maternité des Lilas for my first checkup after leaving Karachi, and he spoke worriedly with Dr. Strouk about the effect of airplanes' compressed air on pregnant women. Dr. Strouk was amazed.

Bussey was promoted to deputy managing editor of *The Wall Street Journal* and moved to Hong Kong to oversee coverage from Asia. A few months after he settled there, the SARS epidemic started.

STEVE LEVINE

Steve LeVine fought his reluctant editors to get back to Pakistan and pursue a journalistic investigation of what happened to Danny. Now he is on book leave from *The Wall Street Journal,* and at Stanford University, Danny's alma mater, Steve is writing about the Caspian Sea, and his book is tentatively titled *Players*. In June 2002 he became the father of a little girl, Alisha, who was born in Tarzana, CA. She is half Kaszakh.

THE PEARLS AND THE DANIEL PEARL FOUNDATION

Shortly after Danny's death became public, Danny's family, friends and colleagues founded the Daniel Pearl foundation (www. danielpearl.com) which promotes cross-cultural understanding through journalism, music, and innovative communications. The first major project of the Foundation has been the Daniel Pearl Music Day—an annual global concert on October 10th, Danny's birthday, in which musical artists include with their concerts a call for tolerance in the spirit of Danny's love of music and commitment to dialogue and humanity.

The idea was inspired by a concert that took place in Tel Aviv on February 22, 2002, a day after the world heard Danny had been murdered. That night, George Pehlivanian, Danny's neighbor and friend from Paris, was scheduled to lead the Israeli philharmonic Orchestra as a guest conductor. Deeply troubled by the news, he was reluctant to perform but, at the last moment, decided to defy the perpetrators by proudly dedicating the concert to Danny.

"As the orchestra played Tchaikovsky's Symphony No. 5, I finally understood the triumph of hope over despair," said Pehlivanian. It was an emotional and triumphant concert, ending with 15 minutes of sustained applause.

The idea spread like a forest fire; evidently the fuel of goodwill around the globe was merely waiting for the right spark. From Moscow to Bangkok, Australia to the United Kingdom, over 100 concerts in 18 countries, with performers such as Ravi Shankar, Elton John and Itzhak Perlman, participated in this global project. Junoon, Pakistan's top rock band, dedicated their performance in Edison, NJ, with the words: "Danny, you will be missed by all of us who still believe that goodness and courage can overcome all injustices."

Other projects launched by the Daniel Pearl Foundation include fellowships that bring Pakistani journalists to work in U.S. newsrooms, a lecture series in journalism and international relations, an essay contest, which challenges teens to write about an incident of hatred, and a series of "Press Under Fire" symposiums reflecting on the risks that journalists face.

ASRA Q. NOMANI

On October 16, 2002, Asra gave birth to her son, Shibli, named after an ancient ancestor who remains famous as one of the greatest Islamic scholars of all time. In June 2003 she published the book that took her to Karachi—*Tantrika: Traveling the Road of Divine Love.*

The Pakistani press continued their relentless attacks on Asra. Not only did they finger her as a spy, but the last article published in Pakistan about her not only listed all of her addresses and phone numbers—it included those of her parents as well.

Asra has begun speaking out on behalf of Muslim women who are considered criminals for having babies out of wedlock. She still carries Merve and Blink around.

CAPTAIN

"What has happened to me personally?" Captain wrote recently. "This case changed me from inside. I couldn't sleep for so many days. Even my kids could feel that there was something terribly wrong with me. This was when I promised myself and Mariane that no matter what it takes, I will bring all of those responsible for Danny's death to justice.

"The mission is not over yet."

Not by any means. Here is what Captain and the other law enforcers have dealt with in Karachi in the wake of Danny's murder:

May 9, 2002: The Sheraton Hotel bombing killed two Pakistanis and twelve French engineers working with the Pakistani navy on a submarine project.

June 14, 2002: The car bombing outside the U.S. consulate killed twelve and injured fifty. Al Qaeda funded the bombing.

September 11, 2002: Ramzi bin Al-Shibh, an Al Qaeda leader, was arrested after a gun battle with Pakistani policemen.

September 21, 2002: Ten more Al Qaeda operatives, including two Algerians, were arrested.

September 25, 2002: Seven Pakistanis working for the nonprofit Institute of Peace and Justice were found murdered.

October 17, 2002: Six parcel bombs, hand-delivered to top law-enforcement officials, exploded around the city. Eight were wounded.

December 15, 2002: Pakistani police thwarted a plot to ram an explosives-laden car into the passing car of a U.S. diplomat. One arrested suspect was linked to the Sheraton Hotel bombing.

December 20, 2002: A chemical storage warehouse used as a bomb-making factory exploded by accident. Five terrorists were killed, including a member of the second cell of Danny's kidnappers—

Asif Ramzi, who was also a suspect in both the U.S. consulate and the parcel bombings.

February 3, 2003: A bomb hidden in a motorcycle exploded near the Pakistan State Oil headquarters. The target: Farooq, Captain's right-hand man, living next door to the headquarters. Farooq survived.

February 22, 2003: Gunmen opened fire outside a Shiite mosque, killing seven worshipers.

May 3, 2003: American authorities uncovered an Al Qaeda plot to fly a small aircraft into the U.S. consulate in Karachi.

In April 2003 Captain received a major award for public service from President Musharraf. The text for the honor reads in part:

In the field of the new wave of sectarian-based terrorism, [Captain] volunteered to take up the highly challenging task of breaking the network and arresting the terrorists targeting the city of Karachi.... [T]hrough continuous monitoring [he] succeeded in locating the whereabouts of highly evasive and notorious terrorists. Then working according to a well thought out plan, he was able to apprehend one of the most wanted terrorists who had been involved in 68 registered cases of sectarian killings in Karachi and various cities in Punjab. His arrest prevented the murder of six prominent personalities on their hit list....

[Captain], in performance of his duty, showed extraordinary diligence, devotion and courage beyond the call of duty and succeeded in arresting some of the most wanted terrorists though meticulous planning, methodical execution and fine leadership. In recognition of his outstanding services in the field of public service, the President of the Islamic Republic of Pakistan has been pleased to confer on [Captain] the award of Sitara-i-Imtiaz.

The recognition meant a great deal to Captain, but it also made him even more of a target. Many of his colleagues had grown twisted with professional jealousy. He was never again allowed contact with Americans, Randall included. He was tailed; his phone and internet accounts were monitored. "Life became miserable," he wrote, a misery intensified by the fact that he was being targeted by the jihadis, as well—especially after he arrested the chief of Lashkar-e-Jhangvi.

"They know who I am, and what damage I have caused them. So they are after my blood, and the life of my family is also in danger. They have made a few unsuccessful attempts on me and my team. So I have had to make a lot of changes in my life—relocated my house, put a halt to a social life. I can't go anywhere without security. In a nutshell, I have lost my independence."

In true Captain-spirit he added this: "But let me tell you, I don't regret even a small bit."

Captain has proclaimed himself Adam's godfather for life.

What Captain Learned

After the Sheraton bombing, the police swept through jihadi groups and picked up, by some accounts, as many as three hundred suspects. Several of those arrested turned out to know a lot about Danny's murder. Through them, we developed a clearer understanding of the cells involved in his kidnapping and death.

We already knew about the first cell, that of Omar Saeed Sheikh and his three accomplices. What we didn't already know we learned in the course of their trial.

The United States requested that Omar be extradited for trial in the U.S., but Musharraf turned them down, hoping to use the trial as an example of the country's crackdown on terrorists. The twists and turns in the trial were endless. Judges were replaced; locations debated. Omar demanded to be tried in a Muslim court, rather than in Pakistan's anti-terrorist court. His lawyer tried to accuse the prosecutor of blasphemy and making statements against Islam. The judge tossed out the accusation. Eventually there were four convictions. Adil,

Suleiman, and Fahad were found guilty and sentenced to life in jail. Omar Saeed Sheikh: death by hanging. Omar's defense lawyer immediately appealed his death sentence, while the prosecutor immediately challenged the life sentences given to the other three. He had wanted death sentences for all four. The cases are on appeal in Pakistan's Supreme Court.

Omar's father, Ahmed Saeed Sheikh, who continues to run a successful wholesale garment business in the East End of London, has declared that "an innocent man has been punished." Omar doesn't seem all that worried about his situation. He has sat in jails before, and he has wound up freed—to return to the kidnapping of true innocents. Anything can still happen, and Omar seems to feel he is living proof of that. As he put it when he was sentenced to death: "We shall see who will die first—either I or the authorities who arranged the death sentence for me."

More trials are in the offing. The authorities have concluded quite a bit about the members of cell number two, the cell responsible for holding Danny in captivity and eventually burying him. One arrested was Naeem Bukhari, the leader of the Karachi branch of Lashkar-e-Jhangvi, who led the way to the compound on January 23. Naeem, also known as Attaur Rehman, was introduced to Omar by a mutual friend from the militant world—a man named Amjat Farouki, aka Haider Farooqi. Haider belongs to Harkat-ul-Jihad-i-Islami and headed up cell number two. Thought to be in his early thirties, he spent six years with Al Qaeda as a chief instructor of Harkat-ul-Jihad-i-Islami training camps in Afghanistan. Omar phoned Haider from Lahore and asked him to find a safe house for important work in Karachi. As of this writing, he is still at large.

Faisal Bhatti also fell into the hands of the police. A man of about twenty-four years of age, he, too, was at the meeting with Omar under the Baloch Bridge, and he admitted standing guard over Danny. Faisal got his training in Lashkar-e-Jhangvi camps in Afghanistan.

The men were all linked to one man who still evades police custody: the wealthy Karachi factory owner Saud Memon, who owned the compound where Danny was held and buried. Memon was the person who authorities believe brought "the three Arabs" who, we came to learn, comprised the third cell—the cell which did the actual killing.

Who exactly is in that group? That still isn't clear. Randall Bennett has always thought they were Saudis. Many others feel they were Yemenis. A Yemeni national who may have been one of the key players of cell number three was arrested in April 2003 in Karachi. On the day of his arrest, Waleed Mohammed bin Attash was in possession of six hundred kilos of explosives. Bin Attash is also in CIA custody; the agency has yet to share information regarding his involvement in Danny's case.

One of the arrested Pakistanis from cell number two has claimed that Khalid Sheikh Mohammad, the third-highest-ranking member of Al Qaeda, was not only one of the Arabic speakers but was the actual executioner. Mohammad was arrested on March 1, 2003, in Rawalpindi, and as of this writing is, as Captain would say, a "guest" of the CIA, being held in an undisclosed location, but whether there is any truth to the charge, we just do not know.

Here's what we do know: Memon drove the three Arab speakers to the hideout on Danny's eighth or ninth day in custody. They brought video equipment. Naeem ordered all the guards out except one, Fazal Karim, who was at the shack from the first day of Danny's captivity. Fazal has been arrested and is the source for much of this.

He has described to police how the Arab speakers videotaped Danny. How Danny, speaking in a language the Urdu-speaking Fazal didn't recognize, probably either Hebrew or French, became agitated while speaking with one of the Arabs. How a local man—Tassadaq Malik, a friend and assistant of Naeem's—was given the job of running the video recorder. How Danny was blindfolded and then, with the recorder running, murdered. How the man running the recorder, perhaps shocked, apparently bungled part of the video. How one of the Arabs yelled at him. How they restarted the recording machine and resumed taping.

Three weeks later, in the lobby of the Sheraton Hotel, a man named Abdul Khaliq, aka Marshall, posing as a reporter from Online Press, handed over a copy of the video to FBI agent John Mulligan, who was also posing as a journalist. The police first grabbed Marshall but then let him go under the mistaken impression that he actually was a journalist. He has since disappeared.

As I write this, President General Pervez Musharraf struggles to retain control over his volatile country. As this book was going to press, yet more Lashkar-e-Jhangvi activists were rounded up. These men do not appear to have been involved in Danny's death, but they pose a serious threat to others in these pages. On July 4, 2003, in Quetta, three gunmen entered a Shiite mosque and killed or mortally wounded forty-eight worshipers. *The New York Times*'s David Rohde described the massacre this way: "Saying nothing, looking 'very relaxed,' walking 'here and there,' in the words of witnesses, the three unidentified gunmen killed and killed and killed here on Friday afternoon." The attack took ten minutes.

Captain's on his way now to investigate Quetta. He says it is an honor.

"Pray for me," he writes.

Letters to Adam and Mariane Pearl

Dear Adam:

I write for those who knew your father by reputation, as the sort of journalist who threw himself into out-of-the-way corners of the world to shed light on peoples and places that too often are presented to Americans in caricature form. Your father painted his subjects whole, in stories that were full of humanity, insight and plenty of wit. Preconceived stereotypes fell away; you caught the people whole.

In this world where America looms so large, both as influence and target, what your father did is the most important journalism I know. . . .

The terrorism that stalks our world will never be defeated by guns alone. It must first be understood. It was in that battle, that battle for understanding, that your father gave his life. I'm grateful for all that he did, and for the example he has set.

Jon Sawyer
Washington Bureau Chief
St. Louis Post-Dispatch

I was moved when President Bush spontaneously asked the members of the Gridiron Club, a Washington-based journalists' organization, to write to Adam about his father. The letters he has received, like this one by Jon Sawyer, are a most precious gift.

Even without being asked, thousands and thousands of people

from all over the world wrote to me, to our son, to Danny's parents, and to his colleagues. Sometimes I could identify the provenance, other times not. People sent emails to *The Wall Street Journal* or letters to the American consulates in their countries, asking them to forward the messages. They wrote in Urdu, Japanese. Some people managed to track down my address and mail me packages—beautiful gifts, many of them handmade, blankets and quilts, booties and angels. Many of the letters offered monetary support. There were more letters and emails than I could ever count or answer individually, but I've read them all.

After this excruciating ordeal, there was nothing I needed more than to be reassured about human nature. I had just experienced how barbaric human beings can be, and I was about to bring a child into the world. Living through the nightmare was like falling down a well. Those letters—your letters—have been the rope that, word by word, allowed me to raise my hopes again and see the light at last.

When Adam grows up, I will have, on the one hand, the terrible tale of his father's murder; and on the other, the voices of men, women, and children from the world over, expressing the full power of human solidarity. Reading each of the letters—just a small selection of which I reproduce here—I could feel the sender grappling to find the words and thoughts that would bring me hope. I am convinced that if we ultimately overcome terrorism and the spread of hatred, it will be because there are millions more on this earth like those who wrote to me.

We call them ordinary people. To me, each one is extraordinary.

Mrs. Pearl,

I wanted to tell you how touched and saddened I feel about your husband's death. I'm not even completely sure why it touched me so deeply, but from the moment I heard of his abduction, I was filled with grief and hope. My days included combing the media for word about him—I felt such anguish about you, too. I can hardly imagine that waiting. I wish with all my heart that he could have come home unscathed.

I just wanted you to know that so many of us—the strangers across the lands—are heartbroken for your loss. I didn't know your husband, but I wish I had. I share his (and your) compassion and humanist views. And despite this awful outcome, I share Daniel's optimism about bringing the world together in peace someday. And I so admire anyone who is willing to "walk the walk" to bring truth to the rest of us about what is happening in these places so far away.

Thank you for sharing so much about Daniel's life. *Thank you* for encouraging him to write even in dangerous places so that we shall all learn more.

My heart, and that of my three daughters and husband, goes to you and your baby. We wish you peace in the years to come, and sunshine in your darkest days.

Anytime you come to Chicago, we invite you to our home.

> With condolences and love,
> Carole Schmidt
> Bloomingdale, IL

* * *

I am an Italian journalist, I am 40 years old, I have a kid born in October. My wife is a journalist too. I worked as a war correspondent in Bosnia. Our family can understand very well—I think—what Mariane felt in these days. We prayed for her. We will pray for Daniel. If we can do something else, please, let us know.

> *Un abbraccio da* Alberto Romagnoli

* * *

While you don't know us, we are deeply grieved by your loss and feel as if we have lost someone from our own family.

Take courage—for something good, however small, will always come out of such a tragedy—or so I believe.

With deep regret for your loss and prayers for Danny,

> Zarina Mehta
> Bombay
> India

*   *   *

Dear Mrs. Pearl and family,

I would like to offer my condolences on the untimely death of Mr. Pearl. May he rest in peace. As a Pakistani, I am ashamed of being one today. His unborn son will come into this world hating us, but is he not justified to hate us? I have no words to say how sorry I am for what happened to Danny. My heart goes out for your family. Danny died for a great cause and he is a martyr. I had hope for him all along and now console myself knowing he is happy up there with his creator and looking down and smiling and longing to see his beautiful unborn son. He will be your guardian angel. People like Danny make this world worth living in. May he rest in peace and God give you the strength you need.

> Sultan, Sara, Ryaan and Raniya

*   *   *

My name is Remy, I'm 16 years old and I live in Holland, I heard the news about Daniel Pearl on the news this morning, I was really shocked when I heard it, it's really sad and it made me angry. I saw the address to send to so that's what I'm doing now, condolences to Mr. Pearl's family and friends, perhaps it's not much but it's better than nothing I think. I wish all of you a lot of strength,

> Remy

*   *   *

Dear Mrs. Dan Pearl:

The news of your husband's death made me cry.

When I heard your response to what those bastards did to your Danny, I cried even more. I am an old man. Eighty-five. Been through lots and lots and have no idea how I managed to stay the course thus far. I wipe my tears and wonder: what can I say to your heartache? Maybe the simple thought that hearing and listening to your voice in anger and hurt made me understand the courage and love of your marriage.

I am sure your new child will absorb the courage of his mother and father and build his life on the tragedy.

Please, forgive me. I had to do this, because at this time, your courage has helped to give mine a boost . . . The enclosed check—double chai, for you and your child, to do whatever you wish to do with it—are a token of my tears. But I hope it does more than what it is. That it perks you up.

It's like a return engagement, because your voice perked up me.

> Sincerely,
> Sam Fink
> Great Neck, NY

*   *   *

Dear Mrs. Pearl,

The enclosed money order was purchased with donations made by friends, family and customers of Deegan's liquor store in Woodhaven, N.Y. We were touched by you and your husband's story, and we hope this relatively small contribution can help out with some baby expenses.

> Best wishes,
> Elizabeth Deegan
> Woodhaven, NY

*   *   *

My heart goes out to you. May God bless Daniel in his heavens. His murder was a senseless act of barbaric behavior that no one accepts. As a Jordanian born to a Muslim family, I feel great shame that Daniel's murderers did their heinous act in the name of Islam. And I am saddened that a man of his caliber and training dies trying to cover the misery and desperation of that part of the World.

Daniel died doing his duty and doing the things that he loves doing. That I hope is great solace for you all.

With sympathy from me and my family,

> Burhan Gharaibeh, Ph.D.
> Rangos Research Center
> Children's Hospital of Pittsburgh
> Pittsburgh, PA

*   *   *

Dear Mariane,

Please accept my gift of this quilt for your son. I was deeply touched by your tragedy and wanted to do something for you. Since we are strangers, I can't console you. We are not friends, so I can't be there for you. I am, however, a quilt maker and nothing says love, in my mind's eye, like a quilt. . . .

It is called "Pearl of Wisdom" because of your strength, courage and grace. These qualities will surely be passed on to your son. From all I have read and seen regarding you and Daniel, this little man, Adam that is, has a wonderful future ahead of him. Hopefully the quilt will bring you both pleasure, security and a bit of comfort. That is my wish. . . .

When I opened the magazine this pattern came from, I knew this was the quilt for you and Adam. No political statement, no patriotic message, just a fun colorful quilt for a new baby. Wrap Adam and yourself in it and consider it a hug from a lady in Austin, Texas, that cares about you and wants nothing but the best for your futures.

> Best wishes, really!
> Kyra H. Loadman
> Austin, TX

*   *   *

To Daniel's family, friends and colleagues,

As a reader of *The Wall Street Journal,* I feel personally hit by such a tragedy. From the images of Daniel I discovered on the BBC News online site some weeks ago at the beginning of his kidnapping, I saw in his eyes, despite his terrible situation, gentleness. I felt that under other circumstances, it would have been a great privilege for me to know him better.

He now has entered the family of dedicated reporters who have paid the highest price in their search of sensitive news for us, readers of the free world. . . .

His memory will not fade away.

Keep Faith

> Jean-Marc Peyron
> Paris, France

*   *   *

Ruth and Yehuda, Tamara and Michelle, Mariane,
Dear Family,

There are no words capable of consoling the clipping of a tree of life of a young person that has all his future ahead of him.

There are no words capable of healing the terrible pain of the murder of your son Daniel, a son that you brought up and who filled your heart with pride with his impressive achievements. Daniel took upon himself a professional and personal mission and with indescribable courage penetrated into the heart of darkness in time of war, in his quest to understand, study and bring before the world community the nature of terror and the struggle against it.

We in Israel feel that Daniel is a piece of our flesh, that the love of his family, his friends and the lovers of peace and freedom in the world will keep his memory alive in hearts.

I am with you in these unbearably difficult moments, feeling your pain and weeping your tears.

> Shimon Peres
> Deputy Prime Minister and Foreign Minister

* * *

We're Thinking of You—"Warm thoughts are offerings of concern from the heart."

> —From the Associates at Wal-Mart Store #2281
> Nancy, Electronics Dept. Mgr.; Ann S.; Jack;
> Cecilia; Valerie; Cheryl in Toys; Sally; Cathy S.;
> Joanice O'Brien; Jean P.; Nancy; Rachael; Rick;
> Lisa Brady; Gale; Betty; Hillary; Jessica; Arriana;
> Tina; Jim in the Photo Lab, among others

> Wal-Mart Store #2281
> West Mifflin, PA

* * *

My name is Lukman Hidayat, an Indonesian moslem. I do really feel very sad to hear about the death of Mr Pearl. My sympathy goes to his family and may God The Almighty give His blessing so that they can endure this heartbreaking unpleasant happening.

> Best Regards,
> Lukman Hidayat

* * *

Dear Sir:

The attached [check] is for Mrs. Pearl.

I am a former newsman, retired on Cape Cod; I like to believe newsmen everywhere will feel compelled to help out.

If you hear Mrs. Pearl is under financial restraints I would appreciate being on a list of those informed; and I will dig down deeper.

Sincerely,
Thomas Turley

*   *   *

Dear Mariane,

I know it is probably not much consolation to you in this dark moment, but please know that my heart, and the heart of a thousand buddhas are with you. No one can know the loss that you feel at this moment, but we give you our tears. . . .

Nam Myoho Renge Kyo
Brenda Thompson
Houston, TX

*   *   *

Me and my class are very sorry your husband/father died. That is why we have raised money [with a raffle] in the Millennium Mall. We have raised about $2,000. We hope you appreciate the money. Your husband was a real American hero.

—Gregg Stevinski,
in one of twenty-six letters
written by the students of
Mrs. Rudolf's fifth-grade
reading class at East
Hampton Middle School,
East Hampton, NY

*   *   *

Gentlepeople—

My son, Philip, is in Afghanistan for *The Christian Science Monitor* and *U.S. News*. We are heartbroken.

> Love, a dad and mom,
> Mr. and Mrs. John R. Smucker
> Alexandria, VA

*　　*　　*

Dear Sir,

My name is CHRISTIAN EMEKA UCHE. I am a Nigerian. I am one of those that read about Daniel Pearl kidnap through CNN website.

I am writing to let you know that you are not the only one affected with his death. I am more than touched when I read about his killing.

Please do accept my condolence and pray that God should help you in this time of grieve.

Also to his wife, I know that you are going through this stress, all I have to say is do bear it and allow God to guide and protect you.

I want you to all to bear the loss.

God bless you.

> From
> Christian Emeka Uche
> Lagos, Nigeria

*　　*　　*

This is to express my sorrow and deepfelt condolences with Daniel Pearl's family and friends. One feels especially for his wife and unborn child, who will be marked by his death more than anyone else.

Mr. Pearl's work speaks of a man trying to explain the complexities of the world to his audience. He tried to enhance the understanding of the subjects he covered, and greatly succeeded in my opinion. His articles were always a pleasure to read, and one could see the marks of a mind well traversed culturally and intellectually.

One way to honor his legacy would therefore be to continue on his path and offer enlightening and in-depth articles, with insight, humor and a humanistic perspective.

Not a small task.

Best,
Henning Gravklev
Oslo, Norway

* * *

To dear Mariane,

Here in Israel as we celebrate the Festival of Purim, it is difficult to find happiness in our hearts as we live in the shadow of terror. We can only pray for better times and a better world.

Meanwhile, please know how all of us here who read about Daniel in the newspapers feel as if we know him a little. Please be well in your pregnancy and have a good and easy birth. We will all be thinking of you when the time comes.

May our children grow up to know a very different reality from the present one.

With love and respect,
Katie and Aryeh Green
Yonatan (aged 14)
Michal (aged 12)
Moriyah (aged 9)
Bet Shemesh, Israel

* * *

Dear Mrs. Pearl,

If it makes you feel better my mom's pregnant to and I know how it feels to lose someone I lost two people that I didn't even know but you knew your husband so at least you can tell your kid about your husband. But I can't tell my kids about the people I lost.

> Sincerely,
> Katie Sorrels
> Indiana

*　　　*　　　*

Mariane Pearl & family:

I am a twenty-nine-year-old woman from Belfast, N. Ireland, and I went to school during the height of the troubles. My mom is Jewish/Croatian. It is through people like Daniel that the world hears the truth . . .

Your family will always be in my heart.

> With best wishes,
> Natalija Harbinson
> Surbiton, Surrey
> England

*　　　*　　　*

On behalf of the International Association of Fire Fighters General President Harold Schaitberger and our entire organization, I send our sincerest condolences to Mrs. Pearl and the staff of the *Journal* over the tragic death of *Wall Street Journal* reporter Daniel Pearl.

Whether it was the loss of 343 FDNY fire fighters in the attack on the World Trade Center or one *Wall Street Journal* reporter killed in Pakistan as a result of a terrorist attack, these were all men doing their jobs the best they knew how and trying to make the world a better place.

Our hearts go out to all of you in the *Journal* family, and particularly to Mrs. Pearl and her unborn child.

May he rest in peace.

> George Burke
> Washington, D.C.

*   *   *

Greetings! My deepest apologies and heartfelt grief for your loss and pain. I'm Shiite, from Karachi, and grew up with my father in jail between 1977–88 for being in the movement for democracy, I cannot fathom your loss but am touched by it, for what it is worth. Your husband's blood is in the likeness of all those who have tried to expose, fight and stand up to oppression throughout history, epitomized by the martyrs of Kerbala, and it shall not be in vain.

I am an architect by profession, and it is my pledge to you to design your husband's memorial (if it already has not been), in the likeness of the architectural heritage of the region, as an indigenous testament to his sacrifice.... May goodness be with you and the memory of the martyrs and sufferers give you strength and make you proud. *Khuda Nigehban!*

Tehmoor Nawaz

*   *   *

Dear Mariane,

The issue of inhumane acts is very personal with us. Three years ago we adopted a child from Brazil. Luciano is a child who lived on the streets of a major city in Brazil. He had been victimized by [an] off-duty policeman who had been hired by merchants to murder street children they considered a nuisance. Without the press and Amnesty International these horrendous acts would have continued. But, because of courageous journalists like Daniel, Luciano survived and is doing well. We don't use the term hero often but it certainly applies to Daniel. He consciously put himself in harm's way to disclose tyrannical acts.

Although we have never met you or Daniel, please know that your courage will live in our hearts forever....

Love, Kathy, John and Luciano Vaden
Greeneville, TN

*   *   *

Dear Mariane,

    . . . I do not know if you wanted it, though I said the Kaddish for Danny.

> Much much love,
> Anne-Marie Dogonowski
> Smorum, Denmark

*   *   *

WISH IT WAS ENOUGH TO KEEP THE WORLD FROM GOING INSANE.

> —note wrapped around a five-dollar bill,
> sent from Brooklyn, NY

*   *   *

Many of those whom are contacting this address probably didn't know Danny Pearl. I am no exception.

However, as with the scores of those who perished in September . . . the epitaph published today on behalf of Danny revealed the ever-slightest glimmer of an individual behind a face that I'll never get to meet—an engaging, opinionated, unique, bright and inquisitive mind. It's these elements to which I'm drawn to engrossing conversations with new acquaintances. And it's the sudden loss of these traits that makes me grieve most.

At the end of the day, perhaps that's all we have: a human connection with another individual. Someone who moves us, who challenges our conventions and consoles when the world comes crashing down around us. I suspect that, for his colleagues, friends and family, Danny was no exception.

> Juli Goins
> Minneapolis, MN

*   *   *

Madame,

I just heard the news of the birth of your son last Tuesday in Paris. I rejoiced and I would like to send you my warmest congratulations and wishes of good health for you and your son.

Like all my countrymen, I have admired your courage after the death, in such revolting circumstances, of your husband. I very sincerely hope that the birth of your child will bring you comfort after this terrible ordeal.

Rest assured that my ministry will be at your disposal for any problem you may encounter with the Pakistani or American authorities.

> Respectfully yours,
> Dominique de Villepin
> Le Ministère des Affaires Étrangères
> France

* * *

I want to express my sadness that this young man has been murdered by terrorists. My prayers go out to his wife, family, friends and co-workers and *WSJ*.

> From the ranch,
> Bobby Leezer
> Magnum Creek Ranch

* * *

Death-Cell
Circle 3
Central Jail
Rawalpindi
Subject: CONDOLENCE
Dear Honourable,

This is to express grief at the sad and untimely death of Mr. Daniel Pearl, the late American citizen and journalist, a victim of Religious Terrorism in Pakistan.

May his soul rest in heavens.

> Sympathizing with the grieved family
> and the Govt. of the USA,
> Dr. Mohammed Younas Sheikh

(Myself a victim of Religious Terrorism by mullahs through abuse of the notorious Blasphemy Law 295/e PPC and threats to due process of law and justice.)

[Dr. Mohammad Younas Sheikh was a professor of homeopathic medicine at a college in Islamabad. He is one of roughly a dozen teachers who were accused by students of blasphemy. His crime: In a class in 2000 he made an innocuous remark about the origins of Islam. Sheikh was convicted and awaits execution, which is mandatory under the blasphemy law.]

*   *   *

Chère Madame,

I am absolutely shattered by what is happening to you and I don't know how to find the proper words of consolation. The ones I reach for seem inadequate. . . . The only thing within my grasp is to invite you to stay at my house for a while if you're considering coming to France.

I am a retired doctor and I live with my husband in the South of France close to Montpellier in a large farmhouse close to the beach.

You would be welcome, we would entertain you, pamper you a bit, cook nice little dishes for you, and surround you with our affection. (I have three children and six grandchildren.)

Though I may not know you, I take the liberty of sending you a kiss—

COURAGE!

> Edmée Finet
> France

*   *   *

Dear all,

My family and I want to send all of you our thoughts and our love at the loss of Daniel Pearl. Our 20-year-old son Andrew is on the U.S.S. *Kitty Hawk,* as an airman in the US Navy. We pray for our military folks daily, that God will keep all of them safe. Daniel has been in our family's prayers (including our 6-yr-old's) since 1/23.

Daniel will NEVER be forgotten in our hearts. Can you please pass along to Daniel's wife and parents, how sorry we are for this senseless killing. We are also sorry for YOUR loss.

Thank you for your time. God Bless

> Regards,
> Sandy, Mike, Kristina, Kimberly Palumbo—
> Round Rock, Texas
> Andrew Yarnish—U.S.S. *Kitty Hawk*—
> Atsugi, Japan

*   *   *

Dear Mr. and Mrs. Pearl,

. . . I've known Danny since eighth grade. Danny and I became good friends at Wildwood Music Camp, where we wrote silly campfire skits together, and we remained friends at Stanford and then again in Washington, D.C., where we worked across the street from each other six or seven years ago.

I don't know if you remember me; we met briefly on a few occasions when my mother and father and I would stop by your house briefly to pick Danny up to take him to music camp. Danny always spoke about both of you with such real love and affection—even as an adolescent when most of us are a bit embarrassed by our parents. . . .

And my heart broke, especially for you, when I heard the news of Danny's murder. I am now a parent, and everything that I would want my children to become I saw in Danny—and I am not talking for a moment about career achievements. I am talking about the ability to truly live life: the ability to experience unrepressed joy; the ability to be thoughtful without being self-absorbed; the ability to see, and add to, the humor in life without adopting the easy distance of a cynic; and the ability to be spontaneous and unforced in relationships with others.

These are the attributes of that rare thing: a fully developed, whole human being. Paradoxically, they also are attributes that we more often see in children than in adults. And those adults who hold on to these attributes all but invariably were raised by parents who loved them without crowding them or trying to live vicariously through them.

When I last saw Danny at a going-away party thrown for him in Washington around 1996, I was struck by how he had held on to the best that was in him as a teenage boy in music camp. And I must admit that I was a bit envious, because it occurred to me that, like a lot of people, I had over the years built up this sort of invisible membrane around myself that I had to push through—against increasing resistance—in order to connect as fully to others as I once had, and even to connect with my own true aspirations. With Danny, there was no such barrier between himself and others or between himself and himself. No wonder people were so drawn to him. . . .

I am convinced from knowing Danny, and from hearing from others who were blessed to know him, that hundreds and hundreds of people, consciously or unconsciously, drew a similar lesson from Danny and were inspired by him to live a better, fuller, more giving life. For enriching me and others in that way, I am confident that I have not only Danny but you to thank.

My thoughts and prayers will continue to be with you.

Sincerely,
Leon Dayan
Washington, D.C.

*   *   *

Dear Mariane,

Wonderful news—Adam is here! We are rejoicing with you and thrilled to know you are both doing well.

I enjoy remembering our visit in Paris and look forward to meeting Adam someday.

President Bush and I send our affection to you both and our hope that these days of beginning bring a new light into your life.

> With warmest wishes,
> Laura Bush
> The White House

*   *   *

Dear Family and Friends of Daniel Pearl,

. . . I woke up thinking about Danny and you at 4:30 this A.M. and tears hit my pillow as I thought of what I might say to you.

I hope that you will eventually get past your grief—I trust that Mrs. Pearl and the baby that is due will have lots of loving support. No doubt the baby will be a world beater.

My husband and I play old-time and Irish music on guitar and mandolin and we will play "Red-Haired Boy" for Danny.

> Best wishes and love,
> Susan Coale
> Highland Park, IL

*   *   *

My husband James W. Barbella died on 9/11 in the World Trade Center. I understand the horror that Danny's wife is going through. This will not end her pain but I hope she knows that there are many people caring about her.

> Sincerely,
> Monica Barbella

*   *   *

Dear Mariane,

Congratulations on Adam's birth. I know your joy is tempered by sorrow. Because my mother was widowed three months before I was born, I have some idea of what you must be feeling and thinking about your boy's future.

My mother worked hard to give me the feeling that I knew my father, that I could be proud to be his son, that my life could honor his memory. Her love gave me the strength and security to handle the emptiness of his absence. I know that your love will do that too.

My thoughts and prayers, and Hillary's, are with you.

Sincerely,
Bill Clinton

*   *   *

Dear Mrs. Pearl,

Enclosed herewith is a letter of condolences from His Highness Shaikh Hamad bin Khalifa al-Thani, Amir of the State of Qatar, on the sad and sorrowful murder of your late husband.

I would like also on this sad occasion to extend to you my personal sympathy. Indeed he was a good friend and I shall miss him a lot. . . .

Few weeks ago, I received the notebooks he promised to send to me. He was a man of his word.

Yours sincerely,
Abdulrahman bin Saud al-Thani
Undersecretary, State of Qatar

Dear Mrs. Pearl,

I was shocked to hear of the brutal and savage murder of your beloved husband. While strongly condemning this barbaric act and all similar terrorist acts, I would like to express to you my sincere condolences and sympathy praying to God the Almighty to rest his soul and grant you and your bereaved family fortitude and solace to overcome this most sad and mournful loss.

> Hamad bin Khalifa al-Thani
> Amir of the State of Qatar

*   *   *

Ten Useful Baby Tips, a few of many offered by Mrs. Brosius's fifth-grade class, Laurin Middle School, Vancouver, WA

Try not to give them too many small round foods. They stick them up their nose.

Don't leave the baby in the car alone. It might be gone when you get back.

Never hit them or they might hit other people.

Don't let them eat peas; they'll stick them up their nose.

If they don't go to sleep, put them in a car seat and go for a ride.

Never take your baby through a major time change. Like from Washington to Texas.

If you bring him to Disneyland, never let him ride the Haunted House because it might be too scary.

If you do get a trampoline, don't let him go on it because he might fall off and hurt himself.

Be sure to keep your money up high because they might swallow it.

Since he is a boy baby, when you change his diapers do it at an angle because for an unexpected reason they tend to have to go when the diaper's off. So watch out!

*   *   *

You don't know me—I'm just one of many people who followed the story of Mr. Pearl's kidnapping in the news this past month.

I was so sorry to learn this morning of his death, and wanted to let his family and friends know that my thoughts are with them. I know this is a very difficult time.

> Tatiana Schwartz,
> Office Manager, MITS
> Michigan

* * *

Dear Pearl Family and Friends,

... It may be of little solace now ... but I do think that Mr. Pearl and all journalists serve the greater good. We owe them our thanks and gratitude for helping to keep the world a free place. When a journalist dies in connection with their job, they die serving us. I thank Mr. Pearl and all journalists for the risk they take. I cannot imagine how different the world would be if they did not take those risks.

> Nathaniel Toll
> Athens, GA

* * *

Dear Madam

I never knew your husband. In fact, I don't read *The WSJ* that often. What is more, I am Turkish—a Muslim. However, I am terribly sorry for this heinous act of crime which goes beyond any kind of religious thinking. ...

I hope that God gives you and your son the strength to push through these hard times. I, as a world citizen, also would like to see the perpetrators of this act of barbarism to see the blade of justice.

Only thing good I can say at the moment is that your husband is now one of those great teachers that teach humanity the importance of free speech and importance of tolerance between cultures.

> Ozgur Altinyay
> Istanbul, Turkey

*   *   *

Dear Mrs. Pearl,

My husband Keith and I met Danny one sunny summer afternoon in Washington, when *The Wall Street Journal* trounced *The New York Times* in softball. After the game, Danny and some of his colleagues and my husband and I went out for drinks, and we had the pleasure of getting to know Danny ever so slightly.

There are plenty of people you meet once and then forget about. Danny wasn't one of them. I remember Danny because he was so clearly, deep down, a really good person. I'm sure you know that far better than anyone, and we grieve with you over your loss of a husband, friend and father to your child.

> With our best wishes for you and yours,
> Robyn Meredith
> Keith Bradsher

*   *   *

I was one of the 52 Americans held hostage for 444 days in Iran from 1979–1981. Please accept my deepest sympathies. I admire what Daniel was doing. Though it's no consolation, I'm certain that his child will grow up with loving knowledge of a father who was kind, generous and a truly dedicated person.

> Barry Rosen
> New York City

*   *   *

Considering we are part of a world that interacts, controls & redefines its own environment I find myself a part of helpless shame that an individual could be killed ruthlessly & unnecessarily. My prayers & heartfelt anguish is with the family of Mr Daniel Pearl.

> Bin Bakshi
> Mumbai, India

*   *   *

Dear Mariane

I am a student from India, deeply troubled by the killing of your husband. I can only say this, if there is a GOD somewhere then he WILL punish those who murdered him. . . . I hope wherever Danny is he is in good hands. I KNOW he will be watching over you and your baby. So please don't ever feel alone. If it means anything, I will be praying for you and your family and all those who have felt his loss. I come from a family of army officers. I was raised as a liberal Jehovah's Witness with a liberal mind and tolerance and forgiveness. I CANNOT accept what has happened to your husband. I think the perpetrators of this disgusting crime should never ever be forgiven.

Please be strong and please don't let hate embitter you. I am with you in your grief . . .

> With all my love and prayers
> Vasundhara Sirnate
> New Delhi

*   *   *

Those of us at Batesville American Mfg. Co. would like to send our condolences to the Pearl family for the tragic loss of Daniel Pearl.

As I watched CNN last night and they announced the loss of Mr. Pearl, I cried. I had prayed that he would be returning to his family. We can ask "why" for the rest of our lives and we will never be able to understand how one human can take the life of another in such a tragic way.

God bless the Pearl family and may they stand the test of time in getting through the loss of such a wonderful person.

> Helen Williamson
> Batesville American Mfg. Co
> Batesville, MS

*   *   *

I am an American journalist living and working in Berlin, Germany. I did not know Mr. Pearl, but I am outraged and sad. I am furious and speechless. Though often disillusioned with my craft, with thoughts of quitting journalism sometimes overwhelming me, I can't allow such senseless violence to erase the words we write, or to silence our voices. I hope family, friends and colleagues know that we all share in the grief and are determined to go on. Our voices will be heard, our pictures will be seen, the truth will be told.

Pilar Wolfsteller
Reuters Television
Berlin, Germany

*   *   *

The Prime Minister of the Grand-Duchy of Luxembourg would like to express his heartfelt sympathies to the family of Daniel Pearl. The atrocious circumstances of his death, as unbearable as they may be to his family and friends, will remain as a reminder for all mankind that freedom is, above all, freedom of expression and of thought. Daniel Pearl was a light in an ocean of shadows. May his light shine on, for us all. To his wife we would like to extend our deepest sympathies for the loss of a husband and a father-to-be. Our thoughts are also with Daniel Pearl's unborn child. May the example of his or her father be a guiding light for life.

Jean-Claude Juncker
Prime Minister of the Grand-Duchy of Luxembourg

*   *   *

It is with great sadness that I learned of Danny Pearl's death. Here in Ireland people have been following the story in the papers and on TV and hoping against all odds for a safe outcome. His soul and his family will be in my thoughts and prayers. RIP

Terry O'Connell

* * *

It was a very very sad moment for all of us here, when we learned of Mr. Daniel's murder. We are very heartbroken at his death, our hearts with his wife, unborn child, family, friends and colleagues.

His murder is an act of evil and we condemn those who committed this crime and these cowardice acts will be punished severely by their own religion. There is no justification whatsoever for their criminal acts.

May God give all of you the will and strength to cope with his loss, and just remember, that he left as a *hero* and he is with *God*.

May God bless all of you, amen.

> Sincerely yours:
> Abdurehman Jewaid Banihamed
> and my entire family and friends
> Ana Banihamed, Ismael Abdurehman,
> Adam Abdurehman, Joseph Abdurehman,
> Salim Rawashdeh, Zaid Jebreel,
> Basim Mustafa, Mohammed Salih,
> Abdu Al-Salam, Mansour Jewaid,
> Mohammed Ali Sulieman, Sameh Jewaid,
> Yousef Jewaid, Wasfi Jewaid, Falah Jewaid

* * *

To *The Wall Street Journal:*

My sincerest condolences on the untimely death of your reporter, Daniel Pearl. His brutal kidnapping and barbaric murder have affected me deeply. Like Mr. Pearl, my brother-in-law, Robert Stethem, was also murdered by terrorists. The senselessness of Robbie's death, and the haunting thoughts of what might have been, are with me still.

May the friends, colleagues, and loved ones of Mr. Pearl take comfort in knowing that he died doing what he loved—being a journalist.

May God bless and comfort you in this time of need, and may Mr. Pearl rest in peace for all eternity.

Ray Sierralta

*   *   *

I, as a Pakistani citizen, would wish to express my sorrow and grief at the death of Daniel Pearl. The public in my country is shocked and horrified at the brutal slaying of an innocent soul and would like to offer condolences to his family, friends and countrymen. Our hearts are with you in the war against terrorism. May Allah help all of us defeat this enemy masquerading as defenders of faith.

Zaki Haq
Karachi, Pakistan

*   *   *

Dear Mrs. Pearl,

Please accept my sincere condolences on the occasion of the tragic death of your husband.

He fell another innocent victim to the people and organizations who made it their profession to commit violence, kidnap, kill and spread terror. International terrorism knows no borders or nationality. It exists in Pakistan and Afghanistan, in the Middle East and in the Balkans, as well as in other areas of the world. Unfortunately, we in Russia have also seen inhuman acts of terrorists who decided to turn a part of our country—Chechnya—into their base. Thousands of people, Russian citizens and foreigners, became victims of their pillaging, brutal acts of terror and hostage taking. That is why we understand and share your sorrow as our own.

It is to fight this global challenge to security and well-being of the people that Russia, the United States and other countries have joined their efforts. We will do everything to root out this evil, eliminate the threat of terrorism, find and neutralize all those who bring death and destruction.

Please, pass my sympathies to Daniel Pearl's parents, to all his relatives and friends, to his colleagues from *The Wall Street Journal*.

> Sincerely,
> Vladimir Putin
> President of the Russian Federation

*   *   *

I know you will receive thousands of emails regarding Daniel Pearl's death but I feel compelled to tell you that I, for one, have followed the story of his abduction very closely. I've prayed for his safe return and watched the news like a mother watches a newborn child at rest. Like his family, until today, I still held out hope for a reunion with his beloved wife.

My heart bleeds for his family, for the senselessness of it all, and for the realization that so much in this world is unexplainable, and simply out of our control. Mr. Pearl's death is a national tragedy. I live in the greatest country on earth, not for its military strength, but for its compassion and tolerance. To see one of our own lose his life to some ill-defined cause, is very sad.

After all is said and done, we realize, once again, that life is truly very fragile. I will pray now for healing for Mrs. Pearl. She will have memories to share with her newborn, and I hope her grief becomes more bearable with the birth of her child. If I knew where to send flowers, I would send a bouquet so large it wouldn't fit in her home. Please let her know that many of us are still grieving with her. It won't ease her pain but it might help her to know that millions of people are with her in spirit.

Patricia DiSiena
Houston, Texas

*   *   *

Mrs. Pearl,

. . . In India we have a saying that "A human being comes to this earth without any possessions and similar is the case when he leaves and soul is the most important thing and as we change clothes the soul changes bodies." So he must have left for heavenly bodies' abode and God too cannot stay without people he loves so he recalls them early to stay with him.

He must have been a great person, now that the whole world has rallied behind his death.

Take care and it will all work out fine.

With regards,
Ravi Dixit

*   *   *

Please accept my sympathies regarding the murder of Daniel Pearl. This unbelievable act of savagery reinforces why we are tackling terrorism head-on. It must be heartbreaking for his family.

Regards,
Alan Taylor
Ayrshire, Scotland, U.K.

*   *   *

Hi there.

My name is Jennifer and I am going to become a journalist. . . . For a very long time I was confused as to what I wanted to do with my life. I wanted a career that was rewarding to me, as well as rewarding to the global community. When Daniel's story began unfolding, I realized what passion and courage journalists like him have. I gained a complete and utter respect for those like Daniel. Journalists, to me, are the first link in the chain of revolution and change. I carry a picture of Daniel in my wallet to remind me of why I finally chose to become a journalist. I hope Daniel's son Adam grows up knowing his father did not die in vain, for I know that I am not the only one whose life was touched by Daniel. I wish Mariane and her new son the best.

Thank you,
Jennifer Taylor
Minneapolis, MN

* * *

I am deeply moved by the fate of Mr. Pearl and really don't understand this horrible crime against him and his family. As a journalist myself and as a human being I strongly denounce such a barbaric act. Never again! My heart reaches out to Mr. Pearl's family and friends and colleagues.

Sincerely,
Werner Pochinger
Austria

* * *

I apologize on behalf of my countrymen on such a coward and shameful act committed on our soil allegedly by our countrymen with your husband.

Many people may have consoled you using various phrases and words. I being a lawyer and social worker, I am well aware of your state. . . .

I know you may be indecisive about your future. I want to reciprocate to your feelings. But I cannot offer any better substitute to your deceased husband still if you think [it] appropriate to live in Pakistan, I am ready and willing to support you and share your sorrow including the esteemed matronial relationship if you desire so.

Regards,
Muhammad Ahmed
(advocate)
Karachi

*   *   *

Dear Mrs. Pearl,

We write to you and your dignified family to express our deepest sympathy on the sad demise of Daniel Pearl. Please allow me to share with you these sad moments as we got to know Daniel the noble man and a great reporter.

We are deeply saddened to learn about the loss of Daniel Pearl's life whom also we share with mutual respect. My grief and pain is all the more augmented when I recall the cheerful and warm friendship that we have had over the last few years. I have always enjoyed and found pleasure in reading his pieces and writings. . . .

Daniel sacrificed his life for not submitting to any pressure in which it will be a doctrine to the community of professional journalism around the world to keep the beacon of truth ever shining and reigning supreme.

We once again extend our heartfelt condolence to you, the family, friends and relatives of the deceased among those whom he would be greatly missed.

Sincerely,
Sultan Bin Zayed Al-Nahyan
Deputy Prime Minister
United Arab Emirates

*   *   *

I sat with my youngest child yesterday as we watched the news confirming Daniel's death. My son, who is 9, is so touched by the tragedy, and has all kinds of questions as to who Daniel was in his life outside that of a journalist. We are all saddened by this loss of life and wonder what evil draws someone to do as they did to Daniel, a man who clearly was a compassionate person. When I see my son, I wonder how future generations will look at the events they have had to deal with since September 11, and how they will shape the world. I pray they do not become callous toward it, but look at the goodness of people as a whole. I have no simple answers for his [questions] as to why Daniel died. I have no simple answers as to why evil exists. I pray for your families that you may find peace.

Debra Leverton

*   *   *

Dear Mariane Pearl,

As a husband and as a father I found myself close to tears when I heard of the death of your husband, Daniel. I still cannot believe it.

As an ordinary decent human being, I did not have to know your husband to feel outraged at his senseless and brutal killing. I cannot see how any cause whatsoever, be it political or whatever, can justify such inhumane acts of brutality. This is not an act against America alone, it is an act against ordinary human beings that love peace and freedom anywhere. . . .

May Almighty God grant you comfort and peace at this very difficult time and may you deliver the child you now carry in perfect health. May God see you through these difficult days. Amen.

James Monday
Banjul
The Gambia

*   *   *

To the family, friends, and colleagues of Daniel Pearl I offer my heartfelt condolences.

Never before have I felt so keenly these words of John Donne:

> "Any man's death diminishes me, because I am involved
> in mankind; and therefore never send to know for whom
> the bell tolls; it tolls for thee."

Because of Mr. Pearl's death, the bell tolls for the world. I did not know Mr. Pearl, but I feel his loss very deeply. However, it is my hope and belief that his spirit of compassion, kindness and creativity will be instilled in some and strengthened in others as a result of the terrible actions taken against him. Please know that you are not alone in your grief.

Sincerely,
Kim Mitchell

*　　*　　*

My deepest condolences on the death of Daniel Pearl. He was everything I inspire to be as a political science student myself. I hope that our comman humanity would bring us togather someday, and stop injustice in both our nations.

Firas Maksad
Beirut, Lebanon

*　　*　　*

Dear Mariane:

I'm a Spanish journalist and my boyfriend has been a war correspondent in Afghanistan. The death of a journalist is always a tragedy. The circumstances in which your husband has been assassinated in Pakistan, while he was carrying out a difficult and courageous task, makes this crime particularly intolerable and one which has impacted heavily on all of the journalists here in Spain. I would like to send condolences and a strong embrace.

> Best Wishes,
> Cecilia Ballesteros

*   *   *

Dear Mrs. Pearl,

All of us here at *The New York Times* were deeply saddened by the tragic news about your husband. He and I never met, but I couldn't let the horror go by without writing you to tell you and the Pearl family how much we all grieve for Danny and for your loss.

All of you are in our hearts and prayers.

> Warmly,
> Arthur O. Sulzberger, Jr.
> New York, NY

*   *   *

Sir,

I myself on behalf of my staff members express heartful shock and grief at the untimely and tragic death of Mr. Daniel Pearl, and condole *The Wall Street Journal* and the bereaved family of the departed soul.

May his soul rest in peace.

> With regards,
> Ramezanali Yousefi
> Regional Director
> Islamic Republic News Agency

*   *   *

Dear Adam,

I have just seen the picture of your beautiful mother, smiling as she holds you safe and asleep in her arms. That photo of mother and newborn has flashed around the globe, and it brought tears to many eyes, including mine. We have awaited your birth as if we were part of your family.

I am a newspaper reporter in Washington. I'm sorry I never met your father, but the world knows him as a brave and heroic man. He was a fine journalist in the best tradition, an idealist who shined the light of truth on the dark places. He wanted to change the world. He did change it. He left us you, the son who will carry his name.

Being a journalist is the reason your dad is not with you and your mother in person, but it is not the defining factor in what he is or was as a father. I believe your father is with you now in spirit and in so many ways you will come to realize as you grow up.

Remember, always, the legion of journalists, your "aunts and uncles," who will be here for you all your life, if you need us, for guidance and support.

And, when you think of the evil that caused your father's death, you must also think of the letters and good wishes from all over the world that celebrated your birth. These are a sign of the will to do what is right and to honor that which is good. Almost all of us have that will within us.

Adam Pearl, you will be like a child in a fairy tale with a magic word—your father's name—that will unlock doors and elicit goodwill throughout your life.

> Sincerely,
> Marsha Mercer
> Media General
> Washington, D.C.

*　　*　　*

Dear Adam,

Welcome to this world! I'm really happy that you are healthy. Your mom is really happy, too. She loves you a lot.

I am so sorry that you did not know your dad. All who knew him say he was a really fine man. He loves you in spirit.

My hope is that the world you enter will be at peace. I will work hard to realize this vision.

All my best Adam. May God bless you.

Sincerely,
George Bush
The White House

P.S. Give your mom a kiss

*   *   *

Dear Mariane,

Please know that all of us here in Littleton, Colorado and in the entire region are inspired by your example even in the midst of your horrible grief. Today in my *daimoku,* I sent heartfelt prayers for Danny, and I felt a huge surge of gratitude well up in my heart for his courage, for the enormity of his mission, and for having the privilege of sharing this planet with him. No, I never knew him personally, but felt, and still feel, a connection to his life, as do so many others. I truly believe that what you said is true; there is an urgent need for all of us, as individuals and as nations, to examine our own responsibility for having created and supported a world that resolves around fear, injustice, and discord. It is time for us to unite in peace, as brothers and sisters, transcending the artificial boundaries of nations. Thank you, Danny, for propelling us in that direction! . . .

Mariane, please know that your grief is in some part our own; it is our desire to share it with you and it is our hope that in sharing it with you, some part of your own sorrow will be diminished. No doubt you and Danny are one in spirit and will without fail be reunited to work together for *kosen rufu* in lifetime after lifetime.

How proud your son will be as he comes of age, both of his father and of you! With so much *daimoku* from your own voice and heart, and so many prayers from all over the world directed at supporting you, how could your child fail to absorb it into his life?

Words seem inadequate to convey what I feel as you bravely conduct yourself as a noble Bodhisattva of the Earth. Thank you so much!! We will all continue to send our prayers for you and for Danny and for the cause of truth and justice for which Danny so brilliantly lived his life.

> With much love and respect,
> Pam Nelson
> Littleton, CO

* * *

Dear Mariane,

I am a 47-year-old woman—psychologist, married mother of 2—who felt compelled to write to you after hearing the news this morning of your husband's death. I cried and prayed deeply for you. I prayed that G-d gives you the strength to cope with this loss, that G-d gives you comfort in your grief, I prayed for the well-being of your unborn child.

My parents are Holocaust survivors and for me to hear that your husband was chosen and eventually killed for being a Jew broke my heart. It is too senseless.

I have never sent a card to someone I've never met before but I had to tell you that I am thinking of you with heartfelt compassion and will continue to pray for you.

> Sheri Noga
> Royal Park, MI

* * *

Dear Mariane,

You and your husband have had a profound impact on our entire family. Our son, David, is a photographer who works worldwide. Your Daniel puts me in such mind of our David.

271

Your grace and pure intelligence through this dark time have been a bright shining light of hope for many, worldwide. As a mother, I have written a hundred "letters"-of-the-mind to you. Please accept our deepest sympathy for your loss and our most joyful gratitude for the gift you have given us all.

With respect,
Suzanne McLain
Fredonia, NY

I am forever grateful to Suzanne McLain, because the card she sent carried the words of a poem by Diane Ackerman called "School Prayer"—words that I have tried, and keep trying, to embody with my whole life:

> "I swear I will not dishonor
> my soul with hatred,
> but offer myself humbly
> as a guardian of nature,
> as a healer of misery,
> as a messenger of wonder,
> as an architect of peace."

Index

www.virago.co.uk

virago

To find out more about Mariane Pearl and
other Virago authors, visit:
www.virago.co.uk

Visit the Virago website for:

- Exclusive features and interviews with authors,
  including Margaret Atwood, Maya Angelou, Sarah
  Waters and Nina Bawden

- News of author events and forthcoming titles

- Competitions

- Exclusive signed copies

- Discounts on new publications

- Book-group guides

- Free extracts from a wide range of titles

PLUS: subscribe to our free monthly newsletter